Better Homes and Gardens®

101
full-size
QUILT
BLOCKS
AND
BORDERS

Better Homes and Gardens® Books
Des Moines, Iowa

Better Homes and Gardens® Books
An imprint of Meredith® Books

101 Full-Size Quilt Blocks and Borders
Editor: Carol Field Dahlstrom
Technical Editors: Susan Banker, Colleen Johnson
Graphic Designer: Gayle Schadendorf
Copy Editors: Debbie Leece, Jill Philby
Editorial and Design Assistants: Judy Bailey, Jennifer Norris, Karen Schirm
Photographers: Hopkins Associates, Scott Little
Technical Illustrator: Chris Neubauer Graphics
Technical Writing: Lila Scott
Project Finishing: Phyllis Dobbs, Jill Mead, Margaret Sindelar
Electronic Production Coordinator: Paula Forest
Production Director: Douglas M. Johnston
Production Manager: Pam Kvitne
Assistant Prepress Manager: Marjorie J. Schenkelberg

Meredith® Books
Editor in Chief: James D. Blume
Design Director: Matt Strelecki
Managing Editor: Gregory H. Kayko

Director, Sales & Marketing, Retail: Michael A. Peterson
Director, Sales & Marketing, Special Markets: Rita McMullen
Director, Sales & Marketing, Home & Garden Center Channel: Ray Wolf
Director, Operations: Valerie Wiese

Vice President, General Manager: Jamie L. Martin

Meredith Publishing Group
President, Publishing Group: Christopher M. Little
Vice President, Consumer Marketing & Development: Hal Oringer

Meredith Corporation
Chairman and Chief Executive Officer: William T. Kerr

Chairman of the Executive Committee: E. T. Meredith III

All of us at Better Homes and Gardens® Books are dedicated to providing you with the information and ideas you need to create beautiful and useful projects. We guarantee your satisfaction with this book for as long as you own it. We welcome your questions, comments, and suggestions. Please write to us at: Better Homes and Gardens® Books, Crafts, RW–240, 1716 Locust Street, Des Moines, IA 50309–3023.

Library of Congress Catalog Card Number: 97-75842
ISBN: 0-696-20739-7

TABLE OF CONTENTS

FOR THE LOVE OF MAKING QUILTS

Welcome to a most lovely collection of extraordinary quilt blocks and keepsake projects—created especially for those who cherish the intricate details and time-honored techniques involved in the art of quilt making.

For anyone who has a passion for quilts, the following pages are beautifully inspiring and full of ideas. More importantly, in your hands lies a fun and imaginative design tool—a hands-on workbook— from which you can successfully recreate each of the blocks and projects to perfection and create your own quilting masterpiece.

ABOUT THE BLOCKS

As you look through the book, you'll see we have chosen to make each of our 80 full-size quilt blocks nine inches square. This easy-to-work-with size makes it possible to interchange your own favorite blocks from the book in many of the quilts and other projects. A nine-inch block can form a natural nine-patch, was often the size used in antique quilts, and combines easily to make small or large bed-size quilts.

Whether pieced or appliquéd, all of the blocks (as well as the fun-finish borders) can be created using templates. To help you make precise templates, all of the patterns provided are finished size. You only need to add the ¼" seam allowance. For sewing ease, you may prefer to strip piece the blocks that are suited to this technique. Whenever possible, we've given instructions for this and other alternative ways to construct the quilt blocks. For additional information turn to pages 212–215.

Our accomplished designers have stitched two color combinations to show how different blocks can look depending on fabric choices. We hope they inspire you to try some creative mixtures of fabric colors and prints. You'll find detailed information on color and design in the back of the book (see page 215).

Throughout the chapters, you'll discover a wonderful collection of both brand-new and antique nine-inch blocks—from ever-popular Country to gorgeous Florals, striking Americana to the whimsical designs in our Just For Fun section. And not only will you find block patterns, but also projects with step-by-step instructions for you to quilt.

ABOUT THE BORDERS

Ranging in width from three to five inches, we've designed 21 borders to help you finish your quilting works of art in grand style. All of our borders have either three-, four-and-a-half-, six-, or nine-inch repeats so you have several options when selecting a border for your quilt.

To further spark your creativity, we've included unique border ideas. Try incorporating a motif from a quilt block as we did on the Stars and Hearts Quilt illustration on page 54. See the Floral Fancies Sampler Quilt on page 5, for an example of combining borders. Also, note that some of the borders in this book turn the corner, others don't. And if you have ever wanted to try using a border pattern as sashing strips in a quilt, look at the illustration on page 10 using the Pieced Pansy floral block and the lovely Pansy Bow border.

DESIGNING A QUILT

With every quilt block design in this book, we've provided a colored illustration of how a bed quilt could be put together using the block. While we've given you just one creative way to construct a quilt using a particular block, there are hundreds of ways you can combine blocks, borders, sashing strips, and set-in corners. Try substituting your favorite nine-inch blocks from one chapter into a favorite illustration in another section.

ABOUT THE PROJECTS

Nothing warms a bedroom quite like a quilt, but there are many other ways to use and display your quilted works of art. From delightful pieces you can wear to room screens, place mats, and tote bags—we've given you options for your quilted pieces along with the complete step-by-step instructions to ensure your success.

As you pick your favorite quilt blocks and try to decide which project you want to create first, enjoy dreaming your way through this design-packed book. Most of all, we hope this exceptional collection tempts your creativity, challenges your talents, and brings you a lifetime of quilting pleasure.

FLORAL FANCIES

Beautiful and flower-garden fresh, we've chosen twenty quilt blocks rich in color and pattern for this chapter and combined all the blocks into our Floral Fancies Sampler Quilt, *below*. Instructions for this quilt are on *page 48*. For more projects to make with quilt blocks from this chapter, turn the page.

POSY ROW BENCH QUILT

WILD ROSE QUILTED ALBUM COVER

6

APPLIQUÉ PANSY PILLOW

☞ FLORAL FANCIES ☜

PROJECTS YOU CAN MAKE

We've created five charming projects using some of the blocks that are in this chapter. From a sweet album cover to a homespun table runner, these projects will give you hours of quilting pleasure. Instructions for making the projects you see here begin on *page 48*. Remember, because all of the blocks in this book are nine inches square, you can interchange any block you wish to create these beautiful projects. When deciding which blocks substitute for each other with the most success, consider whether the block can "stand on its own" or needs to be next to another block like itself to make an interesting pattern. We know you'll have fun mixing and matching all of the blocks you find in this chapter and in this book.

OHIO ROSE TABLE QUILT

SPRING BLOOM TABLE RUNNER

TULIP BOUQUET QUILT BLOCK

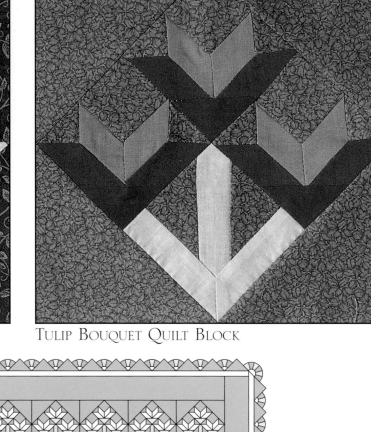

TULIP BOUQUET QUILT BLOCK

How To Construct This Block

Sew A to B; stop stitching ¼"
from end, at the point where B
meets Ar. Sew Ar to adjacent
edge of B, again stitching to
¼" from end. Stitch A and Ar
pieces together; repeat 5 more
times. Sew C to ABAr unit at Ar
edge. Stop stitching ¼" from
end, at the point where C joins
ArA. Stitch a second ABAr unit
to adjacent edge of C, stitching to
Ar edge. Again stop stitching
¼" from end. Sew ArA and ArA
together. Sew D to AAr edges;
repeat 2 more times. Sew F to
each side of E. Sew G to FEF
unit; stop stitching ¼" from end,
at point where E joins GGr. Sew
Gr piece to adjacent side of FEF
unit, again stitching to ¼" from
end. Stitch G and Gr together.
Sew two flower units together.
Sew stem unit to third flower
unit, then stitch these two units
together. Sew H to each edge
of flower block, stitching two
opposite sides first, then
remaining two sides.

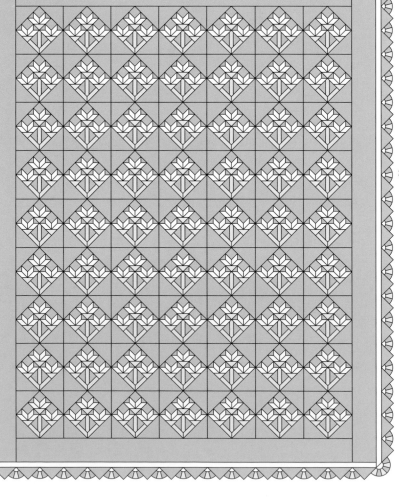

To Make A Bed Quilt

*This quilt is designed
to be a full-size quilt
measuring 78½×96½
inches. We have used a
4½-inch plain border
and the 3¼-inch Fan
border, page 196,
as shown.*

TULIP BOUQUET
Full-Size Block

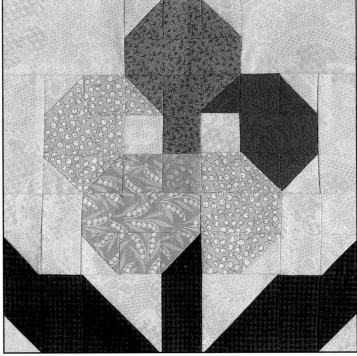

PIECED PANSY QUILT BLOCK

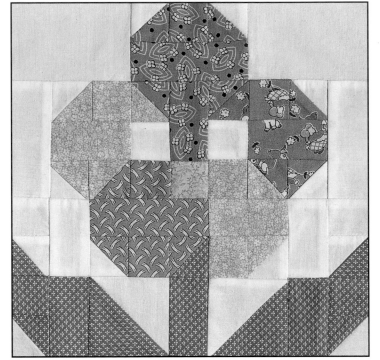

PIECED PANSY QUILT BLOCK

How To Construct This Block

In chosen colors, lay out all pieces in correct position. Be careful of placement. Sew two A's to make a half-square triangle (17 times). Sew two F's to make a half-square triangle (2 times). Sew AA to each side of B, add C to bottom of AABAA. Sew D to each side of AABAAC to make Unit 1. Row 1—Sew AA to each side of B (2 times). Row 2—Sew E to B (2 times). Join Rows 1 and 2 (2 times). Connect two rows with E. Row 3—Sew two AA, three B, two AA. Sew Row 3 to Rows 1, 2. Add C on each side of Unit 2. Row 1—Sew C to E. Row 2—Sew AA, B, AA, B and AA. Sew Row 1 and 2 together. Add E on each side. Horizontally sew B to AA (2 times). Sew BAA to each side of E to make Unit 3. Sew B to AA horizontally (2 times). Sew BAA, E, FF, E, FF, E and BAA to make Unit 4. Sew Units 1, 2, 3 and 4 together.

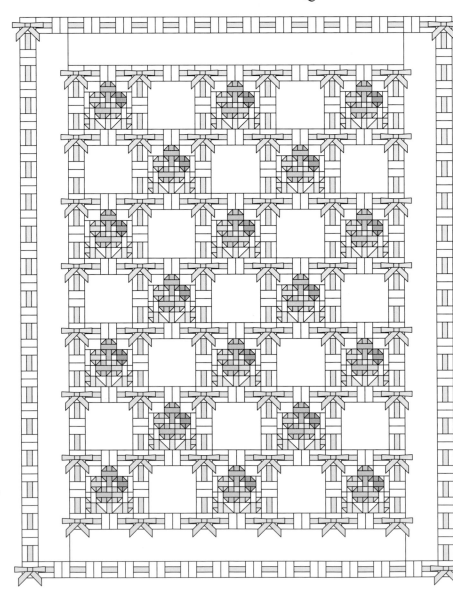

To Make A Bed Quilt

This quilt is designed to be a full- or queen-size quilt measuring 81×105 inches. We have used a 6-inch plain border, the 3-inch Pansy Bow border, page 194, and Pansy Bow sashing strips with plain setting blocks between the pieced blocks. The bows on the Pansy Bow border and sashing strips are three-dimensional.

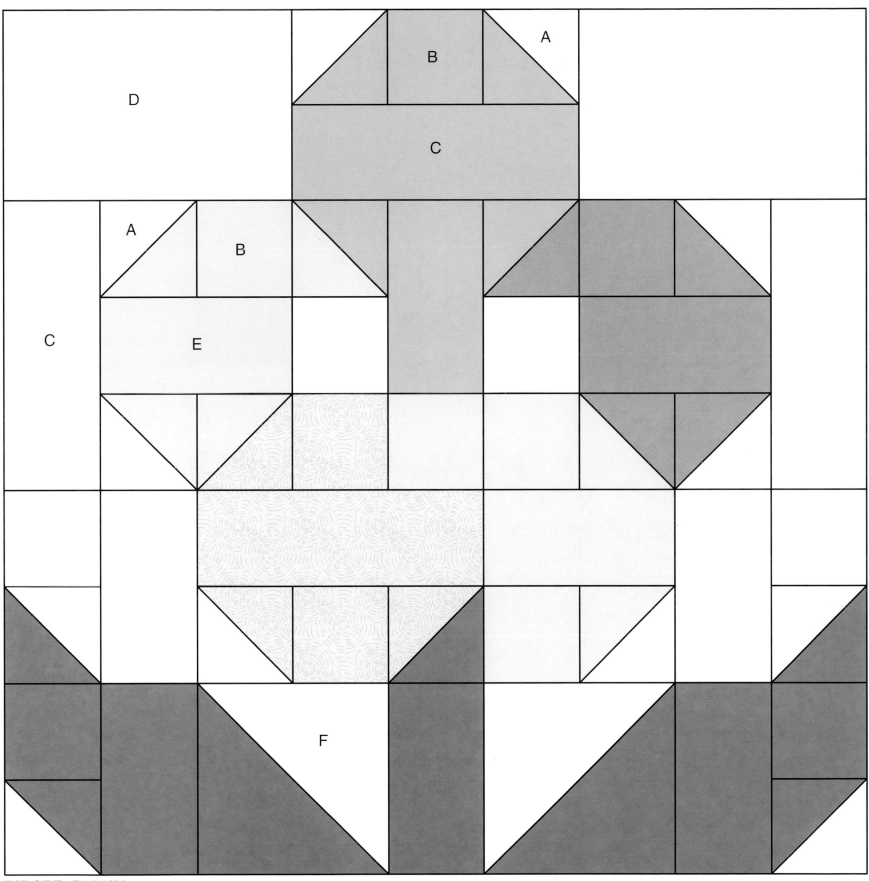

PIECED PANSY
FULL-SIZE BLOCK

FLORAL BASKET QUILT BLOCK

FLORAL BASKET QUILT BLOCK

How To Construct This Block

For appliqué pieces: Mark each pattern piece on the right side of the chosen fabrics. Cut out, allowing a scant ¼" seam allowance. Lay out all pieces to the block according to color and position. Sew A to A (6 times). Sew three AA units together and add one A to the first AA unit to create Diagonal Row 1. Sew two AA units together and add one A to the first AA unit for Diagonal Row 2. Sew A to one AA unit for Diagonal Row 3. Add one A to the top of the AA unit. Sew Rows 1, 2, and 3 diagonally together to make a center unit. Sew D to C; add A (2 times). Sew B to DCA (2 times). Join BDCA to each side of the center unit. Sew E to center unit top. Position F and G pieces, overlapping F on top of G as dotted lines indicate. Appliqué in place with matching threads.

For an alternate fusing method of appliqué, see page 212.

To Make A Bed Quilt

This quilt is designed to be an extra-length full-size quilt measuring 72×108 inches. We have used a 3-inch plain border, the 4½-inch Sawtooth border, page 204, and 3-inch sashing strips as shown.

FLOWER BASKET
FULL-SIZE BLOCK

13

BUTTERFLIES AND BACHELOR BUTTONS QUILT BLOCK

BUTTERFLIES AND BACHELOR BUTTONS QUILT BLOCK

How To Construct This Block

Lay out all pieces in chosen colors. Be very careful of placement. Block A—Make AA unit (2 times). Sew AA unit to B (2 times). Sew AAB to AAB. Sew C to Cr (2 times). Sew CCr to CCr and add D. Set in E (2 times) and AABAAB. *Repeat to make three blocks.* Block B—Sew B to B (2 times). Sew BB to BB (1 time). Sew F to BBBB, add G. Sew F to B, add to BBBBFG. Sew B to G, add to top of BBBBFGFB. Sew A to H, add A (2 times). Sew AHA to B, sew to bottom of unit. Sew B to B, add AHA. Sew AHABB to right side of block. Sew Block A to I, add Block A. Sew I to Block A, add Block B. Sew the two sections together. Add embroidery using running stitches and French knots.

To Make A Bed Quilt

This quilt is designed to be a queen-size square quilt measuring 92×92 inches. We have used a 1½-inch plain border, 1½-inch sashing strips, and setting squares as shown. The blocks are turned on point with plain setting blocks between each grouping of four.

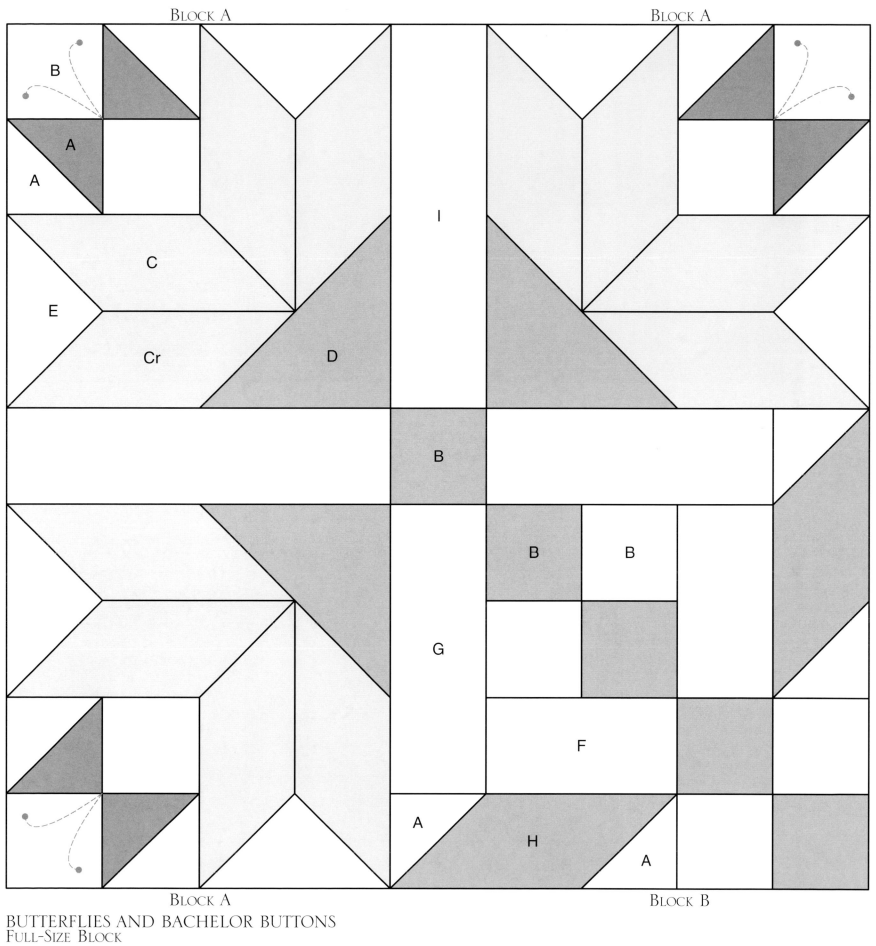

BUTTERFLIES AND BACHELOR BUTTONS
FULL-SIZE BLOCK

IRIS QUILT BLOCK

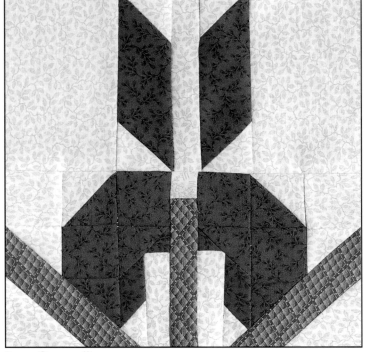

IRIS QUILT BLOCK

How To Construct This Block

Sew B to both ends of A and Ar. Sew C to each outside edge of the BAB and BArB blocks. Join these two units by sewing D for the center strip. Sew F and G together. Set these two units aside. Sew L and I (2 times) and J and K and Jr and K. Sew the JK and JrK units to the LI units, then sew on B and then E (2 times). Sew BB, then add on E, then B (2 times). Sew BBEB to EBJK (2 times). Sew E and B (2 times) and sew to BBE edge of unit. Sew M to N (2 times) and add to bottom of unit. Join two units together with FG for the center strip. Sew bottom to top unit.

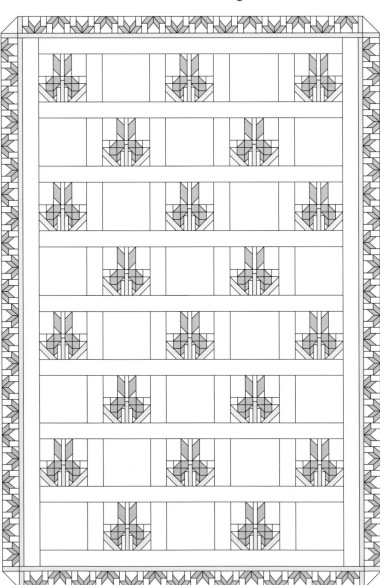

To Make A Bed Quilt

This quilt is designed to be an extra-length twin-size quilt measuring 71×107 inches. We have used a 3-inch plain border, the 4-inch Tulip border, page 206, and 3-inch sashing strips with 9-inch plain setting blocks as shown.

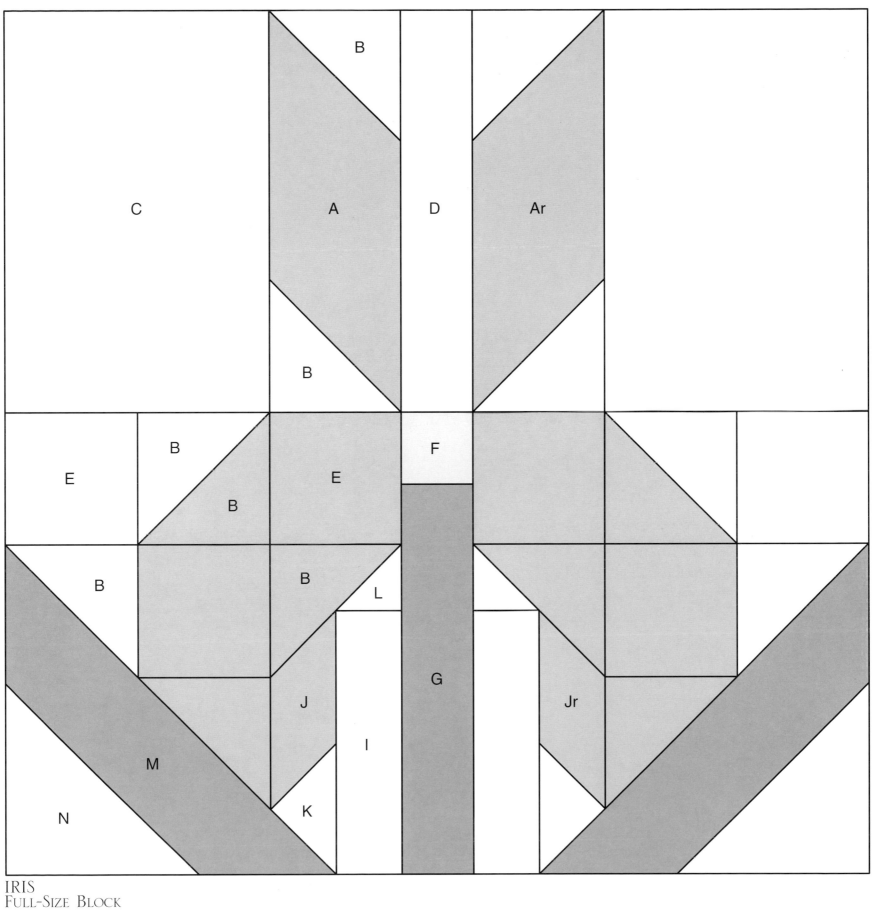

IRIS
FULL-SIZE BLOCK

WILDFLOWERS QUILT BLOCK

WILDFLOWERS QUILT BLOCK

How To Construct This Block

In chosen colors, lay out all pieces in correct position. Be careful of placement. Sew two A's to make a half-square triangle (38 times). Block A: Row 1— Sew B, two AA and B; Row 2—four AA; Row 3—three AA and A; Row 4— B, AA and A. Sew four rows together, add C. Sew E to right side of unit. Sew E to B and sew to bottom of Block A. Block B: Row 1—Sew B, AA and A; Row 2—three AA and A; Row 3—four AA; Row 4—B and three AA, (watch placement). Sew four rows together, add C. Sew D to AA and sew to right side of Block B. Block C: Row 1—Sew B, two AA and B; Row 2—four AA; Row 3—A and three AA; Row 4—A and two AA, (watch placement). Sew four rows together, add C. Sew D to AA and sew to bottom of Block C. Block D: Sew: B to B (2 times), join rows, and add F; sew two AA together, sew to F to make Rows 1 and 2. Row 3—Sew F, B and A; Row 4—two AA and A. Sew four rows together, add C to make Block D. Referring to diagram, sew in a horizontal row, Block A to C and Block B to D. Sew AC to BD.

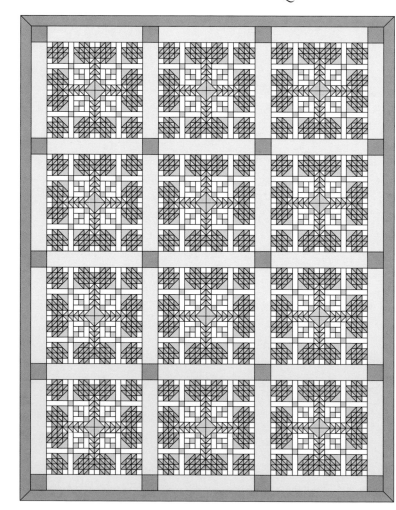

To Make A Bed Quilt

This quilt is designed to be a twin-size quilt measuring 69×90 inches. We have used a 3-inch plain border, a 1½-inch plain border, 3-inch sashing strips, and setting squares as shown.

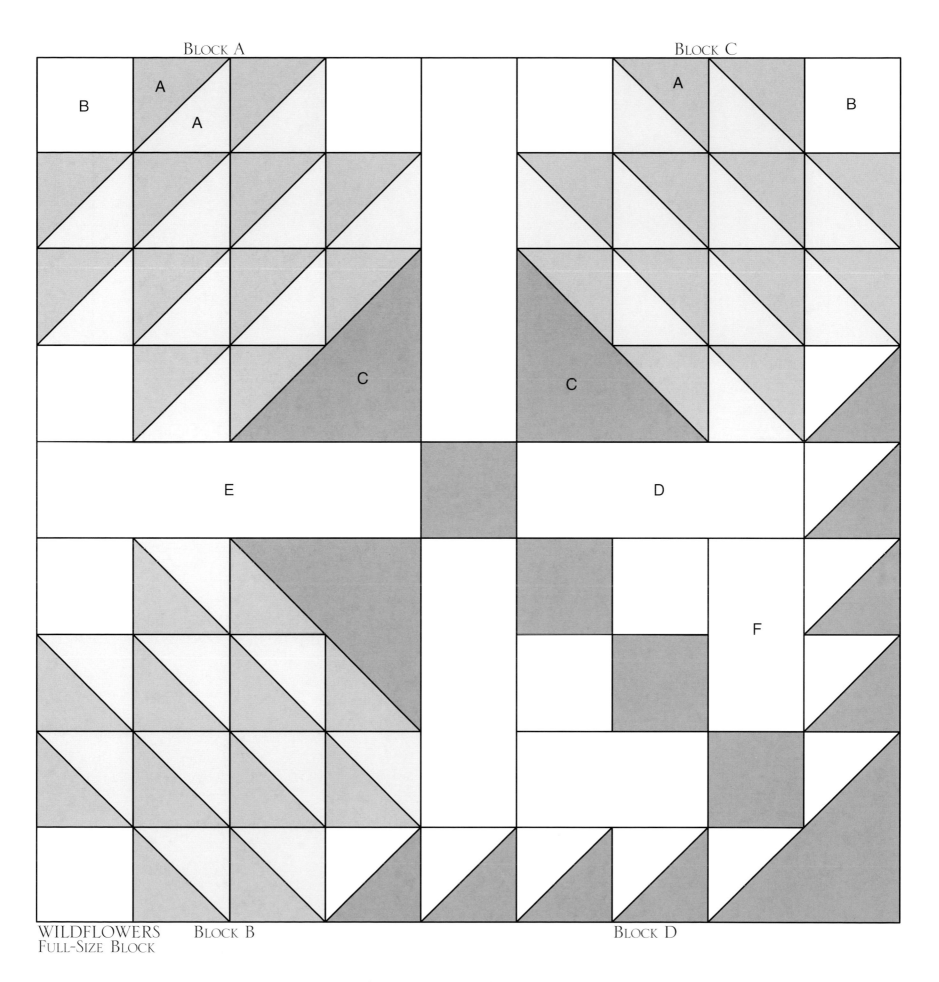

Block A

Block C

B

A

A

A

B

C

C

E

D

F

WILDFLOWERS
Full-Size Block

Block B

Block D

19

FLORAL FANCIES ~ *Appliqué Pansy*

APPLIQUÉ PANSY QUILT BLOCK

APPLIQUÉ PANSY QUILT BLOCK

How To Construct This Block

Mark each pattern piece on right side of chosen fabrics. Cut out allowing scant ¼" seam allowance. Fold a 10" background square in half; then in quarters. Press. Arrange each F piece approximately 1½" in from corners. Layer petals, beginning with A. Add G. Appliqué in place with matching threads. Using two strands of black embroidery floss, add long stitches from center as dotted lines indicate. Add French knot centers on long stitches if desired. Trim block to measure 9½" square.

For an alternate fusing method of appliqué, see page 212.

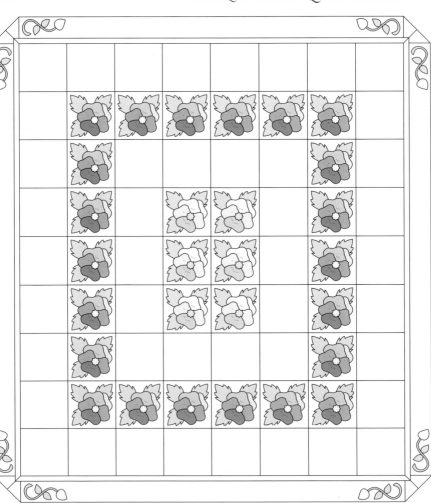

To Make A Bed Quilt

This quilt is designed to be a full-size quilt measuring 82×91 inches. We have used the 5-inch Ivy border in the border corners, page 202, and 9-inch plain setting blocks as shown. We suggest quilting the plain setting blocks with a floral, leaf, or basket motif.

APPLIQUÉ PANSY
FULL-SIZE BLOCK

FLORAL FANCIES ❧ *Thistle*

THISTLE QUILT BLOCK

THISTLE QUILT BLOCK

How To Construct This Block

Row 1—Sew B to A, add B. Row 2—Sew B to three A's, add B. Row 3—Sew five A's. Row 4—Repeat Row 2. Row 5—Repeat Row 1. Sew all rows together. Sew C to unit top. Sew D to unit bottom. Appliqué the pieces onto the background fabric adding E, Er, and F pieces as shown.

For an alternate fusing method of appliqué, see page 212.

To Make A Bed Quilt

This quilt is designed to be a twin-size quilt measuring 72×93 inches. We have used a 3-inch plain border, the 3-inch Checkerboard border, page 195, and 3-inch sashing strips as shown. Color-coordinated pillow shams trimmed with the Checkerboard border would be a nice accessory.

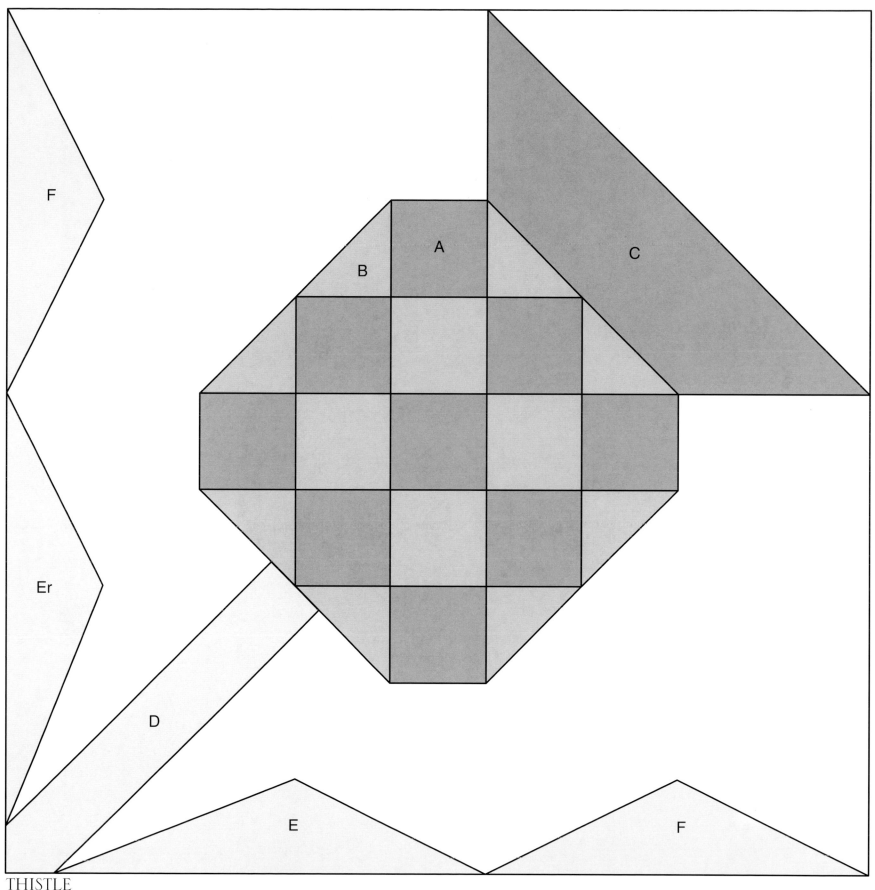

THISTLE
FULL-SIZE BLOCK

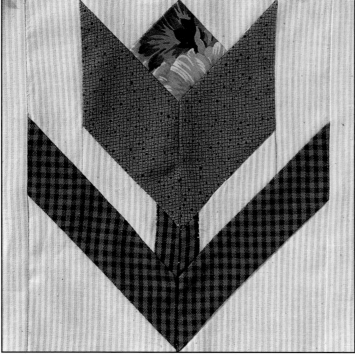

TULIP QUILT BLOCK

TULIP QUILT BLOCK

How To Construct This Block

Sew B to two adjacent sides of A. Sew C to D and Cr to Dr. Then sew CD to E and CrDr to Er. Sew F to CDE unit and Fr to the CrDrEr unit. Then add in the following order: G and Gr pieces, H pieces, and I pieces. Sew one side of the AB unit to the top edge of piece E. Stop stitching ¼" from the end of stitching line at the center point (where the top edges of E and Er join). Repeat on the other side, joining AB to Er. Sew the center seam, stitching from the top down along E, D, and G edges.

To Make A Bed Quilt

This quilt is designed to be an extra-length twin-size quilt measuring 71×107 inches. We have used a 3-inch plain border, the 4-inch Tulip border, page 206, and 3-inch sashing strips as shown.

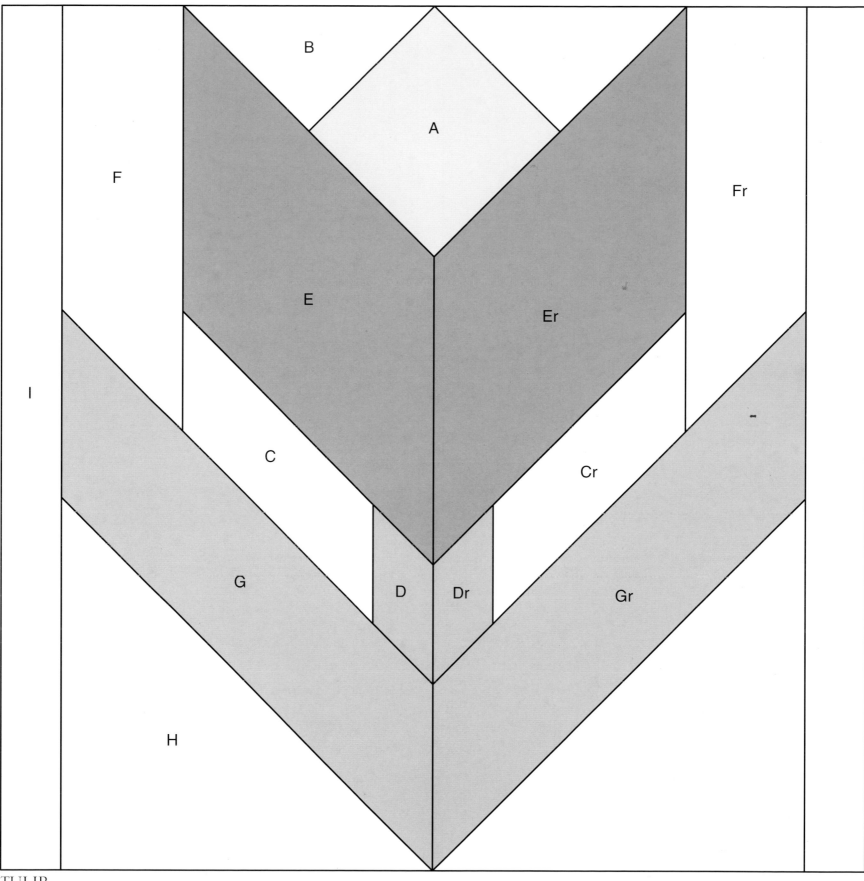

TULIP
FULL-SIZE BLOCK

DAISY AND TULIPS QUILT BLOCK

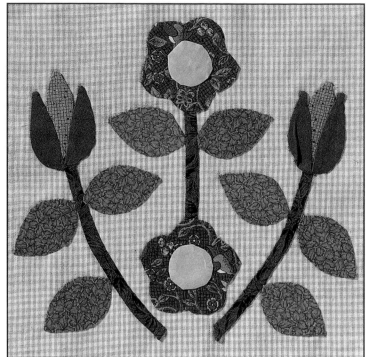

DAISY AND TULIPS QUILT BLOCK

How To Construct This Block

Arrange pieces A through Gr onto background piece. Appliqué C, E, and Er pieces. Appliqué the A pieces, slightly overlapping ends of the C piece. Appliqué the B pieces on top of the A pieces. Appliqué the F pieces, slightly overlapping ends of E piece. Appliqué the G and Gr pieces, slightly overlapping the E, Er, and F pieces. Appliqué the D pieces.

For an alternate fusing method of appliqué, see page 212.

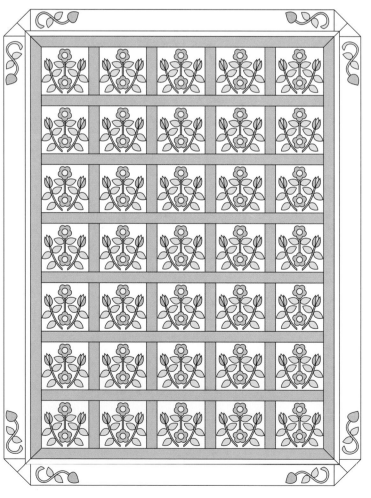

To Make A Bed Quilt

This quilt is designed to be a twin-size quilt measuring 67×89 inches. We have used a 2-inch plain border, the 5-inch Ivy border at the corners, page 202, and 2-inch sashing strips as shown.

DAISY AND TULIPS
FULL-SIZE BLOCK

OHIO ROSE QUILT BLOCK

OHIO ROSE QUILT BLOCK

How To Construct This Block

Mark each pattern piece on the right side of the chosen fabrics. Cut out allowing scant ¼" seam allowance. Fold a 10" background square diagonally in both directions; press. Arrange each piece beginning with A. Position A approximately 7" from the center. Appliqué all pieces in place with matching threads. Trim block to 9½" square.

For alternate fusing method of appliqué, see page 212.

To Make A Bed Quilt

This quilt is designed to be a queen-size square quilt measuring 96×96 inches. We have used a 4½-inch plain border, the 3-inch To the Point border, page 199, and 3-inch sashing strips as shown.

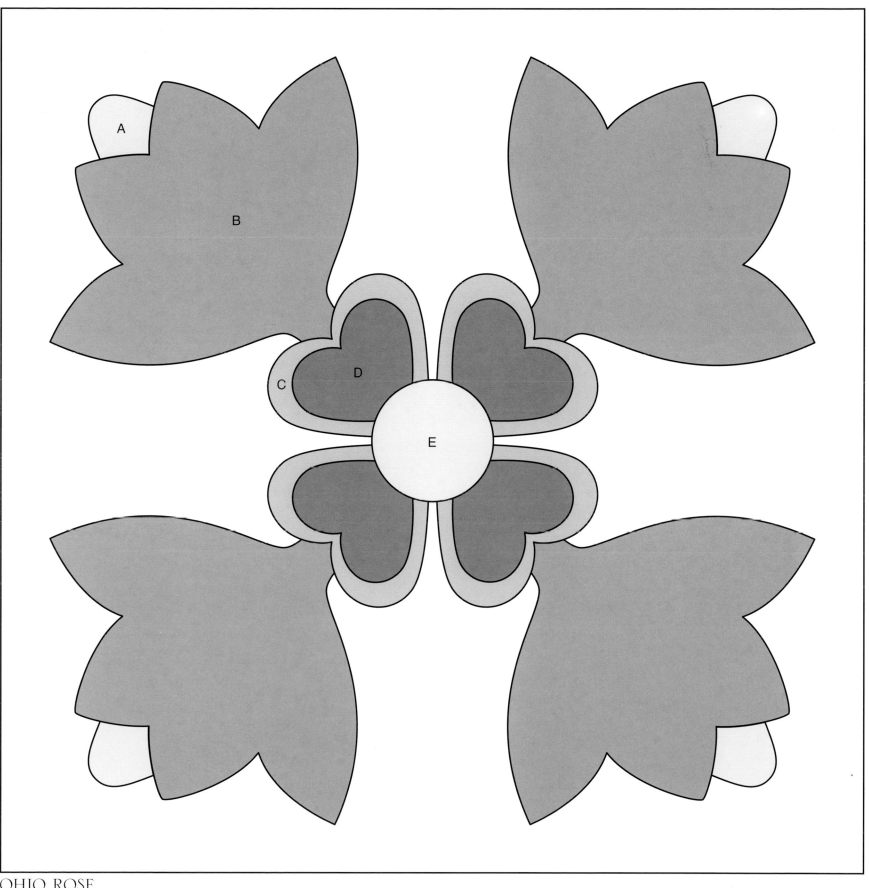

OHIO ROSE
FULL-SIZE BLOCK

MAY BASKET QUILT BLOCK

MAY BASKET QUILT BLOCK

How To Construct This Block

Sew B to A. Sew C to BA. Sew D to CBA. Sew E to DCBA. Sew F to EDCBA. Sew G to FEDCBA. Sew H to I and H to Ir. Sew HI and HIr units to each side of basket. Sew J to basket to complete half of block. Appliqué handle to K. Join the two halves to form a square. Appliqué M and N pieces to K. Add French knots to flower centers.

For an alternate fusing method of appliqué, see page 212.

To Make A Bed Quilt

This quilt is designed to be a queen-size quilt measuring 84½×107 inches. We have used a 6¾-inch plain border, the 4-inch Stripes border, page 205, 4½-inch sashing strips, and setting squares as shown. This block would also work nicely set on point as shown with the Butterflies and Bachelor Buttons block on page 14.

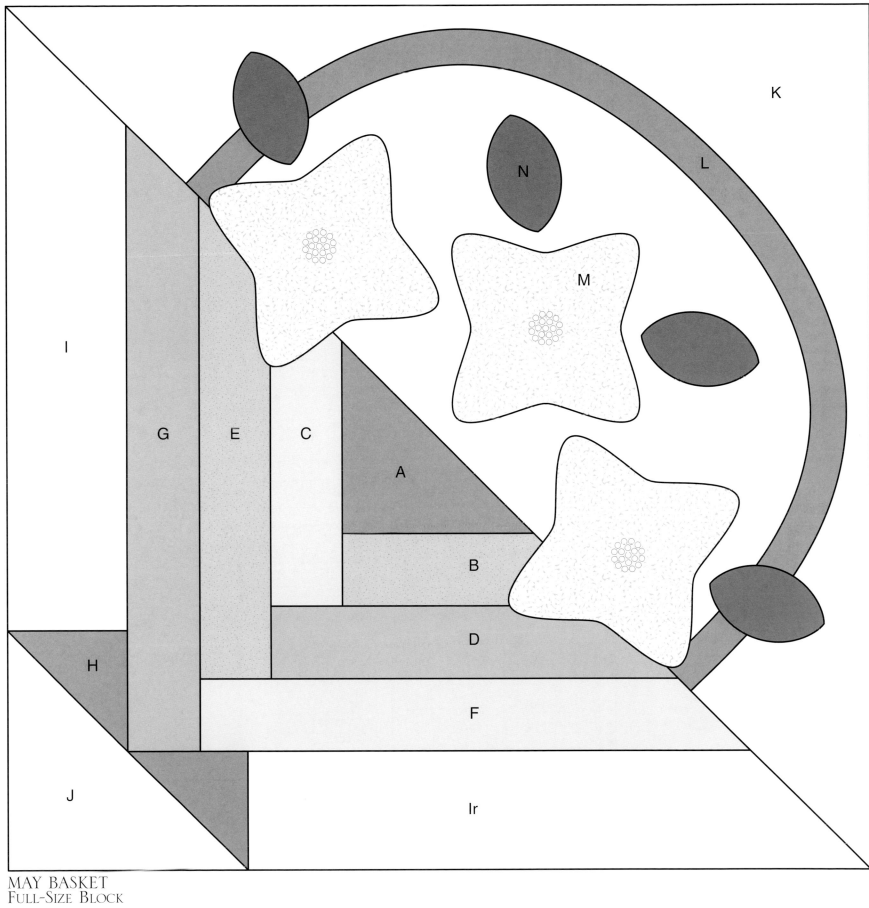

MAY BASKET
Full-Size Block

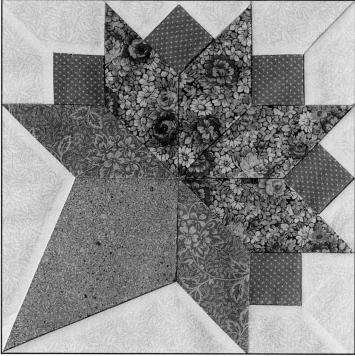

BRIDE'S BOUQUET QUILT BLOCK

BRIDE'S BOUQUET QUILT BLOCK

How To Construct This Block

Sew two A's together (3 times).
Sew D and Dr together
(3 times). Set in B to DDr
(3 times). Set in BDDr to AA
(3 times). Sew one AABDDr to
AABDDr. Sew two C pieces to
B (2 times). Set in one CBC to
the top of the block. Sew F and
Fr to the side of E. Sew FEFr
to AABDDr. Join the top to
the bottom of the block. Set
in CBC.

To Make A Bed Quilt

*This quilt is designed
to be a twin-size quilt
measuring 66×87 inches.
We have used a 3-inch
plain border, 3-inch
sashing strips, and
setting squares
as shown.*

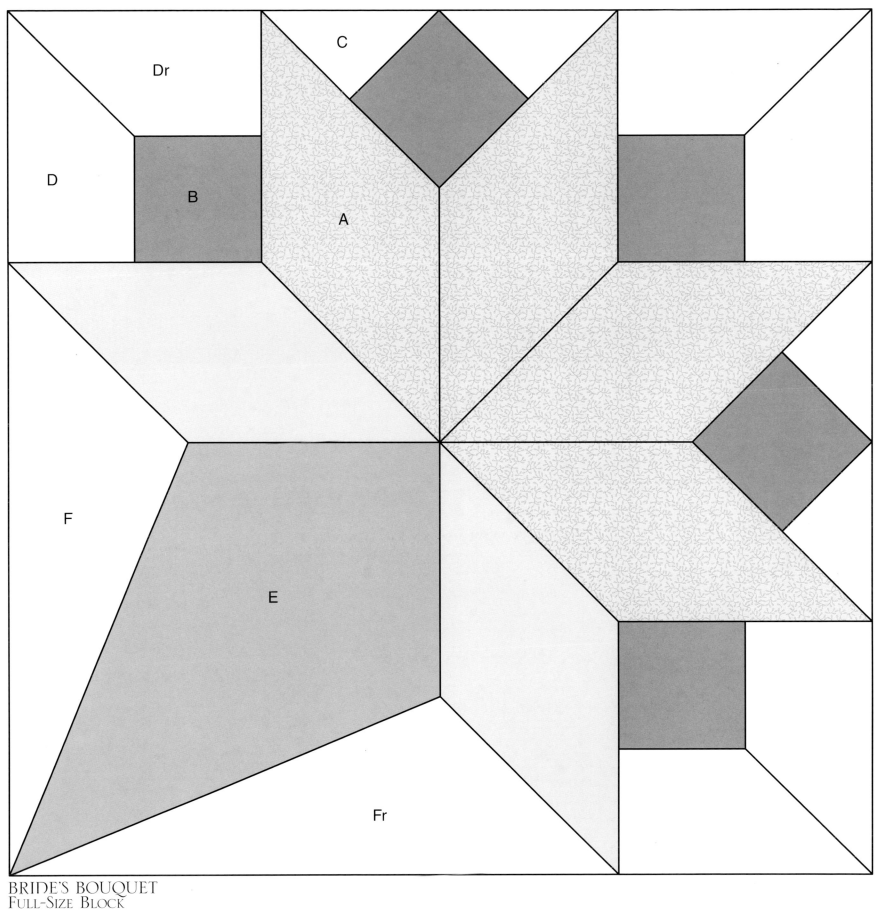

BRIDE'S BOUQUET
Full-Size Block

33

SPRING BLOOM QUILT BLOCK

SPRING BLOOM QUILT BLOCK

How To Construct This Block

Lay out all pieces according to color and position. To A sew one B piece. Sew B to C. Join BC to AB to make a Base Unit. Matching colors, sew a light D to a dark D (10 times). Sew top horizontal Row 1 of two C's, three DD's, one C, and one DD. Sew side vertical row of one C, three DD's, one C, and one DD. Sew E to E (1 time). Sew one EE to the side of the Base Unit. Sew E to C. Add DD to make horizontal Row 5. Sew E to DD. Add C to make Row 6. Sew Row 5 to Row 6. Add F (Row 7). Sew Rows 5, 6, 7 to Base Unit. Sew side vertical Row to the Base Unit. To vertical F add C. Sew FC to the right side of the Base Unit. Sew top horizontal Row 1 to the Base Unit.

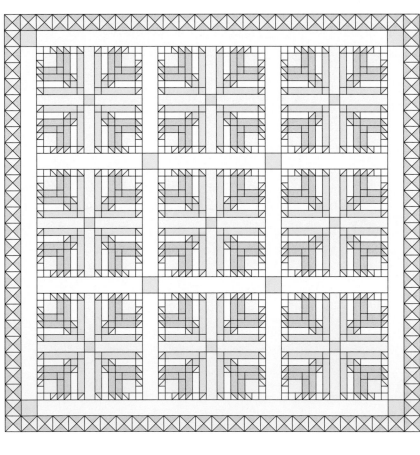

To Make A Bed Quilt

This quilt is designed to be a twin-size square quilt measuring 78×78 inches. We have used a 3-inch plain border, the 3-inch Pie Crust border, page 195, 2- and 3-inch sashing strips, and setting squares as shown.

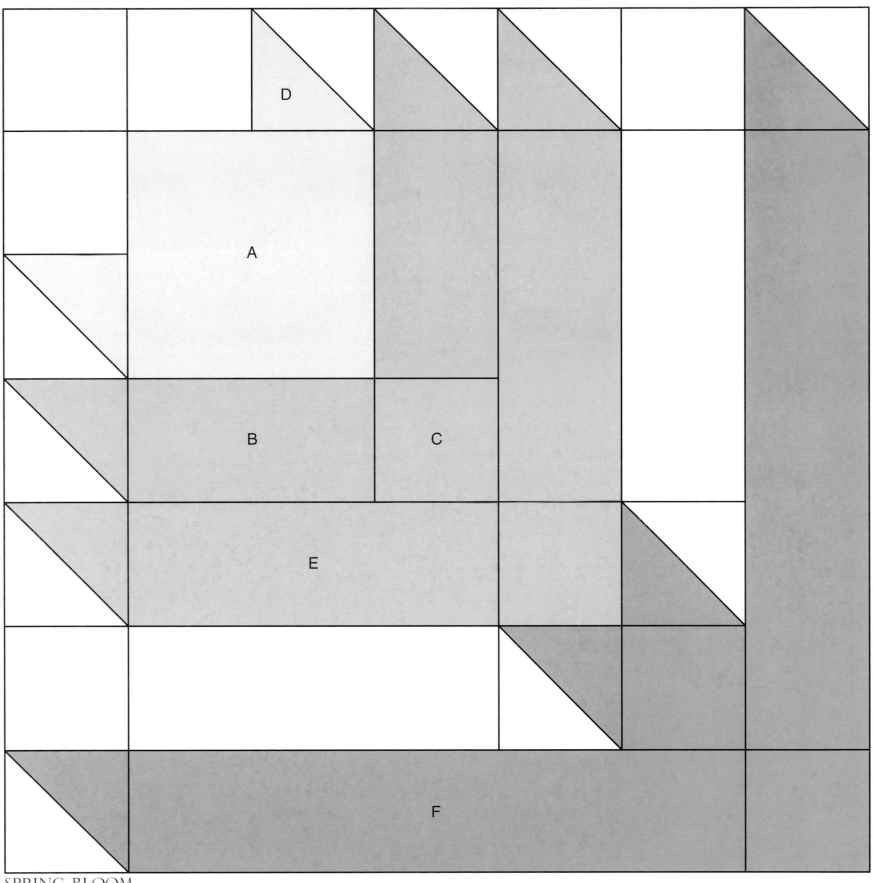

SPRING BLOOM
Full-Size Block

WILD ROSE QUILT BLOCK

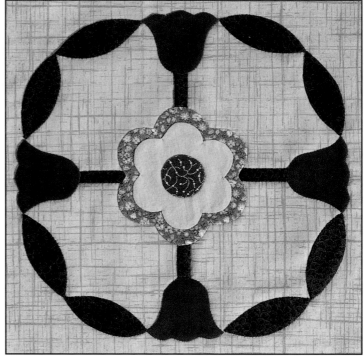

WILD ROSE QUILT BLOCK

How To Construct This Block

Mark each pattern piece on the right side of the chosen fabrics. Cut out allowing scant ¼" seam allowance. Fold a 10" background square in half and then in quarters. Press. Arrange each piece beginning with A. Appliqué in place with matching threads. Trim block to 9½" square.

For an alternate fusing method of appliqué, see page 212.

To Make A Bed Quilt

This quilt is designed to be an extra-length twin-size quilt measuring 69½×105½ inches. We have used a 3-inch plain border, the 3¼-inch Fan border, page 196, and 3-inch sashing strips as shown.

WILD ROSE
FULL-SIZE BLOCK

DOGWOOD QUILT BLOCK

DOGWOOD QUILT BLOCK

How To Construct This Block

Sew two E pieces together
(4 times). Sew D to EE
(4 times). Sew C to Dr
(4 times). Combine CDr and
EED (4 times) to make CDE
unit. Sew B to CDE unit
(4 times). Sew F and Fr to G
(4 times). Sew FGFr to each
side of BCDE (2 times). Sew A
to BCDE unit (2 times). Join
the top and bottom units to the
center section.

To Make A Bed Quilt

*This quilt is designed
to be a twin-size quilt
measuring 75×93 inches.
We have used a 1½-inch
plain border as shown.*

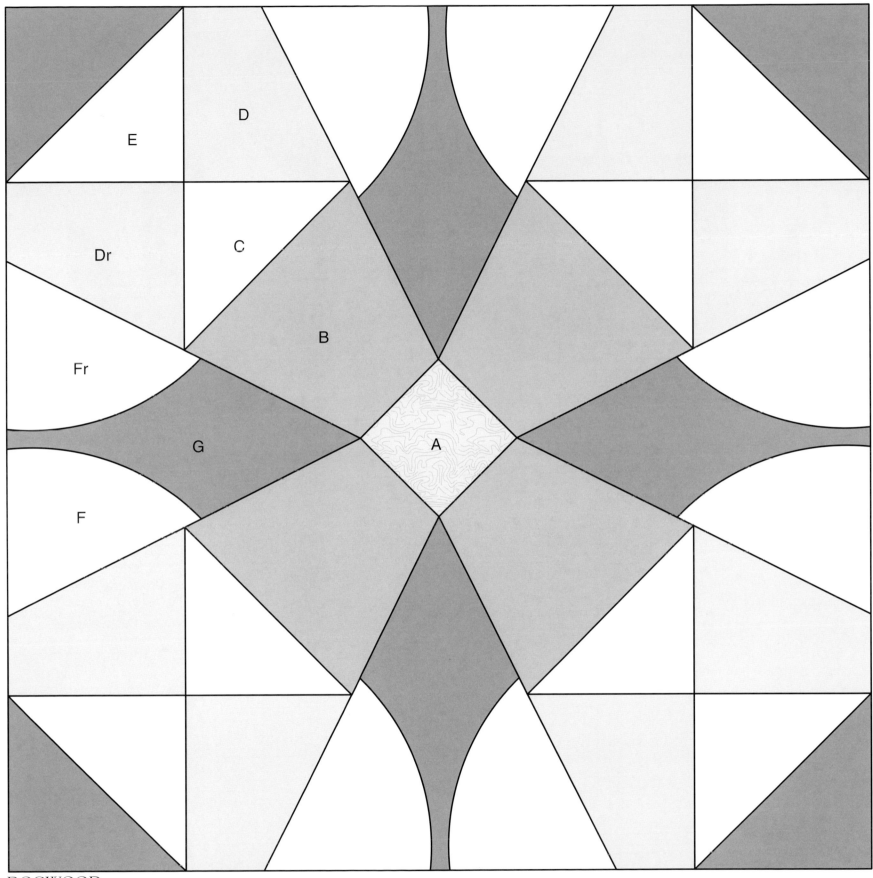

DOGWOOD
FULL-SIZE BLOCK

POSY ROW QUILT BLOCK

POSY ROW QUILT BLOCK

How To Construct This Block

Sew B to A along one side, stopping at seam allowance of A. Sew B to A (3 more times) in counterclockwise direction. Complete seam for first BA. Sew C to B (4 times) to complete square. Make this unit two times. Sew E and F to opposite sides of D (2 times). Sew Er and F to opposite sides of Dr (2 times). Sew EDF and ErDrF units to opposite sides of G (2 times). Join four units to complete block.

To Make A Bed Quilt

This quilt is designed to be a queen-size quilt measuring 81×99 inches. We have used the 4½-inch Sawtooth border, page 204, and 9-inch setting blocks as shown. We suggest quilting the setting blocks with a simple diamond-within-a-diamond motif.

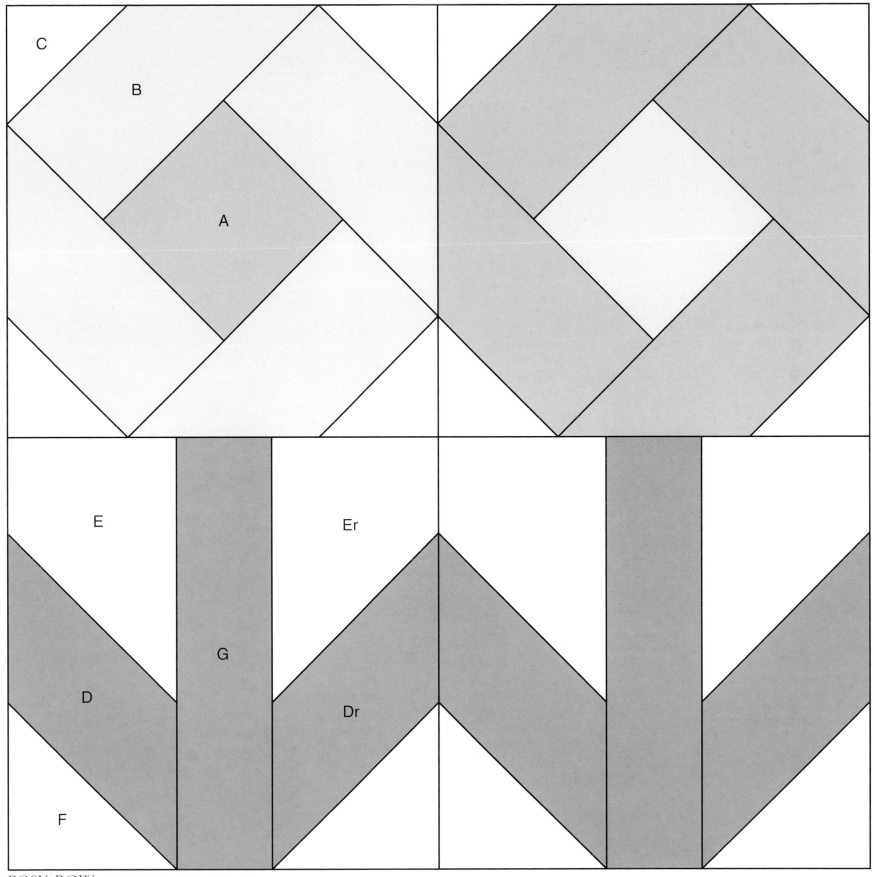

POSY ROW
FULL-SIZE BLOCK

ROSE QUILT BLOCK

ROSE QUILT BLOCK

How To Construct This Block

Appliqué L to I. Sew A to A. Sew A to Br and B to A. Sew C to D. Sew ABr to AA. Sew CD to BA. Sew ABrAA to CDBA. Sew E to F. Sew G to H. Sew EF to GH; add ABrAACDBA. Sew Er to F. Sew G to Hr. Sew ErF to GHr; add I. Sew ErFGHrI to bottom of center unit. Sew J to top and bottom of center. Set in J to each side of center; add K (4 times).

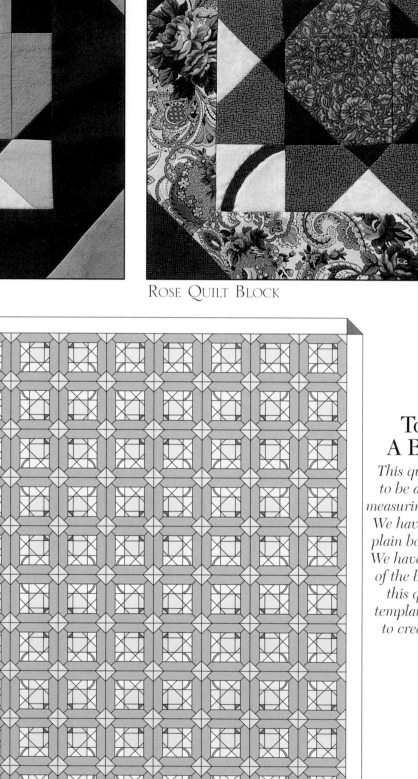

To Make A Bed Quilt

This quilt is designed to be a full-size quilt measuring 78×96 inches. We have used a 3-inch plain border as shown. We have reversed some of the blocks to create this quilt. Reverse templates accordingly to create this effect.

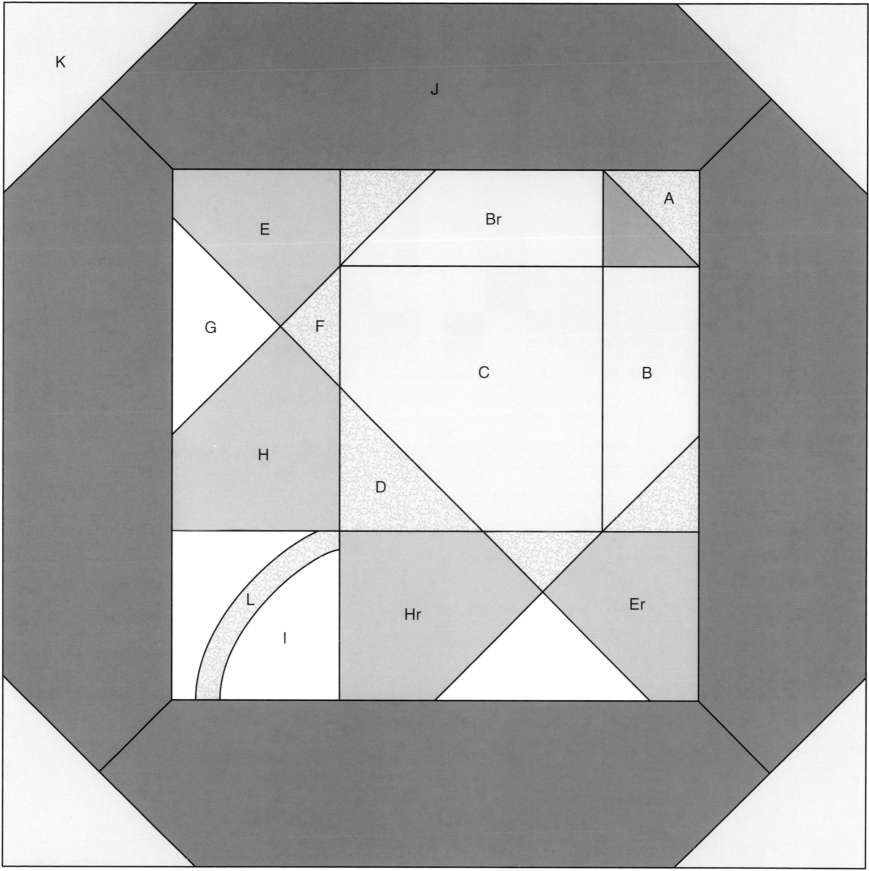

ROSE
FULL-SIZE BLOCK

Flower in the Window Quilt Block

Flower in the Window Quilt Block

How To Construct This Block

Sew A to A (8 times), make four four-patch squares. Sew B to C (4 times). Sew A square to BC (2 times); add A square (2 times). Sew D to E; add D. Sew DED to F. Sew G to H and G to Hr. Set in GH and GHr to each side of DEDF. Sew I to J and I to Jr; add K (2 times). Sew IJK to each side of center unit. Sew BC to each side of center unit. Sew ABC to top and bottom of center unit. Satin-stitch flower detail and use a stem stitch between leaves.

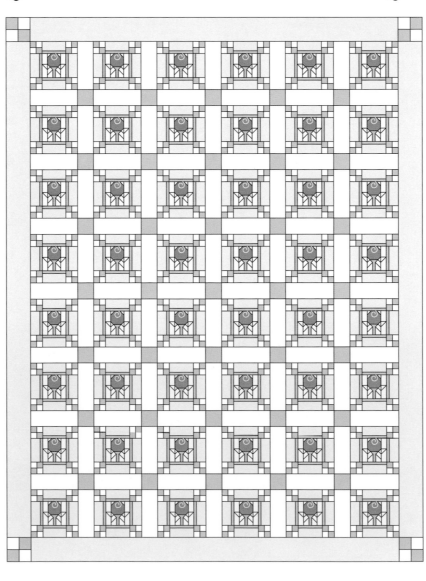

To Make A Bed Quilt

This quilt is designed to be a full-size quilt measuring 78×102 inches. We have used a 4½-inch plain border, 3-inch sashing strips, and setting squares as shown. A four-patch unit is added in each corner.

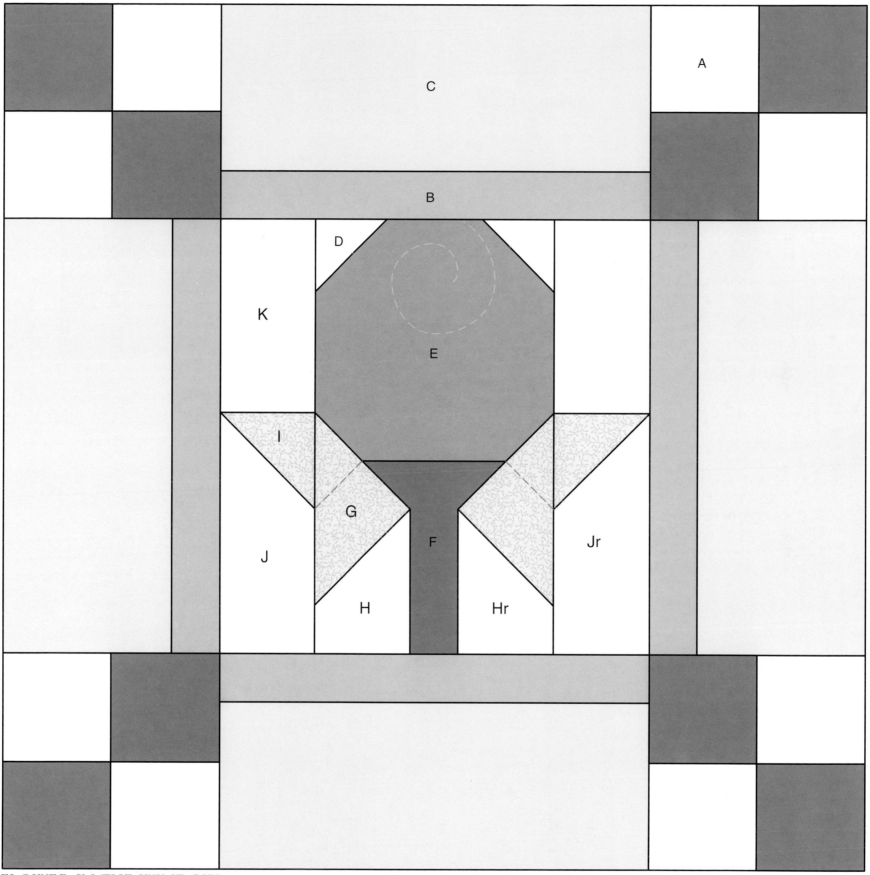

FLOWER IN THE WINDOW
FULL-SIZE BLOCK

FLORAL FANCIES ∞ POPPIES

POPPIES QUILT BLOCK

POPPIES QUILT BLOCK

How To Construct This Block

Sew A to A (8 times). Sew AA to AA (4 times). Sew B to AAAA (4 times); add C (4 times). Sew AABC to D; add AABC (2 times). Sew three D's together. Sew three rows together. Appliqué E, overlap F, and appliqué. Add G and then H. Finish around appliqué edges using blanket stitches, if desired.

For an alternate fusing method of appliqué, see page 212.

To Make A Bed Quilt

This quilt is designed to be a twin-size quilt measuring 69×93 inches. We have used a 3-inch plain border, the 3-inch Checkerboard border, page 195, 3-inch sashing strips, and setting squares as shown.

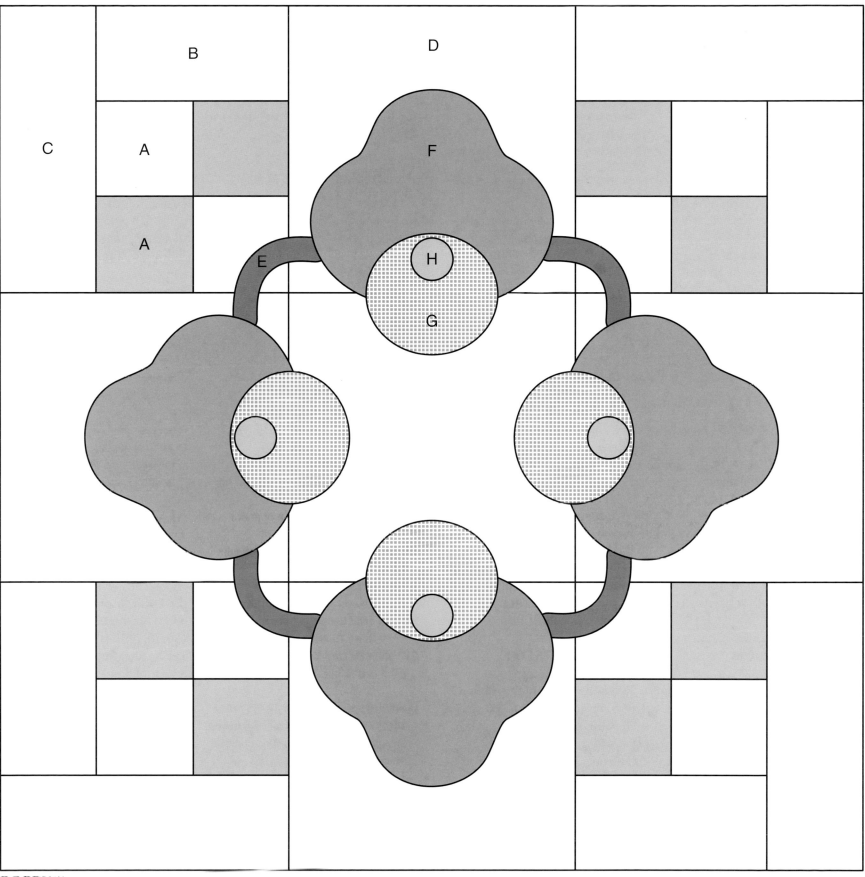

POPPIES
FULL-SIZE BLOCK

FLORAL FANCIES SAMPLER QUILT

As shown on page 5. Finished size: 59×71 inches.

MATERIALS

20—9½" completed unfinished quilt blocks in coordinating colors
Ivy border pattern, page 202; Leaf and Circle border pattern, pages 196–197
1½ yards of solid light green for sashing
30—6" squares of pastel prints
2 yards of solid white for borders
⅔ yard of solid dark green for binding and borders; 3⅔ yards for backing
65×77" quilt batting

Quantities specified are for 44/45"-wide 100% cotton fabrics. All measurements include a ¼" seam allowance unless otherwise specified.

CUT THE FABRIC

To make best use of your fabrics, cut pieces in order listed. These listings include mathematically correct border lengths. You may wish to add extra length to borders now to allow for any sewing differences later. Trim border strips to actual length before adding them to the quilt top. Cut border strips lengthwise (parallel to selvage).

From solid light green, cut:
49—3½×9½" sashing strips

From pastel squares, cut:
30—3½" squares
8 each—Pattern B and Br (Leaf and Circle border)
8—Pattern C (Ivy border)

From white, cut:
2—4½×63½" border strips
2—4½×51½" border strips

From solid dark green, cut:
7—2½×42" binding strips
4—4½" squares for border
8—Pattern B (Ivy border)
8 each—Pattern C and Cr (Leaf and Circle border)
8 each—Pattern D and Dr (Leaf and Circle border)
8 each—Pattern E and Er (Leaf and Circle border)
16—Pattern D (Ivy border)
12—Pattern F (Leaf and Circle border)

ASSEMBLE THE QUILT TOP

1. Lay out 20 blocks in a pleasing arrangement, four blocks horizontally, five rows vertically.
2. Sew one light green 3½×9½" sashing strip to the right side of each block.
3. To the left side of each block that begins each horizontal row, sew one light green 3½×9½" sashing strip.
4. Sew together each horizontal block row. Press seams toward sashing strips.
5. Sew one pastel 3½" square to the right side of 24 light green 3½×9½" sashing strips.
6. For each horizontal sashing row, you will need four sashing strips from Step 5. Join four strips horizontally (6 times). Sew a pastel 3½" square to the left side of each row.
7. Sew the rows together beginning and ending with a sashing row strip. Quilt top should measure 51½×63½" including seam allowance.

MAKE THE SIDE BORDERS

1. Referring to the photograph, *page 5*, position appliqué pieces on each white border strip. Appliqué in place with matching threads.
2. Sew one white 4½×63½" border strip to each side of the quilt top.
3. Sew one dark green 4½" square to each end of two white 4½×51½" border strips. Sew one border to top of the quilt and one to bottom.

COMPLETE THE QUILT

Layer the quilt top, batting and backing. This quilt was quilted by outlining pieces in blocks. The sashing has a curved quilting line with a circle in the center of each pastel square. One of the Leaf and Circle patterns has been quilted in the four dark green setting squares. Bind your quilt.

WILD ROSE ALBUM COVER

As shown on page 6. Finished size: 9¼×20 inches.

We used a 9¼" album cover. (This is a common size for photo albums.) Therefore, a 9½" unfinished quilt block was too small to fit without appliquéing the quilt block to another piece of fabric.

MATERIALS

Purchased photo album 9¼×9¼"
One 9½" completed unfinished Wild Rose quilt block, page 36, in coordinating colors
18×22" (fat quarter) piece of solid tan fabric for cover
18×22" (fat quarter) piece of green print fabric for lining
11×18" (fat eighth) piece of rose print fabric for piping
2 yards of narrow piping cord
4 crystal flower beads; 12 novelty beads
16 gold seed beads; ½" heart charm (from Glass Treasures Mill Hill #12080)
27" chair tie cord with a 3" tassel at each end; 10×21" piece of fleece

Quantities specified are for 44/45"-wide 100% cotton fabrics. All measurements include a ¼" seam allowance unless otherwise specified.

MEASURE THE ALBUM

Open the album flat. Measure the width and length. Add ½" to each measurement for cover size. The album used for this project has a width of 9¼" and a length of 20". Add ½" and resulting measurement is 9¾×20½".

The end flap measurement will be the width and 4" for the length plus ½" seam allowance. The album used for this project measures 9¼" wide and 4" for the length of the end flaps. Add ½" and resulting measurement is 9¾×4½".

CUT THE FABRIC

These listings are mathematically correct for the album used for this project. You may need to change measurements to allow for a different album size.

From solid tan, cut:
1—9¾×20½" rectangle for cover top

From green print, cut:
1—9¾×18½" rectangle for lining—
    (Lining is cut 2" shorter than cover top)
2—9¾×4½" rectangles for end flaps

From rose print, cut:
8×12" rectangle
    (1"-wide bias strips to total 72" in length to cover piping cord)

MAKE THE COVER TOP

The album used for this project is too wide to use a completed unfinished 9½" quilt block. If you choose to sew a block to the top of the cover fabric, you will need to add a border to make the block 9¾" square, unfinished.
1. For this project, the quilt block was appliquéd to the cover fabric before construction was begun. Center the design 1" inside three sides of the 9¾×20½" tan rectangle. See Diagram 1, *page 49*.
2. Layer album cover on top of a piece of fleece; baste. Quilt as desired. The maker of this project machine-appliquéd pieces, echo quilted around the appliqué design, and quilted straight lines 1" apart on the back side of the cover top.
3. Add decorative beads at leaf points and center of flower tops. A heart bead was added to center circle.

MAKE THE PIPING

Cover piping cord with rose print bias strip. Position piping on right side of cover top, at seam line, raw edges away from center. Stitch the piping to top. Trim piping edge to match cover top edge.

COMPLETE THE COVER

1. Cut chair tie cord in half and baste each cut half at center of outer edge of front and back of cover top, on right side of top. The cording rests on top of the piping, cut end in direction of raw edges.
2. Narrowly hem one long side of each green print 9¾×4½" end flap. Sew one end flap, right sides together, to each end of album cover. Clip seam allowance and corners. Do not turn.
3. Lay 9¾×18½" green lining, right sides together, on cover top. It will be on top of wrong side of end flaps that were sewn in Step 2. Center lining on top with equal distance from each end. Sew lining to album cover along top and bottom edges.
4. Turn lining right side out. Turn end flaps right side out.
5. Slip cover over album. Tie closed with tassel cords.

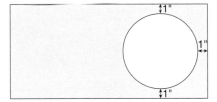

Diagram 1

POSY ROW BENCH QUILT

As shown on page 6. Finished size: 19×43 inches.

MATERIALS

Three 9½" completed unfinished Posy Row quilt blocks, page 40, in coordinating colors
1½ yards of yellow print for sashing, back, and ruffle

⅛ yard solid green
⅛ yard white print
3¼ yards of piping cord
18 decorative buttons
16×40" piece of batting

Quantities specified are for 44/45"-wide 100% cotton fabrics. All measurements include a ¼" seam allowance unless otherwise specified.

CUT THE FABRIC

To make best use of your fabrics, cut pieces in order listed.

From yellow print, cut:
20×42" rectangle
  (4½"-wide bias strips to piece a 4½×216" strip for ruffle)
1—15½×39½" rectangle for back
2—3½×39½" sashing strips
4—3½×9½" sashing strips

From solid green, cut:
4—2×21" strips

From white print, cut:
4—2×21" strips

MAKE THE QUILT TOP

Referring to the photograph on *page 6* for placement, lay out three blocks and four 3½×9½" sashing strips in a horizontal row. Sew the blocks and strips together. Add a 3½×39½" sashing strip to top of row and one to bottom of row. Your top should measure 15½×39½" including the seam allowance.

MAKE THE PIPING

1. Align the long edges of a 2×21" green strip and a 2×21" white print strip. Join the strips. Press the seam allowance toward the green strip. Repeat with the remaining strips to make four units. Join the four units lengthwise to make a strip that measures 12½×21". See Diagram A at *right*.
2. Trim left-hand edge of strip. Cutting from left-hand edge, cut

into 2"-wide segments. Sew the segments together to make a strip that measures 2×118".
3. Cover the piping cord with the green and white strip. Position the piping on the right side of the quilt top, at seam line, raw edges away from the center. Stitch piping to the top. Trim the piping edge to match quilt top edge.

MAKE THE RUFFLE

Fold a 4½×216" yellow bias strip in half lengthwise with the wrong sides together and press. Fold the ruffle in half and mark the halfway point. Gather raw edges. Place the halfway mark at the center top of the quilt front, on top of the piping. Overlap end edges of ruffle at the center of the bottom of the quilt top. Adjust the gathers evenly around the top and stitch.

ASSEMBLE THE QUILT

Layer the quilt top and quilt back, right sides together, with batting underneath.
Note: It is helpful to pin ruffle very tightly to quilt front, out of seam line, to avoid catching ruffle in stitching.
1. Stitch the front to the back, leaving an opening for turning. Trim the corners and seams. Turn right side out. Stitch the opening closed and quilt as desired.
2. Add decorative buttons to each flower center and at the corners of the blocks.

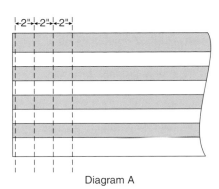

Diagram A

APPLIQUÉ PANSY PILLOW

As shown on page 7. Finished size: 14×14 inches, not including ruffle.

MATERIALS

One 9½" completed unfinished Appliqué Pansy quilt block, page 20, in coordinating colors
15" square of pink print
1¼ yards of purple print
2 yards of piping cord; 4 yards of flat lace
15" square of batting
14" pillow form; embroidery floss

All seam allowances are ¼" wide.

CUT THE FABRIC

From purple print, cut:
12×18" rectangle
  (1½"-wide bias strips to total 60" in length to cover piping cord)
1—14½" square for backing
4—6½×42" strips, piecing to make a total of 4 yards for ruffle

PREPARE THE BLOCK

Center the pansy design on a 15" square of pink print. Following directions for the construction, *page 20*, machine satin-stitch around the design with matching thread. Add petal lines using embroidery floss. Add French knots to the center of the pansy with embroidery floss. Layer the block and batting. Baste. Quilt as desired. Trim the block and batting to measure 14½".

ASSEMBLE THE PILLOW

1. Cover the piping cord with a bias strip. Position the piping on the right side of the pillow front, at the seam line with raw edges together. Stitch the piping to the pillow. Trim piping raw edge to match the pillow edges.
2. Fold ruffle strip lengthwise, wrong sides together, and press. Place the bottom edge of lace at the fold line. Stitch lace in place around outside edge of ruffle.

3. Fold the ruffle in half and then fold it again into quarters. Mark each fold and gather the ruffle, placing the marked quarter at each side center on the front of the pillow front, on top of the piping. Overlap the end edges of the ruffle and stitch. Place the pillow back on top of the ruffle and stitch the front to the back, leaving an opening for turning.

Note: It is helpful to pin the ruffle very tightly to the pillow front, out of the way of the seam line, when sewing the pillow front to the pillow back, to avoid catching the ruffle in the stitching.

4. Trim the corners and turn right side out. Insert the pillow form. Stitch the opening closed.

OHIO ROSE TABLE QUILT

As shown on page 7. Finished size: 15×15 inches, not including binding.

MATERIALS
One 9½" completed unfinished Ohio Rose quilt block, page 28, in coordinating colors
½ yard of white print for border and backing
⅛ yard of blue print
⅛ yard of green print
⅛ yard of pink print
⅛ yard of yellow print
16" square of batting
Optional—white rayon twist thread

All seam allowances are ¼" wide.

CUT THE FABRIC
From white print, cut:
1—16" backing square
8—Pattern C (To the Point border, page 199)
8—Pattern Cr (To the Point border)
16—Pattern E (To the Point border)

From blue print, cut:
8—Pattern D (To the Point border)

From green print, cut:
16—Pattern A (To the Point border)

From pink print, cut:
16—Pattern B (To the Point border)

From yellow print, cut:
2—2×42" strips for binding

ASSEMBLE THE BORDER
Assemble the border pieces into To the Point border as instructed on *page 199*. Make a total of four complete borders and a total of four complete four-patch corner units.

ADD THE BORDERS
To two opposite sides of the quilt center, sew a border strip. To the remaining two border strips, sew a four-patch setting square to each end. Sew one strip to the top of the quilt and one to the bottom of the quilt.

COMPLETE THE QUILT
Layer the top, batting, and backing. Baste and quilt as desired. The quilt-maker machine-quilted with outline stitching using white rayon twist thread. Bind your quilt.

SPRING BLOOM TABLE RUNNER

As shown on page 7. Finished size: 15×46¾ inches.

MATERIALS
Two 9½" completed unfinished Spring Bloom quilt blocks, page 34, in coordinating colors
¾ yard of cream print fabric
¼ yard of rose print fabric
1⅜ yards of backing fabric
19×50" piece of batting

Quantities specified are for 44/45"-wide 100% cotton fabrics. All of the measurements include a ¼" seam allowance unless otherwise specified in the instructions.

CUT THE FABRIC
From cream print, cut:
1—14" square, cutting it diagonally twice in an X for a total of four setting triangles
1—9½" square for center block
12—2×9½" border strips

From rose print, cut:
3—2×42" binding strips
3—2⅜" squares, cutting each in half diagonally for a total of six triangles
4—2" squares

From backing fabric, cut:
1—18×49" rectangle

ASSEMBLE THE TABLE RUNNER
1. Sew one cream print 2×9½" border strip to the left side of each of the three blocks. Add one to the opposite side of the blocks.
2. Sew one 2" square to one end of a 2×9½" border strip. To the opposite end of the border strip, sew one rose print triangle. Repeat this for a total of four border strips. Sew one completed border strip to each remaining side of the two Spring Bloom blocks. Refer to Diagram 1 which is shown at *right* for the correct placement.
3. To the remaining two 2×9½" border strips, add one rose print triangle on one end.
4. Sew one border strip from Step 3 to one cream print setting triangle. Refer to Diagram 1 again for the correct placement. Repeat for a second setting triangle.
5. Referring to the Diagram, lay out the blocks and setting triangles. Sew the setting triangles to each block. Press the seams toward the setting triangles.
6. Sew the pieces together in diagonal rows as shown.

COMPLETE THE TABLE RUNNER
Layer the table runner, batting, and backing. Quilt as desired. The maker machine-quilted in the ditch. Finish the Spring Bloom Table Runner with binding.

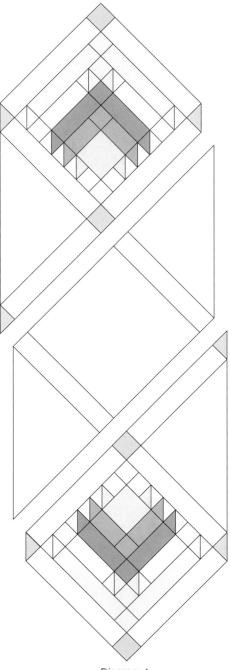

Diagram 1

COUNTRY CLASSICS

Full of homespun charm, our Country Classics Sampler Quilt
showcases all twenty blocks in this chapter. Instructions for this quilt are on *page 94*.
For projects to make with some of the blocks in this chapter, turn the page.

☞ COUNTRY CLASSICS ☜

PROJECTS YOU CAN MAKE

On these two pages you'll find some clever ways to use your 9-inch Country blocks. You'll find Christmas stockings to sew, an antique quilt to recreate, a great jacket to wear, a tote bag to carry, and a valance full of hugs and kisses. Whatever you choose to piece and quilt, we're sure our projects will please you. Remember, the blocks can be used in so many ways—we know you'll have fun personalizing your own quilting projects with your favorite 9-inch blocks. Instructions for all of the projects you see here start on *page 94.*

COUNTRY CHRISTMAS STOCKINGS

HEARTS AND GIZZARDS TOTE BAG

PINWHEEL JACKET

ANTIQUE COUNTRY CORNERS QUILT

HUGS AND KISSES VALANCE

53

STARS AND HEARTS QUILT BLOCK

STARS AND HEARTS QUILT BLOCK

How To Construct This Block

Sew B to A (4 times). Sew B to adjacent edge of each AB unit. Sew one BAB unit to one side of C then sew second BAB unit to opposite side of C to form center section. Sew D to one end of each of the remaining two BAB units. Sew second D to opposite ends of BAB units for side sections. Sew one side section to center section, then sew second side section to opposite side of center section. Sew E to one side of block, then sew E to opposite side. Sew F pieces to top and bottom edges of block. Appliqué G (heart pieces) onto A pieces, overlapping onto E and F pieces.

For an alternate fusing method of appliqué, see page 212.

To Make A Bed Quilt

This quilt is designed to be a twin-size quilt measuring 70×95 inches. We have used a 3-inch plain border as shown with corner setting squares appliquéd with a single heart. The blocks are turned on point and alternate with plain setting blocks.

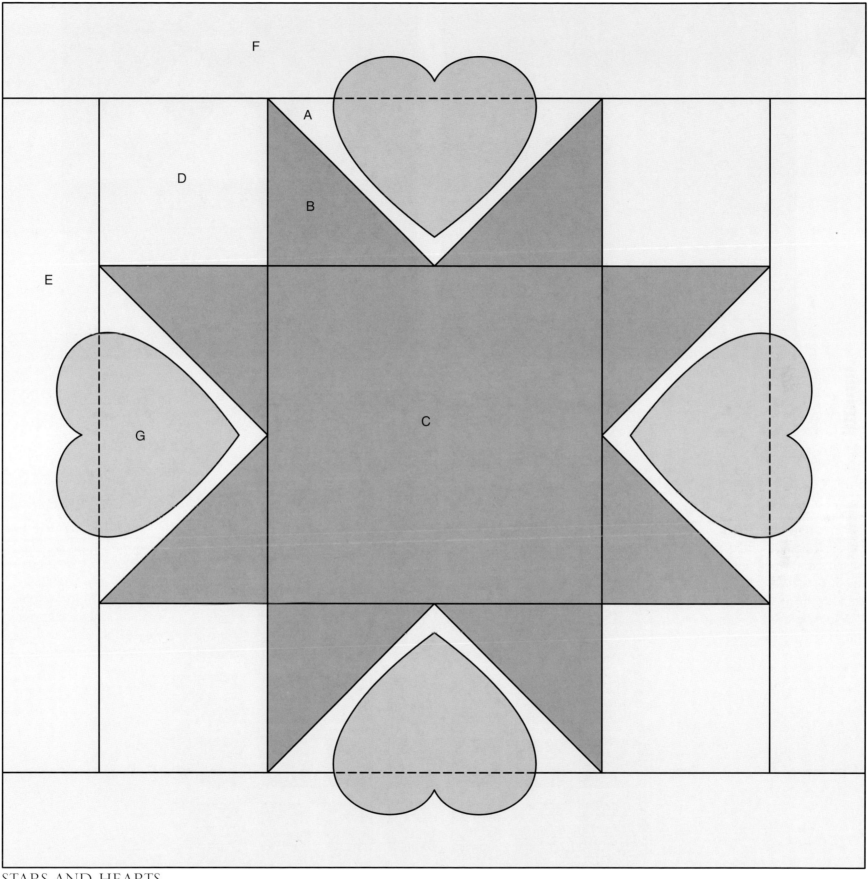

STARS AND HEARTS
FULL-SIZE BLOCK

COUNTRY CLASSICS ⟡ *BASKET VARIATION*

BASKET VARIATION QUILT BLOCK

BASKET VARIATION QUILT BLOCK

How To Construct This Block

Sew A to A (5 times). Sew three AA units together; add A. Sew two AA units together; add A. Sew C to 2AA,A. Sew C2AA,A to 3AA,A to make Unit 1. Sew B to each side of Unit 1. Sew E to each side of D. Sew EDE to Unit 1. Sew F to A (2 times). Sew G to FA (2 times). Sew GFA to A; add GFA. Sew to Unit 1.

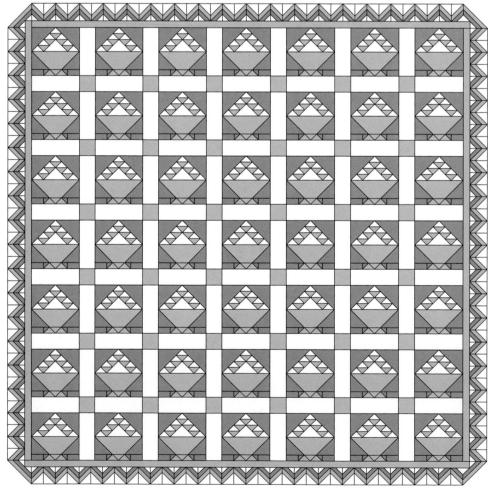

To Make A Bed Quilt

This quilt is designed to be a queen-size square quilt measuring 90×90 inches. We have used the 4½-inch Chevron border, page 201, 3-inch sashing strips, and setting squares as shown.

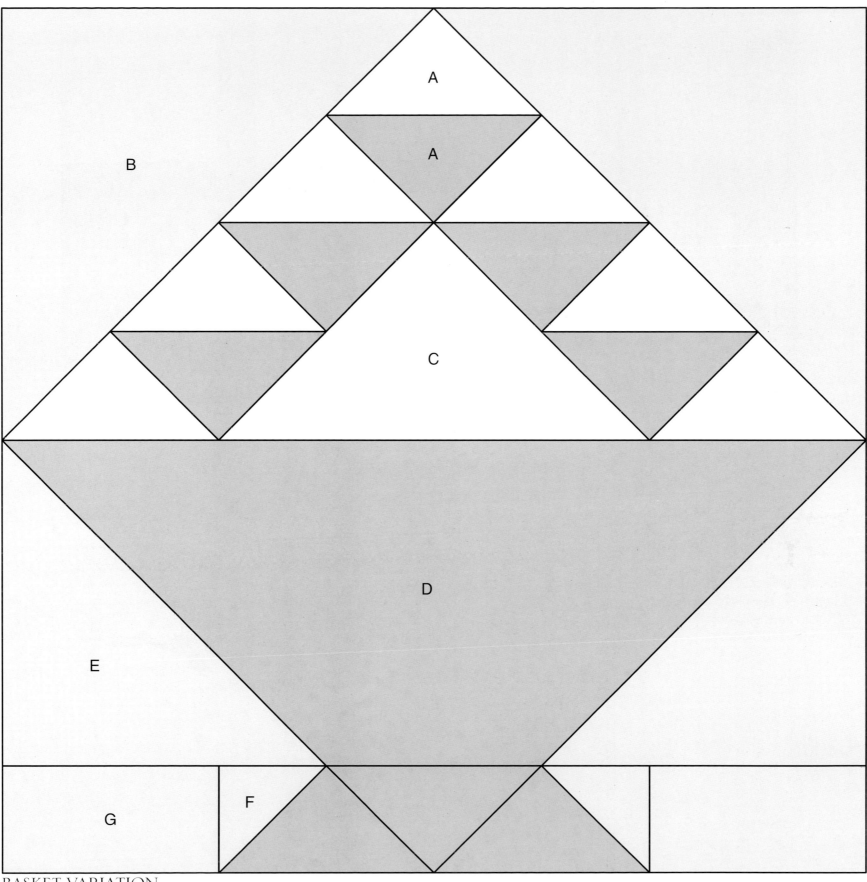

BASKET VARIATION
FULL-SIZE BLOCK

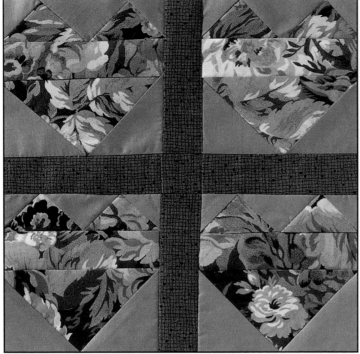

FOUR HEARTS QUILT BLOCK

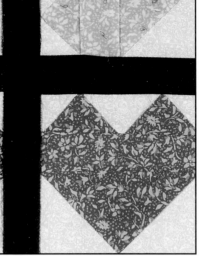

FOUR HEARTS QUILT BLOCK

How To Construct This Block

Sew A to B (8 times). Sew AB to A; add AB (4 times). Sew C to ABAAB (4 times). Sew E to D (4 times); add E (4 times). Sew EDE to ABAABC (4 times) to make heart. Sew G to edge of two hearts (2 times). Sew G to F; add G. Sew GFG between two sets of hearts. Rotate any heart unit 90 degrees as desired.

To Make A Bed Quilt

This quilt is designed to be a twin-size quilt measuring 72×94 inches. We have used a 2-inch plain border, a 10-inch plain border, a 3-inch plain border, and 2-inch sashing strips as shown. We suggest quilting the 10-inch plain border with heart motifs.

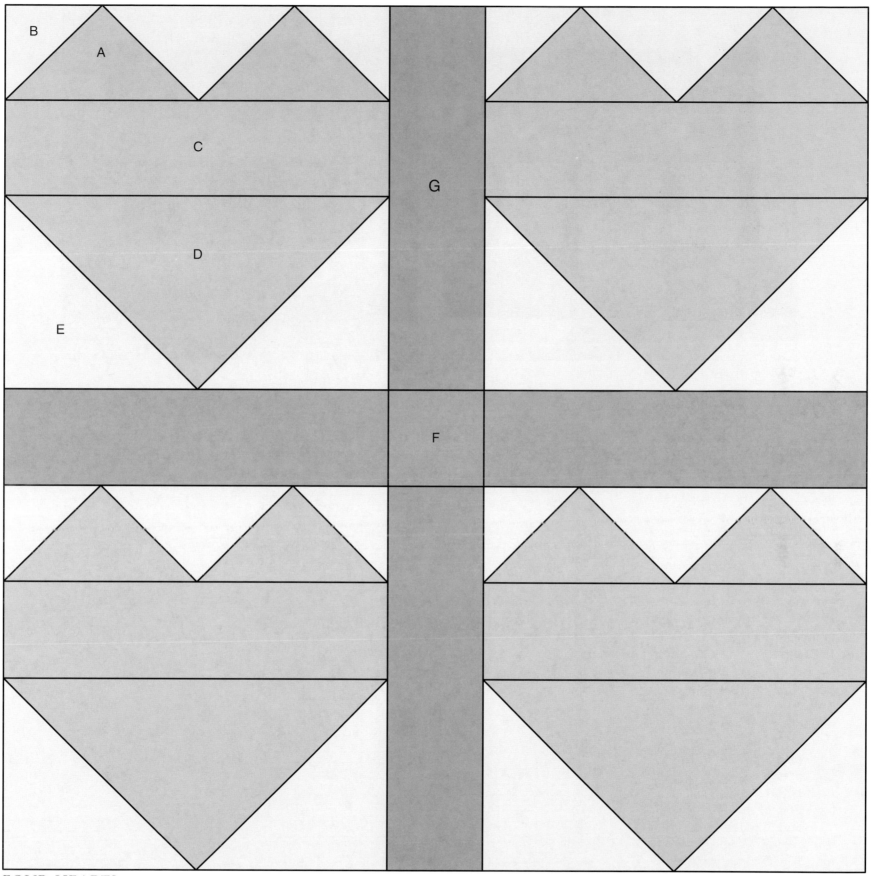

FOUR HEARTS
FULL-SIZE BLOCK

COUNTRY HOUSE QUILT BLOCK

COUNTRY HOUSE QUILT BLOCK

How To Construct This Block

Sew B to C. Sew B to Cr. Sew BC and BCr units to each diagonal edge of A. Sew D to bottom edge of A. Sew F to E (2 times). Sew G to each side of two EF units. Sew an EFG unit to one edge of H, then sew remaining EFG unit to the opposite side of H. Sew this EFGH unit to D edge of first unit to form house unit. Sew B to B (2 times). Sew BB unit to I (2 times). Sew one BBI unit to one edge of house unit, then sew remaining BBI unit to opposite edge. Sew K to J, then sew another K to the opposite edge of J. Sew this strip to bottom of house unit. Sew B to each of the two diagonal edges of L. Sew M to left edge of BLB and N to right edge. Sew this unit to KJK edge of house unit. Sew O to top edge of house to complete the block.

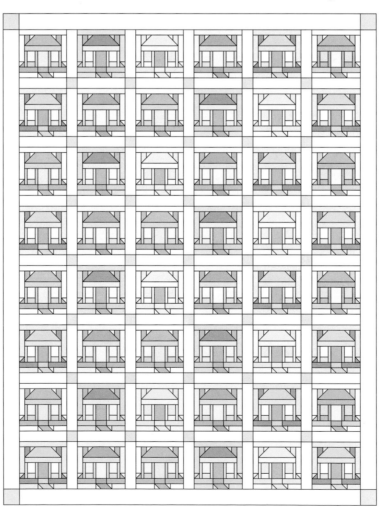

To Make A Bed Quilt

This quilt is designed to be a twin-size quilt measuring 70×92 inches. We have used a 3-inch plain border, 2-inch sashing strips, and setting squares as shown.

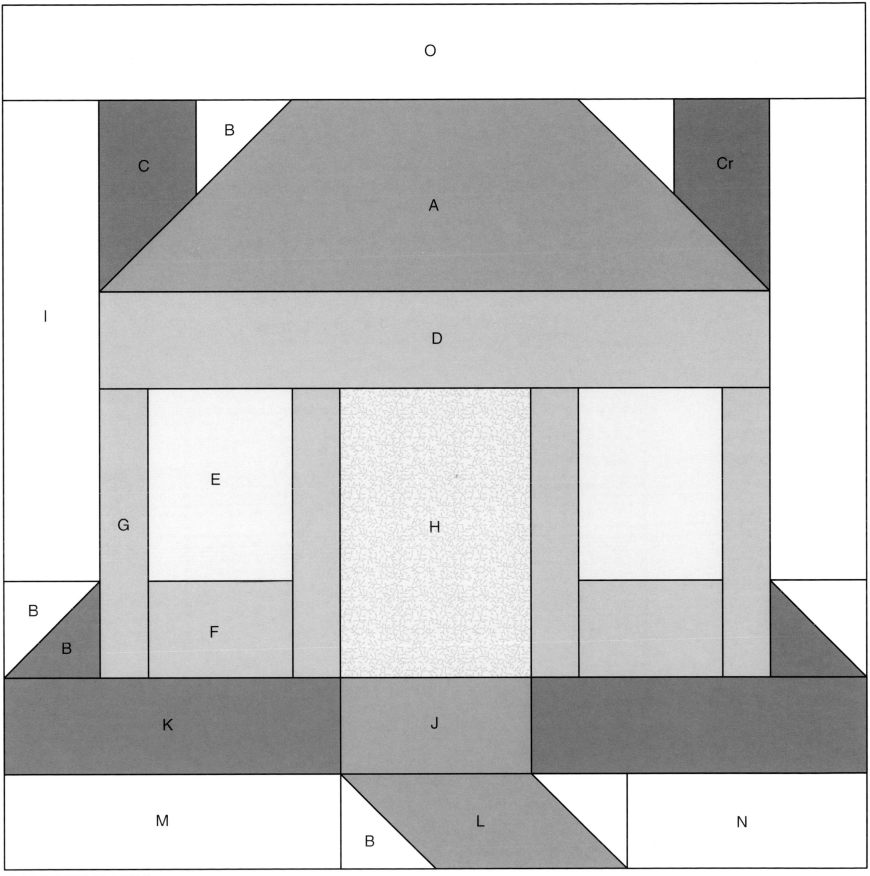

COUNTRY HOUSE
FULL-SIZE BLOCK

JACOB'S LADDER VARIATION QUILT BLOCK

JACOB'S LADDER VARIATION QUILT BLOCK

How To Construct This Block

Make AA unit (6 times). Make BBB unit (9 times); combine three BBB units to make nine-patch (3 times). Sew two AA units with B unit on one end (2 times) for top and bottom strips. Sew two AA units with B unit in the center for center strip. Sew top and bottom strips to center strip.

To Make A Bed Quilt

This quilt is designed to be a queen-size square quilt measuring 91×91 inches. We have used a 2-inch plain border, the 3-inch Checkerboard border, page 195, 3-inch sashing strips, and setting squares as shown.

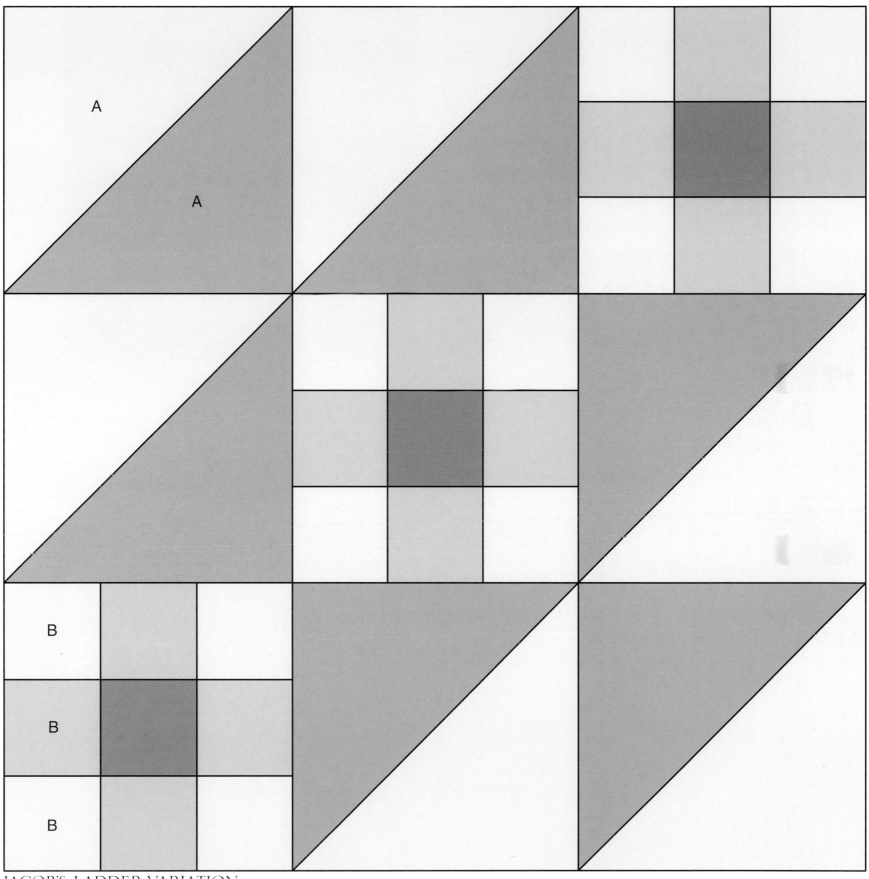

JACOB'S LADDER VARIATION
Full-Size Block

MAPLE LEAF QUILT BLOCK

MAPLE LEAF QUILT BLOCK

How To Construct This Block

Sew B to B (2 times). Sew C to C (4 times). Sew CC to CC (2 times). Sew (2)CC to D (2 times). Sew F to E; add F. Row 1—Sew A to CCD; add BB. Row 2—Sew CCD to A; add A. Row 3—Sew BB to A; add FEF. Sew rows together.

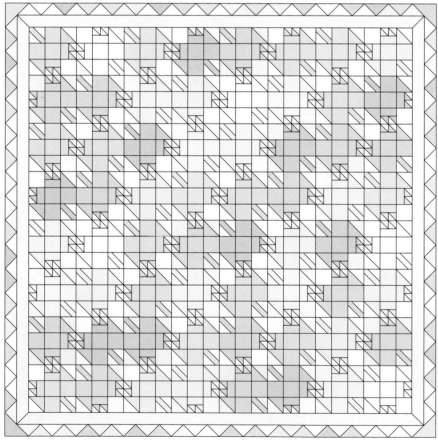

To Make A Bed Quilt

This quilt is designed to be a full-size square quilt measuring 81×81 inches. We have used the 4½-inch Sawtooth border, page 204, as shown and turned every other block to create alternating diagonal rows.

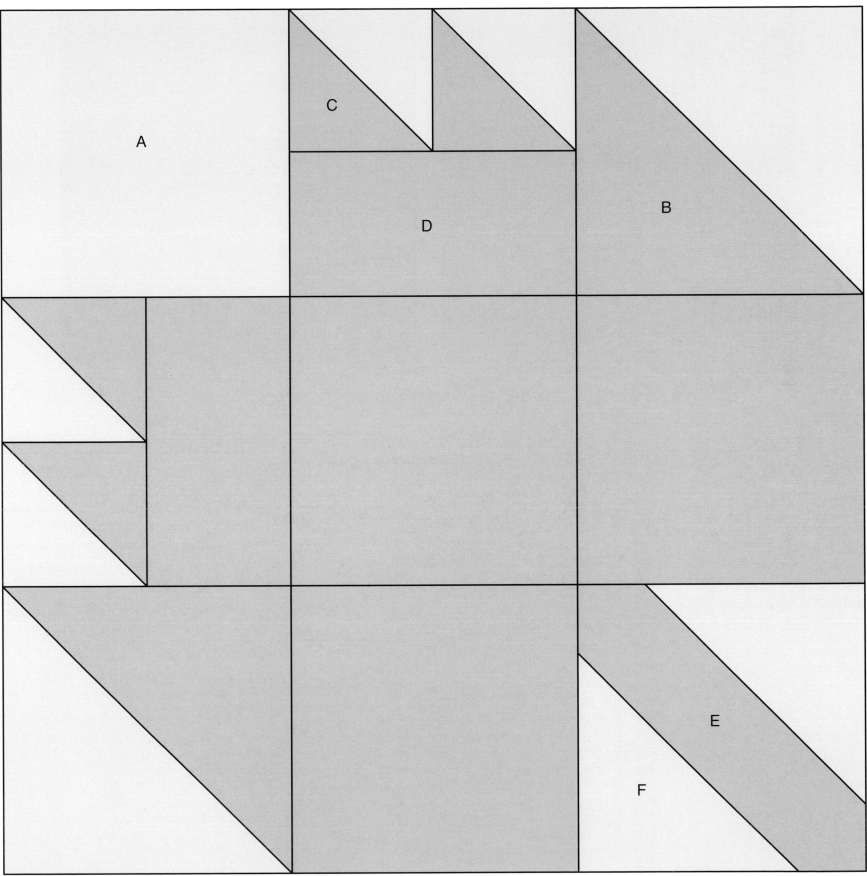

MAPLE LEAF
FULL-SIZE BLOCK

INS AND OUTS QUILT BLOCK

INS AND OUTS QUILT BLOCK

How To Construct This Block

Sew A to A (8 times). Sew AA to AA (4 times). Sew three B strips together (4 times). Sew AAAA unit to BBB unit (2 times). Sew a second AA unit to opposite edges of BBB units to form side strips. Sew a BBB unit to C, then sew a second BBB unit to opposite side of C for center strip. Sew a side strip to center strip. Sew remaining side strip to opposite side of center strip to complete block.

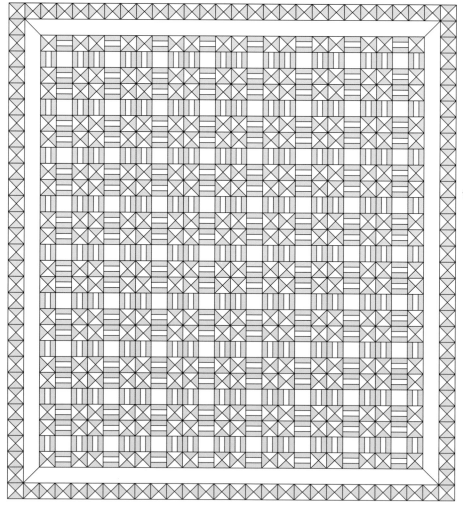

To Make A Bed Quilt

This quilt is designed to be a full-size quilt measuring 84×93 inches. We have used a 3-inch plain border and the 3-inch Pie Crust border, page 195, as shown.

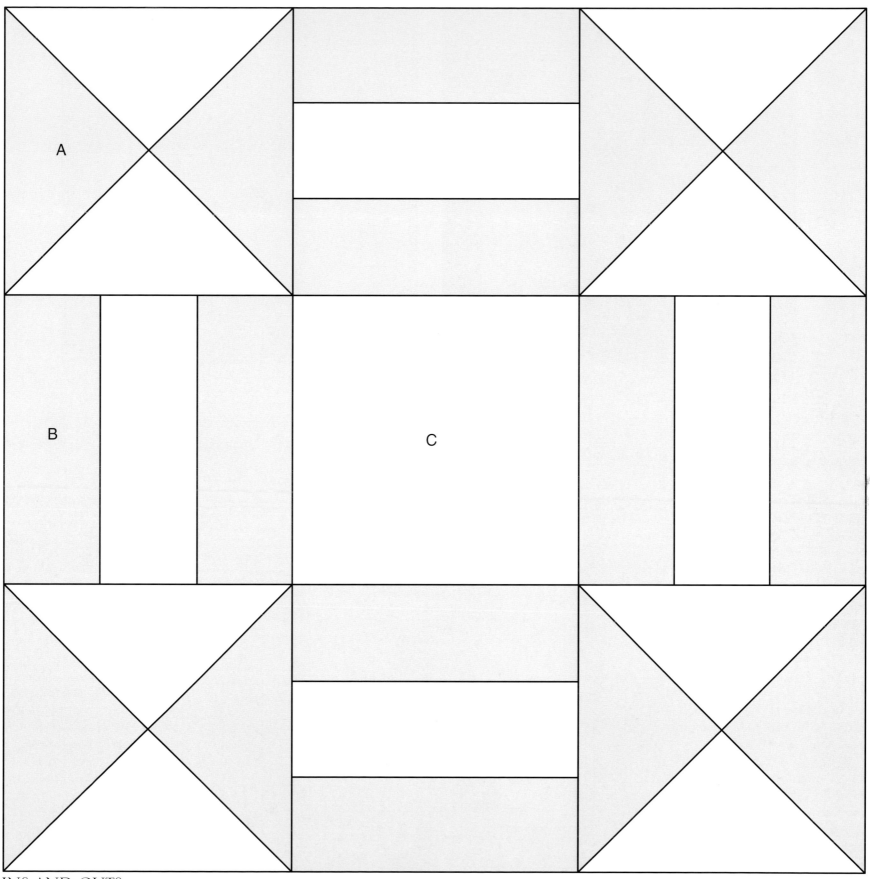

INS AND OUTS
FULL-SIZE BLOCK

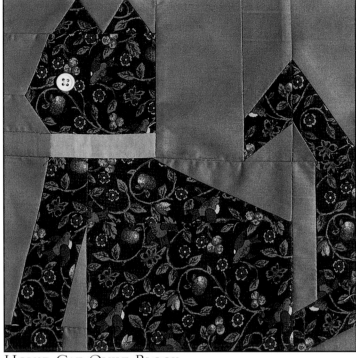

HOUSE CAT QUILT BLOCK

HOUSE CAT QUILT BLOCK

How To Construct This Block

Sew A to A and sew a third A to B. Sew these two units together along A edges. Sew C to end of this strip attaching to A edge. Sew E to D, ending stitching ¼" from end that will form nose point of D. Sew F to D, again ending stitching ¼" from end forming nose point. Sew E and F together. Sew first strip with ears to top of EFD unit. Sew G to H, then sew this strip to bottom of EFD unit. Sew O to right edge of this unit. Sew I to J, then sew M to opposite side of J. Sew K to L, then sew N to opposite side of L. Sew IJM unit to KLN unit, then sew this unit to O edge of first (head) unit. Sew R to P, then sew Q to opposite side of P. Sew S to T, then sew ST unit to bottom of RPQ unit. Sew U to V, then sew UV unit to W. Sew X to Y, then sew XY unit to Z. Sew AA to opposite side of Z. Sew RPQ (leg) unit to left edge of the UVW unit. Sew XYZAA (tail) unit to right edge of UVW unit. Sew this completed unit to bottom of head unit to complete block. Sew on button eye if desired.

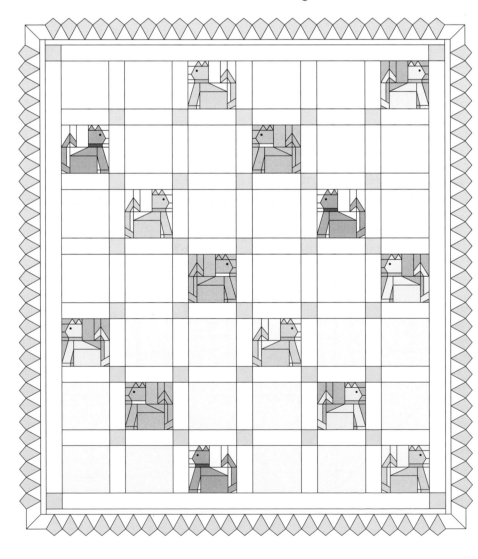

To Make A Bed Quilt

This quilt is designed to be a full-size quilt measuring 85×97 inches. We have used a 3-inch plain border, the 5-inch Sawtooth and Diamond border, page 211, 3-inch sashing strips, and setting squares as shown. We have used 9-inch setting blocks between the blocks. Reverse templates as needed to face cat in the opposite direction.

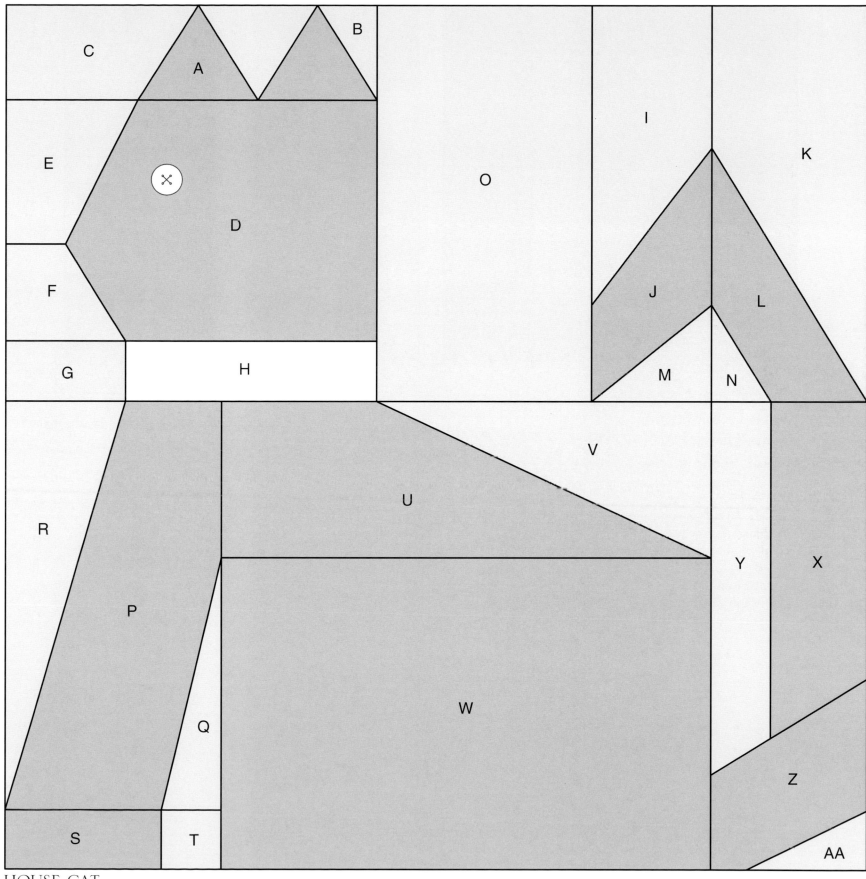

HOUSE CAT
FULL-SIZE BLOCK

COUNTRY PINWHEEL QUILT BLOCK

COUNTRY PINWHEEL QUILT BLOCK

How To Construct This Block

Use template or cut 3⅛"
squares in half diagonally to
equal two A triangles. Cut a
total of 16 dark A triangles and
16 light A triangles. Sew one
light A to one dark A together
along long edges. Make a total
of 16 AA units. Join the AA
units together into two rows,
then add the next two rows to
make block.

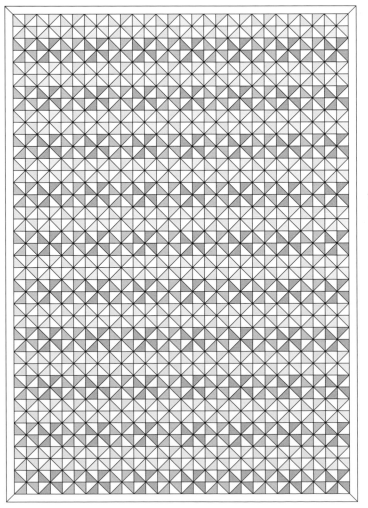

To Make A Bed Quilt

*This quilt is designed
to be a twin-size quilt
measuring 66×93 inches.
We have used a 1½-inch
plain border
as shown.*

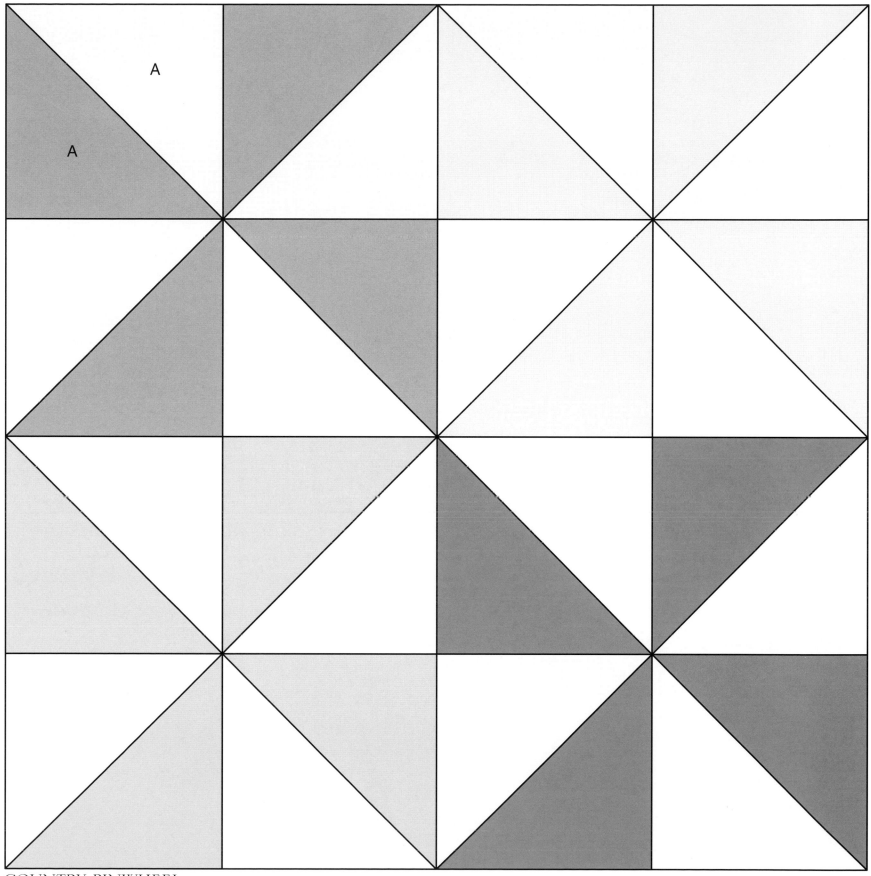

COUNTRY PINWHEEL
FULL-SIZE BLOCK

COUNTRY DECISION QUILT BLOCK

COUNTRY DECISION QUILT BLOCK

How To Construct This Block

Lay out all pieces in correct position, watching placement carefully. Sew A to B (4 times). Sew AB to C (4 times). Sew C to C (4 times). Sew CC to F (4 times). Sew CCF to G (4 times). Sew two C's to H (8 times). Sew CCFG to CCH (4 times) to make Unit. Sew CCH to I (4 times). Sew CCHI to Unit (4 times). Sew a Unit to ABC (2 times); add a Unit (2 times). Sew ABC to F; add ABC. Sew ABCFABC to connect the Units.

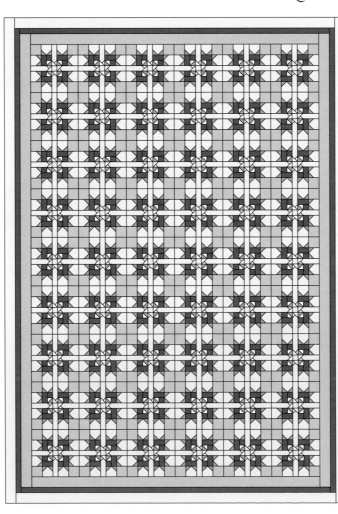

To Make A Bed Quilt

This quilt is designed to be a twin-size quilt measuring 64×91 inches. We have used 2-, 1-, and 2-inch plain borders as shown.

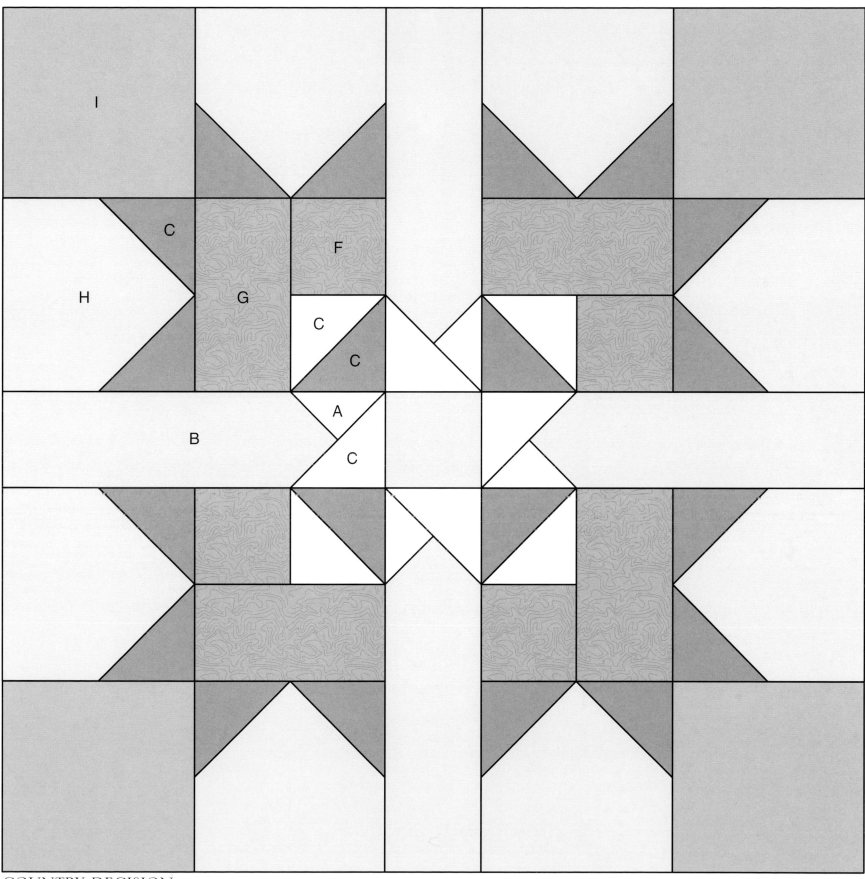

COUNTRY DECISION
FULL-SIZE BLOCK

RECTANGLE HEART QUILT BLOCK

RECTANGLE HEART QUILT BLOCK

How To Construct This Block

Sew C to D. Sew Cr to D; add F and Fr. Sew CDF and CrDFr units together; set in I. Sew A to B (2 times). Sew AB to center unit. Sew AB to A. Sew ABA to center unit. Sew E to side of ABA. Sew H to side of AB. Sew G (2 times) to center, add J (2 times). Sew K to center (2 times). Sew L to each side of center. Sew M to L; add M (2 times). Sew MLM to top and bottom of center.

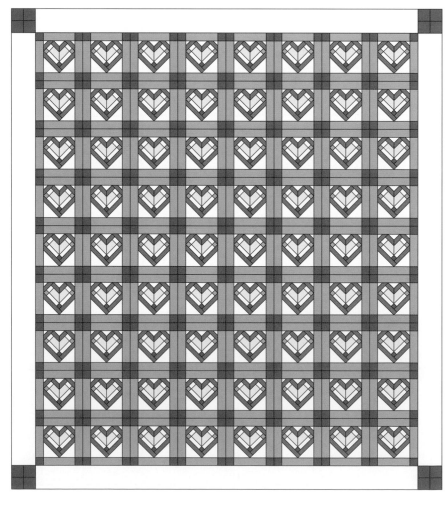

To Make A Bed Quilt

This quilt is designed to be a full-size quilt measuring 81×90 inches. We have used a 4½-inch plain border as shown with four-patch setting squares in the corners of the border.

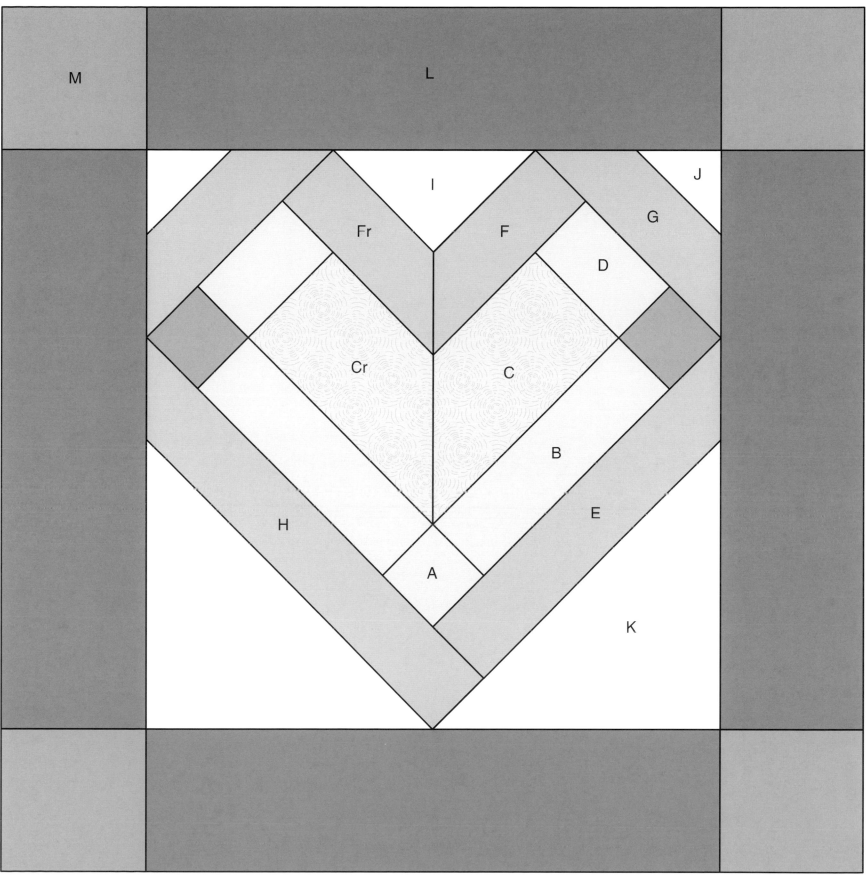

RECTANGLE HEART
FULL-SIZE BLOCK

PATCHES QUILT BLOCK

PATCHES QUILT BLOCK

How To Construct This Block

Sew B to each side of A. Sew B to top and bottom of A. Sew C to top and bottom of AB. Sew C to each side of AB. Sew D to D (8 times). Sew two DD units together (4 times). Sew another D to the D strip so that each of four strips has five D pieces sewn together. Sew a D strip to each side of previously completed block, sewing to two opposite sides first, then to remaining two sides. Sew E to each corner of block.

To Make A Bed Quilt

This quilt is designed to be a twin-size quilt measuring 72×81 inches. We have used the 4½-inch Sawtooth border, page 204, as shown.

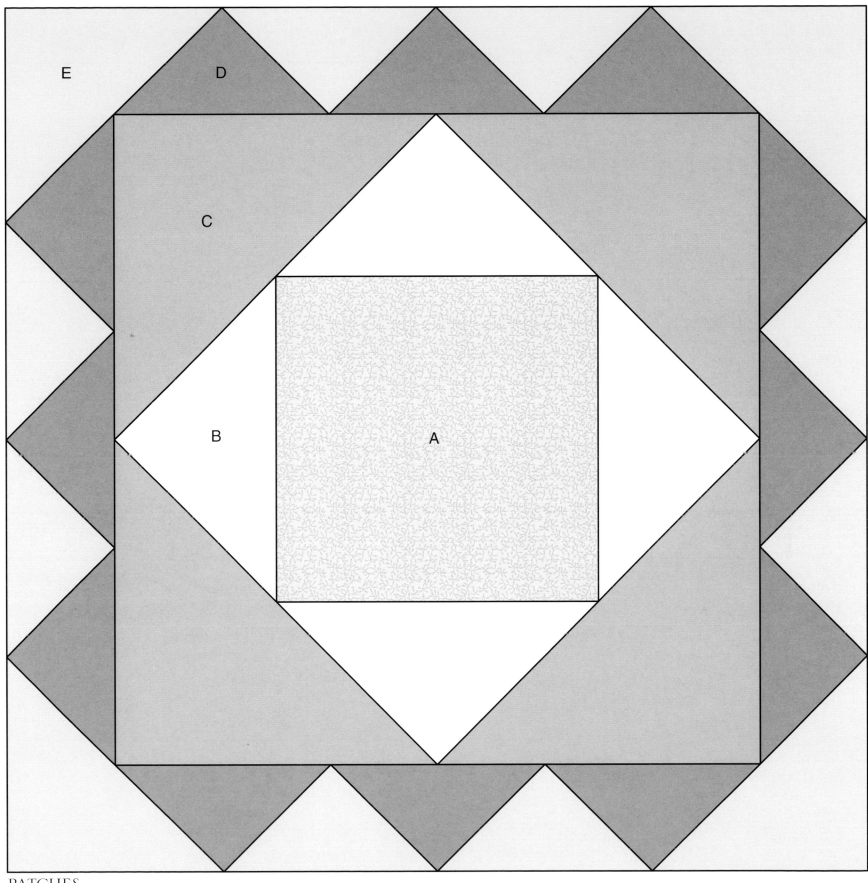

PATCHES
FULL-SIZE BLOCK

INDIAN CORN QUILT BLOCK

INDIAN CORN QUILT BLOCK

How To Construct This Block

Lay out all pieces according to color and position. Sew A to A (13 times). Row 1—Sew horizontally B, AA, C, AA, B, C, and AA. Row 2—Sew horizontally three B's, AA, C, AA, B, and AA. Row 3—Sew four B's and A. Row 4—Sew AA, four B's, and A. Sew Row 3 to Row 4. Add D. Sew vertically B to AA. Add to left side of F. Sew BAAF to right side of Rows 3 and 4. Sew vertically AA to B. Add to left side of C. Add D. Row 5—Sew horizontally A, four B's, and A. Row 6—Sew horizontally A, two B's, AA, B, and A. Sew Row 5 to Row 6. Add D to right side of Rows 5 and 6. Sew AABCD to the left side of Rows 5 and 6. Sew G to G. Vertically sew C to AA. Vertically sew AA, B, and AA. Join the two units. Add E, GG, and G. Horizontally sew A to C. Sew AC to D. Add ACD to right side of G.

To Make A Bed Quilt

This quilt is designed to be a twin-size quilt measuring 72×93 inches. We have used a 3-inch plain border, the 3-inch Checkerboard border, page 195, and 3-inch sashing strips as shown.

INDIAN CORN
Full-Size Block

HEARTS AND GIZZARDS QUILT BLOCK

HEARTS AND GIZZARDS QUILT BLOCK

How To Construct This Block

Cut four A triangles from one color. Cut four A triangles from a second color. Appliqué two matching B's onto opposite color A (8 times). Sew two A (opposite color) triangles to make a square (4 times). Sew two squares together (2 times). Sew two rectangles together to make a block.

To Make A Bed Quilt

This quilt is designed to be a twin-size quilt measuring 66×75 inches. We have used two 3-inch plain borders as shown.

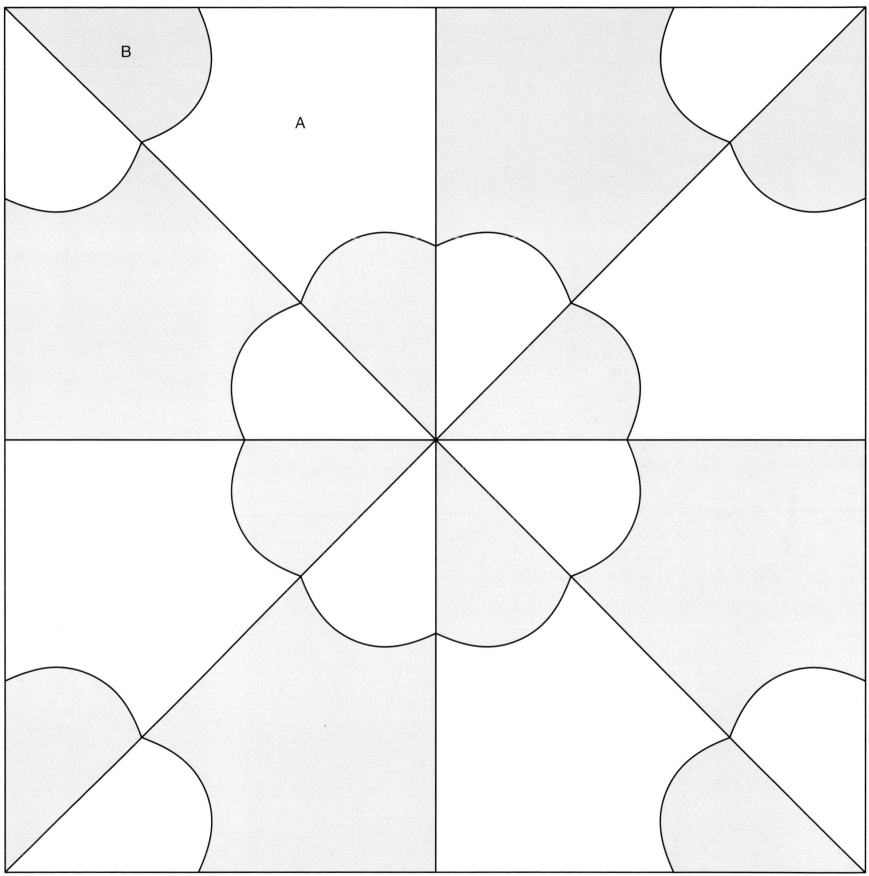

HEARTS AND GIZZARDS
Full-Size Block

AMISH CROSS QUILT BLOCK

AMISH CROSS QUILT BLOCK

How To Construct This Block

Make BB unit (8 times). Sew A piece to BB unit (4 times). Sew BB unit to A piece (4 times). Sew AB units to BA units (4 times) forming corner AB squares. Join two AB squares together with C piece in between (2 times) to form top and bottom rows. Sew two C pieces with D square in between for the center row. Sew top and bottom rows together with the center row in between.

To Make A Bed Quilt

This quilt is designed to be a twin-size quilt measuring 63×90 inches. We have used a 4½-inch plain border and setting squares as shown.

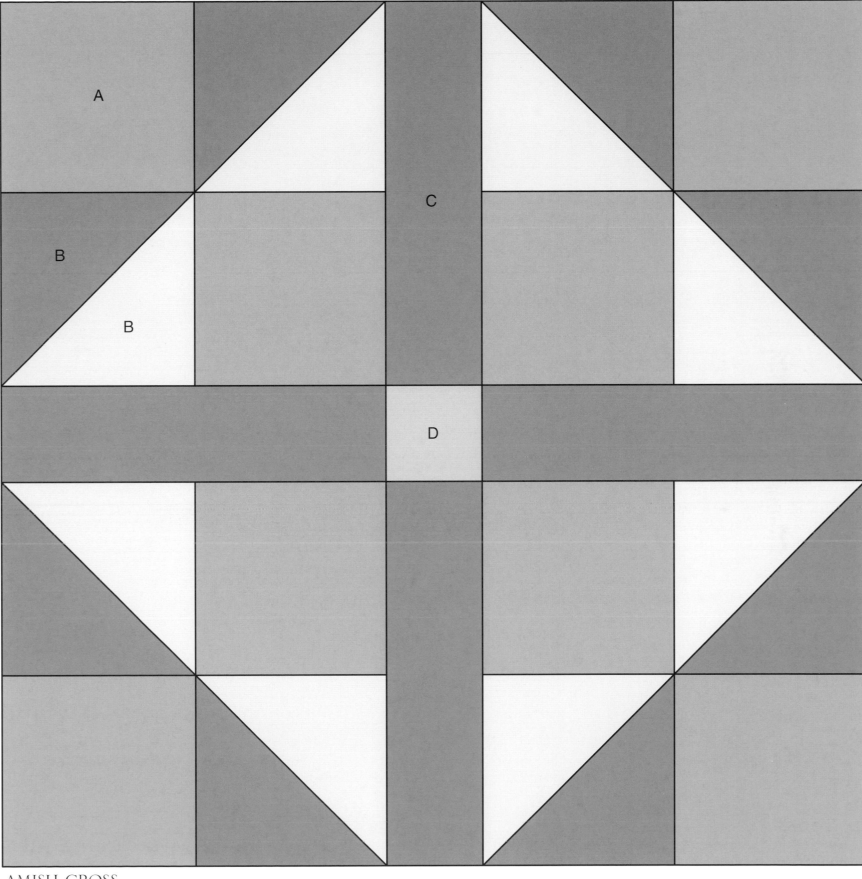

AMISH CROSS
FULL-SIZE BLOCK

HUGS AND KISSES QUILT BLOCK—X

HUGS AND KISSES QUILT BLOCK—O

How To Construct This Block

Sew A pieces together to make nine-patch center. Sew BB unit (4 times). Sew the A pieces together to make four-patch (4 times). Sew two A four-patch units together with BB unit in between (2 times). Sew two BB units together with A nine-patch in between. Sew two ABA rows together with BAB row in between. Sew C piece to two opposite sides of assembled AB block. Sew ACA unit (2 times). Sew ACA strips to top and bottom of assembled ABC block.

Note: Depending on color arrangement, the block will appear to either resemble an "O" or "X" motif—thus a hug or a kiss.

To Make A Bed Quilt

This quilt is designed to be a full-size quilt measuring 81×99 inches. We have used two 4½-inch plain borders and setting squares as shown.

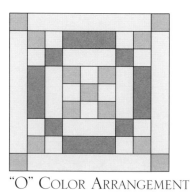

"O" COLOR ARRANGEMENT

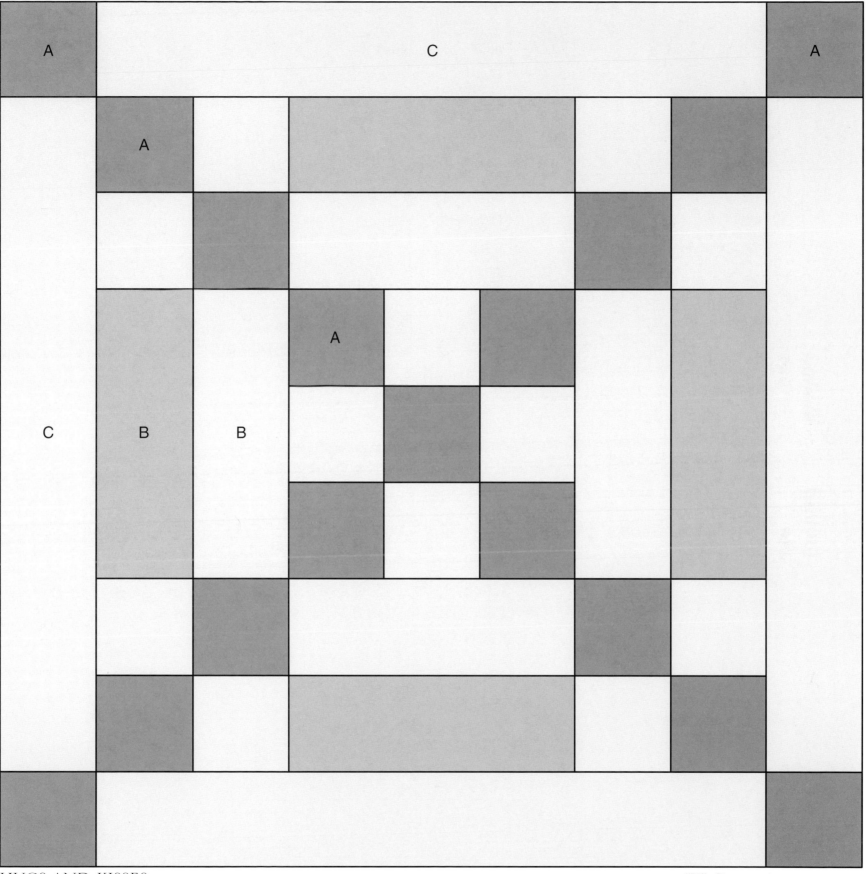

HUGS AND KISSES
FULL-SIZE BLOCK

"X" COLOR ARRANGEMENT

TREES IN A CORNER QUILT BLOCK

TREES IN A CORNER QUILT BLOCK

How To Construct This Block

Sew A to A (4 times). Sew A to AA; add A (4 times). Sew C to B; add C (4 times). Add A unit to CBC to make a tree (4 times). Sew E to D; add E (4 times). Sew one tree unit to EDE; add one tree unit (2 times). Sew EDE to F; add EDE for center row. Sew three rows together.

To Make A Bed Quilt

This quilt is designed to be a twin-size quilt measuring 69×87 inches. We have used a 4½-inch plain border and the 3-inch To the Point border, page 199, as shown.

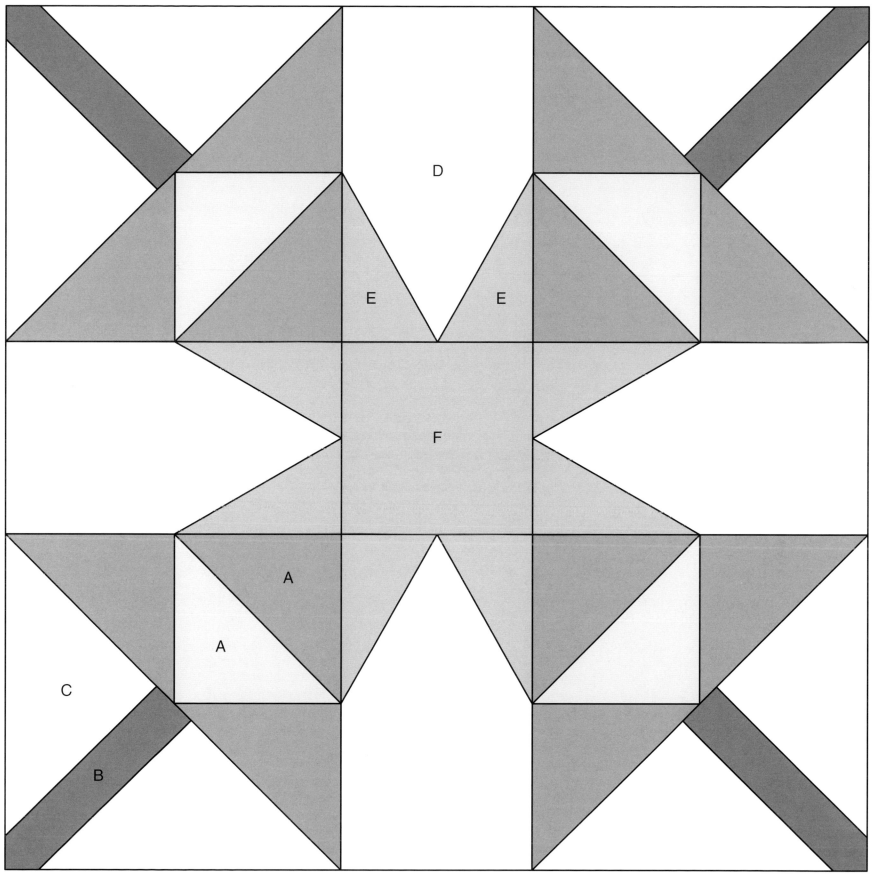

TREES IN A CORNER
FULL-SIZE BLOCK

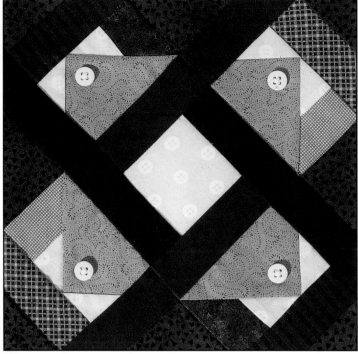

WOVEN RIBBONS QUILT BLOCK

WOVEN RIBBONS QUILT BLOCK

How To Construct This Block

Sew one B to side of one D (4 times). Sew BD to C (4 times). Add B to other side of CBD unit (4 times). Sew E to BCBD (4 times). Sew F to BCBDE (4 times). Sew G to FBCBDE (4 times). Sew H to each side of two units. These will become two opposite corner units. (The remaining two units will become the end units of the center square.) Sew four J pieces around center square A, setting in corners where necessary; add end units to opposite sides of center square. Sew one corner unit to center unit; add remaining corner unit to opposite side of center unit to complete the block.

To Make A Bed Quilt

This quilt is designed to be a twin-size quilt measuring 66×93 inches. We have used a 1½-inch plain border as shown.

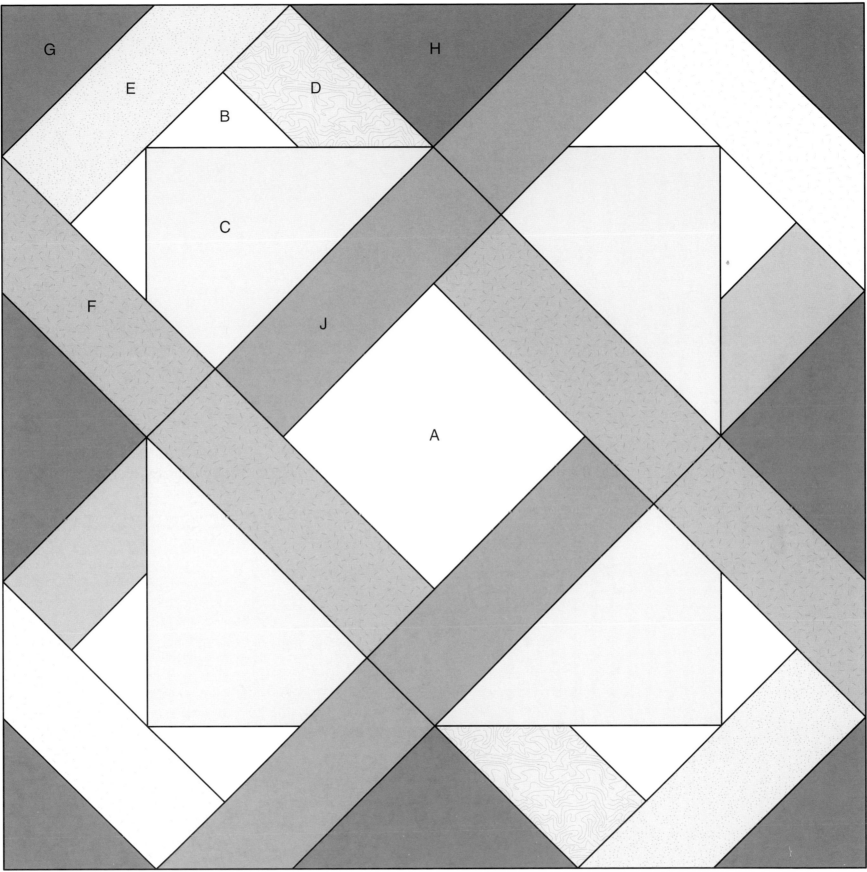

WOVEN RIBBONS
FULL-SIZE BLOCK

COUNTRY CORNERS QUILT BLOCK

COUNTRY CORNERS QUILT BLOCK

How To Construct This Block

Sew A to A (2 times). Sew together. Sew B to B (16 times). Add three BB units to each side of AA unit. Add five BB units to top and bottom of block.

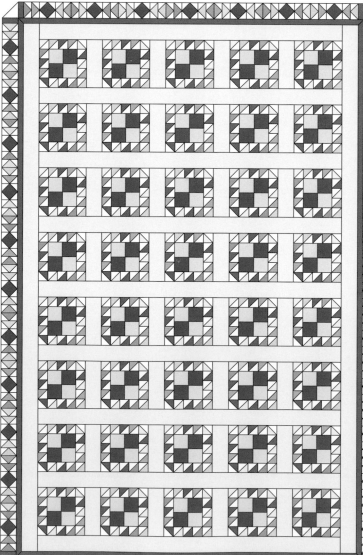

To Make A Bed Quilt

This quilt is designed to be an extra-length twin-size quilt measuring 71×107 inches. We have used a 3-inch plain border, the 4-inch Eclectic border, page 200, and 3-inch sashing strips as shown.

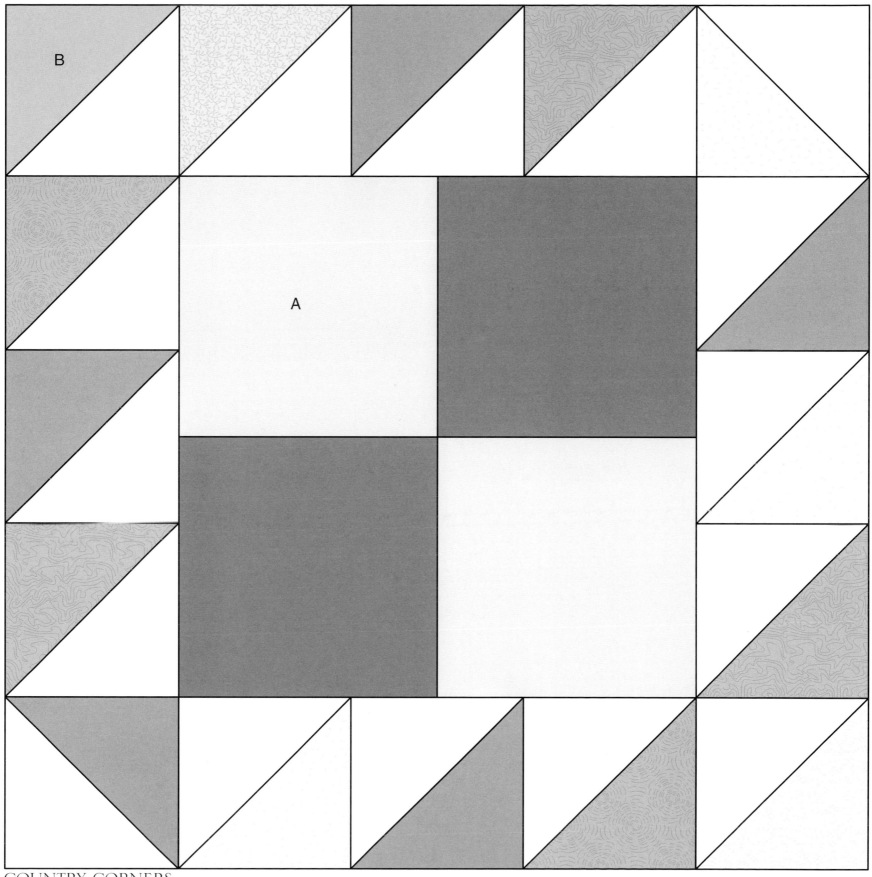

COUNTRY CORNERS
FULL-SIZE BLOCK

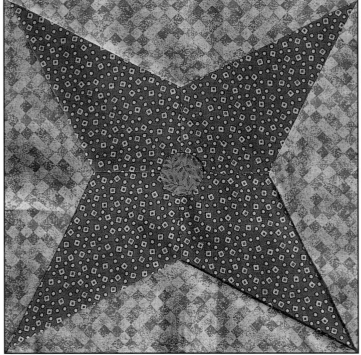

FOUR-POINTED STAR QUILT BLOCK

FOUR-POINTED STAR QUILT BLOCK

How To Construct This Block

Sew B to each side of A (4 times). Sew BAB unit to BAB unit (2 times). Join two halves to make block. Sew button at center if desired.

To Make A Bed Quilt

This quilt is designed to be a full-size quilt measuring 78×96 inches. We have used the 3-inch Diamond border, page 198, as shown.

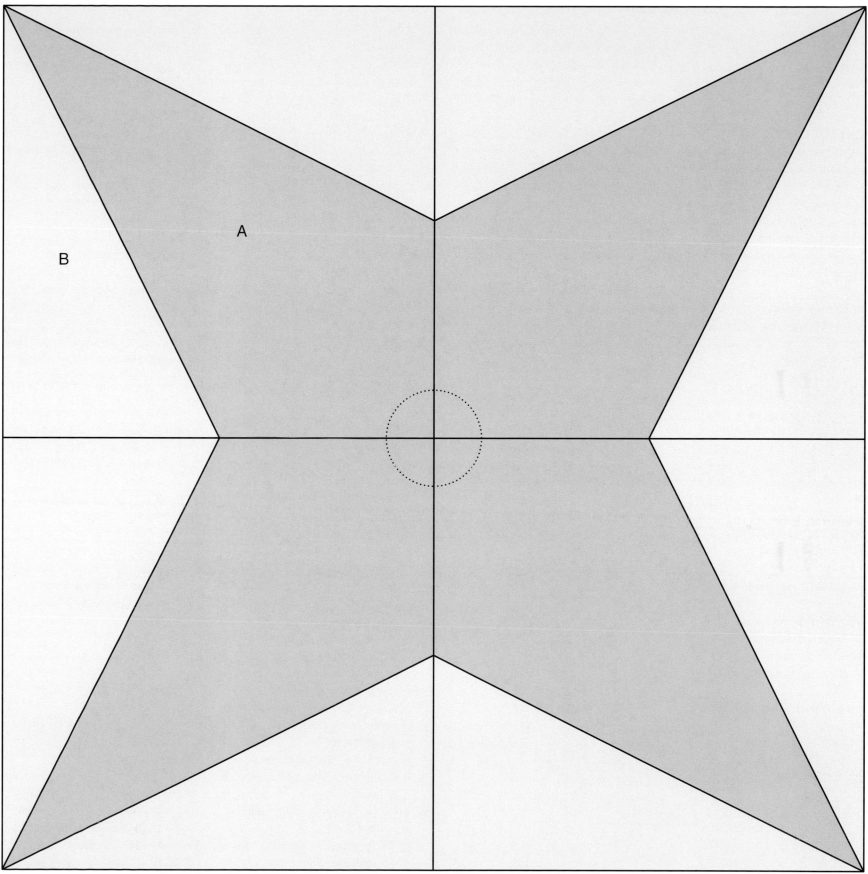

FOUR-POINTED STAR
FULL-SIZE BLOCK

COUNTRY CLASSICS SAMPLER QUILT

As shown on page 51. Finished size: 55¼×66½ inches.

MATERIALS

20—9½'' completed unfinished quilt blocks in coordinating colors
2 yards solid blue for sashing, border, and binding
1¼ yards total of assorted tan, gold, rust, brown, and green prints
⅓ yard of gold print for border
3⅓ yards for backing; 60×72'' quilt batting

Quantities specified are for 44/45''-wide 100% cotton fabrics. All measurements include a ¼'' seam allowance unless otherwise specified.

CUT THE FABRIC

To make the best use of your fabrics, cut the pieces in the order listed *below*. For this project, cut sashing strips lengthwise (parallel to selvage).

From solid blue, cut:
6—2¾×47¾'' sashing strips
25—2¾×9½'' sashing strips
7—2½×42'' binding strips
98—Pattern C (Stripes border, page 205)

From assorted prints, cut:
94—Pattern A (Stripes border)
4—Pattern B (Stripes border)
4—Pattern Br (Stripes border)

From gold print:
6—1⅜×42'' strips
  Piece to make:
  2—1⅜×49½'' border strips
  2—1⅜×60¾'' border strips

ASSEMBLE THE QUILT TOP

1. Lay out 20 blocks in a pleasing arrangement, four blocks horizontally, five rows vertically.
2. Sew one 2¾×9½'' sashing strip to the right side of each block.

3. Sew to the left side of each block that begins each horizontal row, one 2¾×9½'' sashing strip.
4. Sew each horizontal row together. Press all of the seams toward the sashing strips.
5. Sew one 2¾×47¾'' sashing strip to the bottom of each horizontal row. Sew one 2¾×47¾'' sashing strip to top of the first row. Press the seams toward sashing strips.
6. Sew each row together. The quilt top should measure 47¾×60'' including seam allowances.

ASSEMBLE THE TOP AND BOTTOM BORDERS

1. Sew 21 Pattern A's together for the top border.
2. To left Pattern A, sew one Pattern Br.
3. To right Pattern A, sew one Pattern B.
4. Set in 22 Pattern C triangles.
5. Sew one 1⅜×49½'' gold border strip to pieced Pattern A strip to make the top border.
6. Sew 21 Pattern A's together for the bottom border.
7. For the bottom border, Pattern A points will be positioned pointing down. To left Pattern A, sew one Pattern B. To right Pattern A, sew one Pattern Br.
8. Repeat Steps 4 and 5 to complete the bottom border.

ASSEMBLE THE SIDE BORDERS

1. Sew 26 Pattern A's together two times for the two side borders. The points of Pattern A will point out from the quilt on each side.
2. To the left side border, sew to the top of Pattern A, one Pattern B. To the bottom of the border strip, sew one Br to the last Pattern A.
3. To the right side border, sew to top Pattern A, one Pattern Br. To the bottom of the border strip, sew one B to last Pattern A.

4. Set in 27 Pattern C triangles to each side border.
5. Sew one 1⅜×60¾'' gold border strip to each pieced Pattern A strip.
6. Sew a border strip to the top and one to the bottom of quilt top, starting and stopping ¼'' from each side. Sew each side border strip to the quilt top, again starting and stopping ¼'' from top and bottom.
7. Miter corners of the border. The quilt top should measure 55¾×67'' including seam allowances.

COMPLETE THE QUILT

Layer quilt top, batting, and backing. This quilt was quilted with outline stitching and X's in sashing. Bind quilt.

PINWHEEL JACKET

As shown on page 52.

All materials and directions are given for making a ladies jacket in sizes 6/8—16/18. Larger sizes: add to strip sizes in proportion to total amount of pieced fabric required.

MATERIALS

Assorted scraps of off white, tan, gold, brown, and black prints, plaids and checks for four 9½'' quilt blocks
½ yard of black plaid for fabric No. 1
⅜ yard of black plaid for fabric No. 2
⅜ yard of black and tan stripe for fabric No. 3
¼ yard of black plaid for fabric No. 4
¼ yard of black plaid for fabric No. 5
¼ yard of black plaid for fabric No. 6
⅛ yard of black plaid for fabric No. 7 for sleeve insets
⅛ yard of tan gingham for fabric No. 8
¼ yard of black print for fabric No. 9 for band
3½ yards foundation fabric (will not be visible)
3½ yards lining; ¼ yard black ribbing
¼ yard of fusible interfacing
Smoke-colored monofilament thread
Covered raglan shoulder pads
Tissue paper for drafting pattern

Quantities specified for 44/45''-wide 100% cotton fabrics. All measurements include a ¼'' seam allowance unless otherwise specified.

CUT THE FABRIC

To make best use of your fabrics, cut pieces in order listed *below*.

From assorted scraps, cut:
96—Pattern A (Country Pinwheel block, page 71)

From black plaid No. 1, cut:
2—16×15'' pieces for jacket back
1—16×15'' piece for jacket right front

From black plaid No. 2, cut:
2—16×10'' pieces for jacket back
1—16×10'' piece for jacket right front
1—2×36½'' piece for jacket left front

From black and tan stripe No. 3, cut:
2—16×10'' pieces for jacket back
1—16×10'' piece for jacket right front

From black plaid No. 4, cut:
4—5×12'' pieces for sleeves

From black plaid No. 5, cut:
4—8×12'' pieces for sleeves

From black plaid No. 6, cut:
4—5×12'' pieces for sleeves

From black plaid No. 7, cut:
4—2×12'' pieces for sleeves

From tan gingham No. 8, cut:
1—4×36½'' piece

From black print No. 9, cut:
2—4×42'' pieces for band

From foundation fabric, cut:
1—14½×36½'' piece for left front
1—16×34'' piece for right front
2—16×34'' pieces for back
4—12×17'' pieces for sleeve

From fusible interfacing, cut:
2—3×42'' pieces for band interfacing

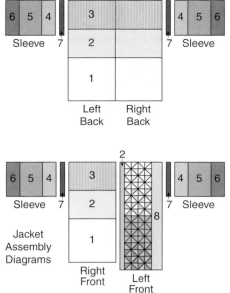

Sleeve 7 | Left Back | Right Back | 7 Sleeve

Jacket Assembly Diagrams

Sleeve 7 | Right Front | Left Front | 7 Sleeve

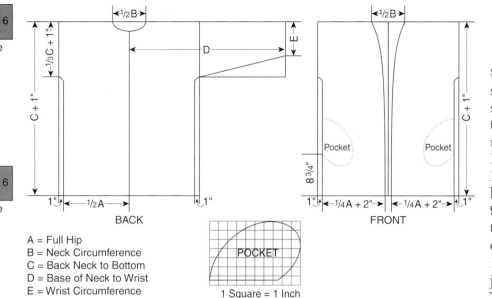

A = Full Hip
B = Neck Circumference
C = Back Neck to Bottom
D = Base of Neck to Wrist
E = Wrist Circumference

POCKET
1 Square = 1 Inch

ASSEMBLE THE BLOCKS AND JACKET SECTIONS

1. Cut and assemble four 9½" pinwheel blocks. Refer to the directions for the Country Pinwheel block shown on *page 70.* Sew together four pinwheel blocks vertically. The piece should measure 9½×36½" including the seam allowance. This piece will be the jacket left front.

2. Referring to Jacket Assembly Diagrams, *above,* lay out the pieces for the left and right front, left and right back, and four sleeves as indicated. Sew together the pieces for each section. The left front should measure 14½×36½" including the seam allowance. The right front and each back piece should measure 16×34" including the seam allowance and each sleeve should measure 12×17" including the seam allowance.

LAYER THE JACKET AND QUILT

1. Layer and pin together the left front section and the left front foundation piece.

2. Machine-quilt the left front through both layers of the fabric, stitching in the seam lines with a smoke-colored monofilament thread on the top and standard sewing thread in the bobbin.

3. Pin and baste the right front, each back, and the four sleeve sections to their respective foundation pieces.

MAKE THE PATTERN

Take and record the following measurements:
Full hip _____"—A
Neck circumference at base _____"—B
Back neck to bottom of jacket _____"—C
Base of neck to wrist _____" D
Wrist circumference _____"—E

CUT THE JACKET PIECES

From prepared sections, cut:
1—left front
1—right front
1—left back
1—right back
4—sleeves (reverse two patterns)

From lining fabric, cut:
2—fronts (reverse one pattern)
2—backs (reverse one pattern)
4—sleeves (reverse two patterns)
4—pockets (reverse two patterns)

ASSEMBLE THE JACKET AND LINING

Note: Use ½" seam allowances throughout the jacket and lining construction, unless otherwise stated in the instructions.

1. With right sides together, sew the center back seam of jacket. Press the seam open. Topstitch ¼" on each side of seam.

2. With right sides together, sew fronts and back at shoulder seams of jacket. Press seams open.

3. With wrong sides together, fold 2×12" black plaid No. 7 in half lengthwise and press. Raw edges matching, pin to the arm opening edge of sleeve and baste in place. Repeat with the remaining three strips. With right sides together sew shoulder seam of sleeve. Repeat with the second sleeve. Press the seams open.

4. With the right sides together, sew sleeve to jacket. Repeat with second sleeve. Press the seams open.

5. Sew pockets to each side seam of all sections using a ¼" seam. Press the seams toward open pocket.

6. With right sides together, sew underarm/side seams of jacket. When approaching a pocket opening, use short reinforcement stitches. Then change the machine to longest stitch and machine-baste pocket opening closed. Lock stitch and resume the regular stitch length for remaining seam line.

7. Sew around the pocket using a ¼" seam, beginning and ending at reinforcement/backstitches of side seam. Clip the seam allowances above and below the pocket.

8. Reinforce underarm seams by stitching a seam ⅛" from first stitching using short stitches. Clip the underarm seam allowances, but not through reinforcement seam. Press pockets toward center front. Remove the machine basting holding pockets closed.

9. Repeat Steps 1 through 4 and 6 through 8 with the lining pieces, omitting the pockets.

10. With wrong sides together, pin jacket lining to inside of jacket. Turn up the jacket hem 2". Hem in place. Turn up lining hem 2½". Hem in place.

11. With right sides together, sew neck bands across one short end. This makes center back seam. Press seam open.

12. With the wrong sides together, fold neck band in half lengthwise and press. Turn one long edge of the band under ½" to the inside and press. Fuse interfacing to the wrong side of band.

13. With right sides together, pin the unpressed edge of the band to front opening of jacket, matching the jacket center back seam with the neck band center back seam. *Note: The band will be longer than the front opening of the jacket.* Beginning at the bottom of one jacket hem, sew band to the front opening. End at the opposite bottom jacket hem. Trim and grade the seam allowances; clip the seam allowance around the neckline.

14. Trim bottom ends of the band to ½" below the bottom edge of jacket. With right sides together, fold the band in half and sew across each end of the band at the lower edge of jacket. Clip the corners, grade seam allowances. Turn band and press.

15. Edgestitch or hand-sew the band in place.

16. Fold a 6"-wide strip of ribbing in half and pin-fit around the wrist or lower arm. With right sides

together, sew short ends of the cuff piece together, forming a circle. Press the seam open. With wrong sides together, press the cuff in half, matching cut edges. Divide each cuff into fourths, marking with pins. Divide the cuff of the sleeve into fourths using the sleeve seams as halfway marks. Match pins of cuff and sleeve. Sew, stretching the cuff as needed to fit. Finish raw seam allowances or enclose seam allowance between lining and jacket.

17. Try on the jacket. Position the shoulder pads at the correct location. Sew in the shoulder pads. *Hint: If you cannot find ribbing in a color you need, check out the men's clothing department. Men's socks make good, sturdy cuffs and generally a seam does not need to be added.*

COUNTRY CHRISTMAS STOCKINGS

As shown on page 52. Finished size: 11½×17½ inches.

We have made the Christmas stocking in both the Country Pinwheel (page 70) and Jacob's Ladder Variation (page 62).

MATERIALS
A fat quarter measures 18×21".

For each stocking:
Three 9½" completed unfinished quilt blocks in coordinating colors
1 fat quarter of plaid for stocking back
½ yard of coordinating fabric for lining and cuff
12×18" rectangle for piping
1⅓ yards of small piping cord
Fleece; interfacing (optional)
Trim: buttons, ribbon, bell, cording

All seam allowances are ¼" wide.

CUT THE FABRIC
From plaid, cut:
1 stocking back

From coordinating fabric, cut:
2 stocking patterns; one will be reversed for the lining
1—10½×17¾" strip for cuff
1—1¼×6" strip for loop

From second coordinating fabric, cut:
Enough 1½"-wide bias strips to total 46" in length for piping

From fleece, cut:
2 stocking patterns

PREPARE THE BLOCKS
Sew two blocks together, vertically. Add a third block to the left side of bottom block, horizontally. (See Diagram 1, *below.*) Only a small portion of third block will be used.

ASSEMBLE THE STOCKING
1. Lay fleece onto the wrong side of the front and back stocking. Baste and quilt if desired. The maker chose not to quilt the stocking.
2. Piece the 1½" bias strips to total 46" in length. Cover the piping cord with the bias strip. Position the piping on the right side of the stocking front, at the seam line with the raw edges together. Stitch the piping to the stocking, beginning at

the top side edge and continuing to the other top side edge of the stocking. Trim the piping to match the stocking edge.
3. With the right sides together, sew the front to the back. Clip the seams and press. Turn stocking right side out.
4. Stabilize the cuff with interfacing, if desired. Sew the 10½×17¾" strip together at the short ends. This will form the back seam of the cuff. Press the seam open. Press the cuff in half lengthwise with the wrong sides together.
5. Position the cuff over the top of stocking with raw edges together. Position the seam at the back of the stocking. Fold the piping toward the front as you stitch the cuff to the stocking.
6. Press a ¼" hem lengthwise on each side of the 1¼×6" strip for a loop. Fold in half lengthwise, press, and topstitch along the edge. Fold the loop in half. Baste the raw edges together at the top of the cuff behind the piping at the stocking back side seam.

ASSEMBLE THE LINING
1. With the right sides together, sew the lining front to the lining back, leaving an opening in one side seam for turning. Clip and press the seams open.

2. Slip stocking into the lining, right sides together, matching seams. Sew around the top edge and trim. Turn to right side by pulling the stocking through lining side seam opening. Stitch opening closed. Press lining to the inside of stocking. Turn cuff down over top of the stocking.
3. Add trims as desired.

HUGS AND KISSES VALANCE

As shown on page 53. Finished size: 12×29 inches.

MATERIALS
Three 9½" completed unfinished Hugs and Kisses quilt blocks, page 84, in coordinating colors:
2 blocks stitched in X version
1 block stitched in O version
1 yard border print fabric
⅜ yard backing fabric

Quantities specified are for 44/45"-wide 100% cotton fabrics. Measurements include a ¼" seam allowance unless otherwise specified.

CUT THE FABRIC
From border print, cut:
1—3½×29½" border strip
2—1½×9½" sashing strips
4—1½×20½" tie strips

From backing fabric, cut:
1—12½×29½" piece for back

MAKE THE VALANCE
1. Sew three blocks together in a horizontal row. Position O version block in the center of the row.
2. To each side of the row, sew one 1½×9½" sashing strip.
3. Sew the 3½×29½" border strip to the bottom of the row. Press the seam toward the strip.

MAKE THE TIES
1. Press a ¼" hem on each long side of each 1½×20½" tie strip. Fold in

CHRISTMAS STOCKING PATTERN

1 Square = 1 Inch

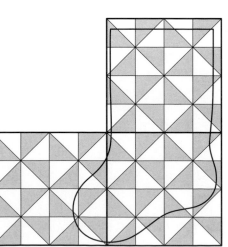

Diagram 1

half, wrong sides together; press. Fold in tie ends; press. Topstitch.

2. Fold each tie in half. Place evenly across valance top, the folded edge against the raw edge of the valance top and the ties hanging over the front of the blocks. Baste.

COMPLETE THE VALANCE

With the right sides together, stitch front to back leaving an opening for turning. Trim corners; turn right side out. Stitch opening closed. Tie a knot in ends of each tie.

HEARTS AND GIZZARDS TOTE BAG

As shown on page 52. Finished size: 15×15 inches.

The maker of the tote bag did not line the entire bag body with fleece, only the front block and handles were lined.

MATERIALS

One 9½" completed unfinished Hearts and Gizzards quilt block, page 80, in coordinating colors
½ yard of gold print
⅛ yard of light gold
1 yard of brown; ⅜ yard of fleece
1¼ yards of small piping cord

All seam allowances are ¼" wide.

CUT THE FABRIC

From gold print, cut:
1—15½" square
4—3½" squares
3—1½×15½" strips
2—2½×18½" strips

From light gold, cut:
4—3½×9½" strips

From brown, cut:
2—15½" squares
6—1½×15½" strips
3—3½×15½" strips

1—12×18" rectangle, cutting it into enough 1½"-wide bias strips to total 42" in length for piping

From fleece, cut:
1—12½" square
2—2×18½" strips

ASSEMBLE THE TOTE FRONT

Stitch, right sides together, one light gold 3½×9½" strip to the top and bottom of completed quilt block. Press seams toward block. Sew one gold print 3½" square to each short end of a light gold 3½×9½" strip. Repeat for a second border unit. Stitch a border to each side of quilt block. Press seam toward border. Layer tote front and a 12½" square of fleece. Baste and quilt tote front. The quilt maker machine-quilted around the pieces of the front.

ASSEMBLE THE TOTE BAG

1. Sew a brown 1½×15½" strip lengthwise to a gold print 1½×15½" strip. Sew a brown 1½×15½" strip to opposite side of the gold print strip, to make one boxing strip. Repeat with the remaining strips for a total of three boxing strips.

2. Join the three boxing strips on the short side to make a boxing strip 3½×45½" including the seam allowance. With right sides together and in one continuous seam, beginning at top of tote front, stitch the boxing strip to front, stopping ¼" from bottom corner. Pivot fabric without moving the needle and continue sewing around the bottom, again stopping ¼" from corner and continuing up opposite side. In the same manner, join the boxing strip to the gold print 15½" back square.

3. Piece the brown bias strips to make a 42" strip. Cover piping cord with bias brown strip. Position the piping on top of the tote bag, right sides together, raw edges together.

Stitch piping to top edge of the tote bag. Trim the edge seam of piping to match the tote bag edge.

HANDLES

Press a ¼" hem lengthwise on each side of two 2½×18½" gold print strips. Layer strips with fleece, press each strip in half lengthwise, and stitch, wrong sides together. Position each handle, right sides together on top of the piping, 4" from center of the boxing strip. (See Diagram 1, *below.*) Baste in place.

LINING

In the same manner as before, join the short sides of the three brown 3½×15½" strips to form a boxing strip, 3½×45½" including the seam allowance. Stitch boxing strip, right sides together, to front and back 15½" brown lining squares, leaving an opening in one seam for turning.

FINISHING THE TOTE BAG

Slip tote bag into lining, right sides together, matching seams. around top edge. Trim and clip the seams.

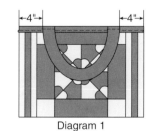
Diagram 1

Turn the bag right side out. Stitch opening in lining seam closed.

ANTIQUE COUNTRY CORNERS QUILT

As shown on page 53. Finished size: 61×85 inches.

The maker of this quilt had trouble with the templates. She may have cut them off a little each time she used them. The blocks are not the same size. This is where sashing

becomes very useful. It is much easier to join odd sizes together with sashing. The easiest method is to choose the smallest block and just cut all others the same size. Some points are cut off, but it is a way to salvage multi-sized old blocks and a beautiful quilt can be the result.

The maker also placed her half-square triangles in different directions in each block. The directions that follow will be for the same placement in each block. However, if some go differently, the quilt will still result in a pleasing mixture as in this antique quilt. This is a place to have fun and use up all those scraps of fabric.

MATERIALS

4⅛ yards total of assorted light, medium, and dark print and solid scraps for blocks
3½ yards total of muslin for blocks and binding
2½ yards of solid blue for sashing and borders
3¾ yards of backing fabric
67×91" piece of batting

Quantities specified are for 44/45"-wide, 100% cotton fabrics. All measurements include a ¼" seam allowance unless otherwise specified.

SELECT THE FABRIC

The quilt-maker usually chose two identical solids and two identical prints for the center of each block. She also used a random mixture of prints. This gave the old quilt a beautiful mix of prints and color.

CUT THE FABRIC

To make the best use of your fabrics, cut the pieces in the order that follows on *page 98*. Cut the border strips and long sashing strips lengthwise (parallel to selvage). The list includes mathematically correct border lengths. You may wish to add extra length to the border strips now to allow for any sewing differences later.

From assorted prints and solids, cut:
140—Pattern A (Country Corners block, page 91)
560—Pattern B (Country Corners block)

From muslin cut:
560—Pattern B (Country Corners block)
8—2×42" strips for binding

From solid blue, cut:
4—3½×81½" sashing strips
2—2½×81½" border strips
2—2½×61½" border strips
30—3½×9½" sashing strips

ASSEMBLE THE BLOCK

1. To make one block, you will need two light A squares, two medium or dark A squares, 16 muslin B triangles and 16 print B triangles.
2. With right sides together, sew a light A square and a medium or dark A square together. Press seam allowance toward darker square. Repeat for remaining two A squares.
3. Sew the two groups of squares together, matching opposite colors together. *Note: Seams will interlock and will then easily match up.*
4. With the right sides together, lay a print B triangle on a muslin B triangle. Sew together on the long side. Press the seam allowance toward the print triangle. Repeat for a total of 16 triangle square units. *Note: When sewing a number of triangles together, forming half-square triangles, it is easier to chain-piece all the sets together. Keep all the pieces in the same position with the muslin fabric on top. Cut the sets apart; press seam allowance toward darker triangles. See Diagram 1, above right.*
5. Lay out the triangle squares from Step 4 around four squares from Step 3 in a pleasing arrangement. See Diagram 2, *above right.*

6. Referring to Diagram 2, sew three side triangle squares together, sew this set to one side of the center of the block. Repeat with the other three side triangle squares. Press seam allowance toward center squares. Sew each group of five triangle squares together and sew one group to the top of the block and one to the bottom. Press seam allowance toward triangle squares.
7. Repeat Steps 1 through 6 for a total of 35 blocks. The blocks should measure 9½" square including seam allowance.

ASSEMBLE THE QUILT TOP

1. Referring to the photograph, *page 53,* or the Quilt Assembly Diagram, *right,* lay out seven blocks vertically with six 3½×9½" solid blue sashing strips.
2. Sew together the pieces in a vertical row. Press seam allowance toward the sashing strip.
3. Repeat Step 1 and 2 to make five vertical rows.
4. Join the rows by adding a 3½×81½" solid blue sashing strip between each row. Press the seam allowance toward the sashing strips.
5. Sew a solid blue 2½×81½" border strip to each side of quilt top. Then add one solid blue 2½×61½" border strip to the top and bottom of quilt top. Press the seam allowance toward the border strips.

COMPLETE THE QUILT

Layer the quilt top, batting, and backing. This quilt is quilted 1½" diagonally through sashing and borders. Large squares have been quilted with an X on each square, outline quilted ¼" inside outer edge of the blocks and ¼" outside four center squares. Bind the quilt.

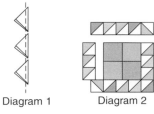

Diagram 1   Diagram 2

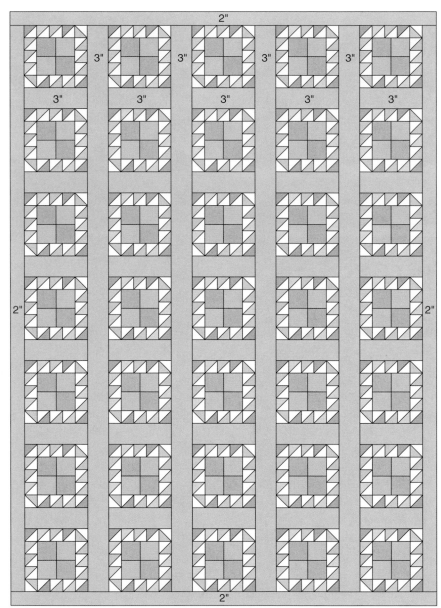

Quilt Assembly Diagram

AMERICANA

True to the red, white, and blue, we've chosen twenty outstanding quilt blocks and combined them in this star-studded Americana Sampler Quilt. Instructions for making this sampler quilt are on *page 142*. Turn the page for more projects to make using some of the blocks in this chapter.

AMERICANA CHAIRBACK CUSHIONS

PICNIC BASKET COVER

AMERICANA

STARS AND STRIPES PLACE MAT

ANTIQUE LOG CABIN QUILT

PROJECTS YOU CAN MAKE

We've used some of our quilt blocks to create and re-create this array of all-American decorative pieces—chairback cushions, a true-blue tablecloth, a patriotic picnic basket cover, and even an antique red, white, and blue log cabin quilt. We know you'll find this striking collection of blocks and projects to your liking. Remember, because all of the blocks are nine inches square you can combine and recombine the blocks to personalize your own celebration! Instructions for all the projects seen here begin on *page 142.*

JEWEL STAR TABLECLOTH

101

PIECED EAGLE QUILT BLOCK

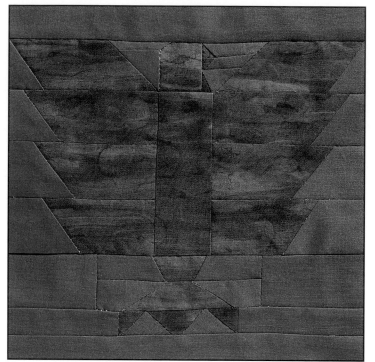

PIECED EAGLE QUILT BLOCK

How To Construct This Block

Sew A to B, and second A to C. Sew D to E. Sew AB and AC strips together. Sew on DE strip. Sew this to right edge of H. Sew F and G together then sew to left edge of H. (In sewing these units together, sew F edge to H, stopping stitching ¼" from point where G is attached. Sew G and H seams together.) Sew I to J and Ir to Jr. (Note: The I pieces have two slanted edges. The edge with the shortest slant is the outside edge.) Sew IJ units to head unit. Sew L to K and Lr to Kr, then N to M and Nr to Mr. Sew P to O and Pr to Or. Sew LK unit to NM unit, then add PO unit. Repeat with LrKr, NrMr, and PrOr strips. Sew these to each side of Q. Sew previously completed strip with head to top of wing and body unit. Sew S and Sr to each slanted edge of R, and U and Ur to each slanted edge of T. Sew these two strips together and then sew V to each end on SU edges. Sew this to bottom edge of wing and body unit. Sew X to W and W to remaining W. Sew these two units together, then sew remaining X to W edge. Sew Y to each end, then sew this to bottom of body unit. Sew Z to top and bottom edges to complete the block.

To Make A Bed Quilt

This quilt is designed to be a full-size quilt measuring 75×87 inches. We have used the small block from the Stars and Stripes border, page 197, for the 3-inch plain sashing strip and border accents. Plain 9-inch setting blocks are surrounding the center six eagle motifs.

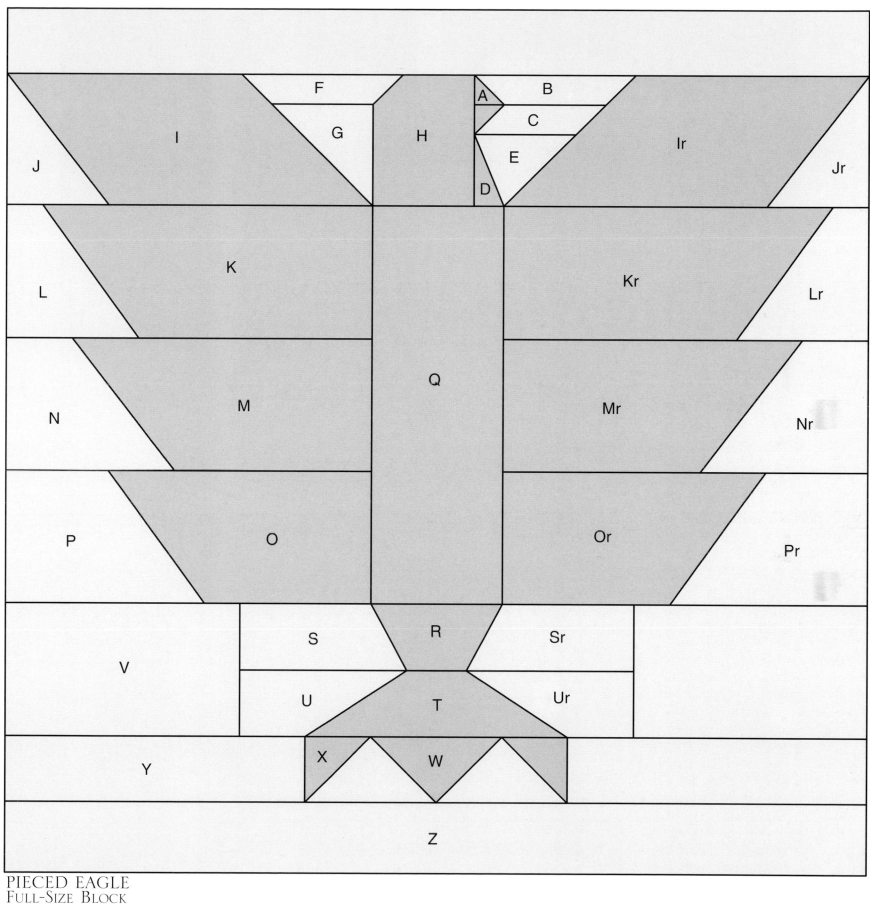

PIECED EAGLE
FULL-SIZE BLOCK

EIGHT-POINTED STAR QUILT BLOCK

EIGHT-POINTED STAR QUILT BLOCK

How To Construct This Block

Sew A to Ar (4 times). Sew one short edge of C to A, stopping the stitching at seam line. Reposition edges and sew adjacent edge of C to Ar, starting stitching at seam line (4 times). Stitch two AArC units together, then stitch the remaining two AArC units together. Stitch these two units together to form a star. Stitch one edge of B to A edge, stopping stitching at seam line. Reposition edges and continue stitching adjacent edge of B to Ar edge, starting stitching at seam line. Repeat, stitching each B piece to AAr edges, being careful not to stitch through AAr seam lines. Sew a D strip to two opposite edges of star unit. Sew E to remaining two edges. Sew G to F (2 times). Sew Gr to F (2 times). Sew H to remaining G and Gr pieces (4 times). Sew HG and HGr units to GF and GrF units (4 times). Sew two GFH units to two opposite edges of star unit. Stitch two GGrFH units to remaining two edges of star unit to complete the block.

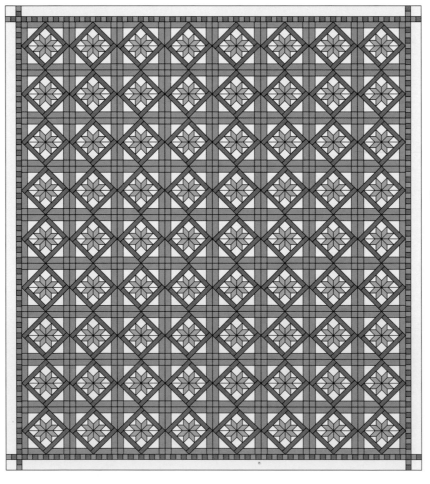

To Make A Bed Quilt

This quilt is designed to be a full-size quilt measuring 78×87 inches. We have used the 3-inch Checkerboard border, page 195, as shown.

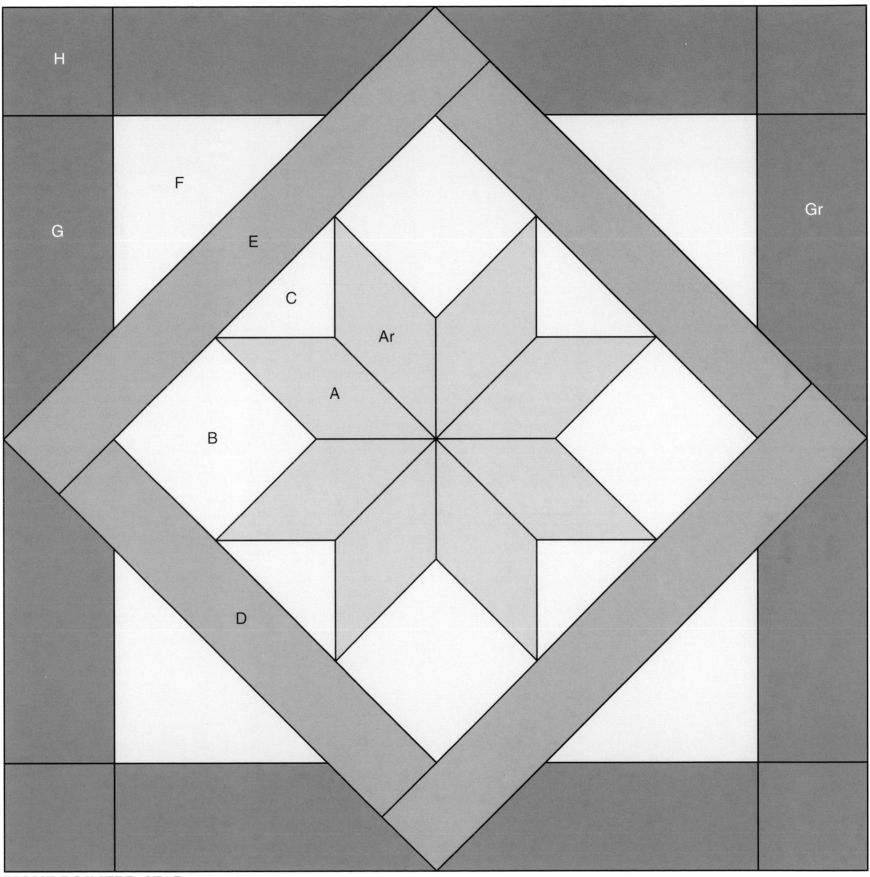

EIGHT-POINTED STAR
Full-Size Block

FIREWORKS QUILT BLOCK

FIREWORKS QUILT BLOCK

How To Construct This Block

Star unit: Sew B to A (4 times); add B (4 times). Sew C to BAB (2 times); add C (2 times). Sew BAB to D; add BAB. Sew CBABC to opposite sides of BABDBAB. Repeat (4 times). Stripe unit: Sew three E's together (4 times). Sew a star unit to opposite sides of a stripe unit (2 times) for Rows 1 and 3. Sew a stripe unit to opposite sides of a star unit for Row 2. Sew Rows 1, 2, and 3 together.

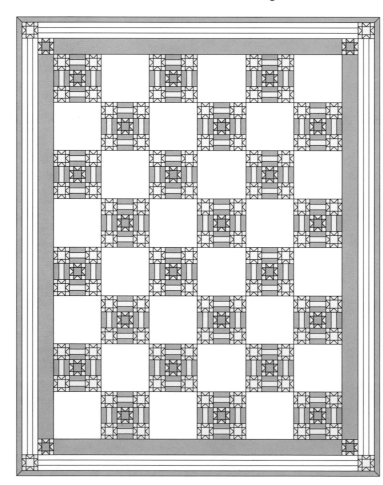

To Make A Bed Quilt

This quilt is designed to be a twin-size quilt measuring 68×86 inches. We have used a 3-inch plain border and four 1-inch plain borders. One corner star from the nine-patch block is used in the corners of the borders. We suggest quilting stars in the plain setting blocks we've placed between the pieced blocks.

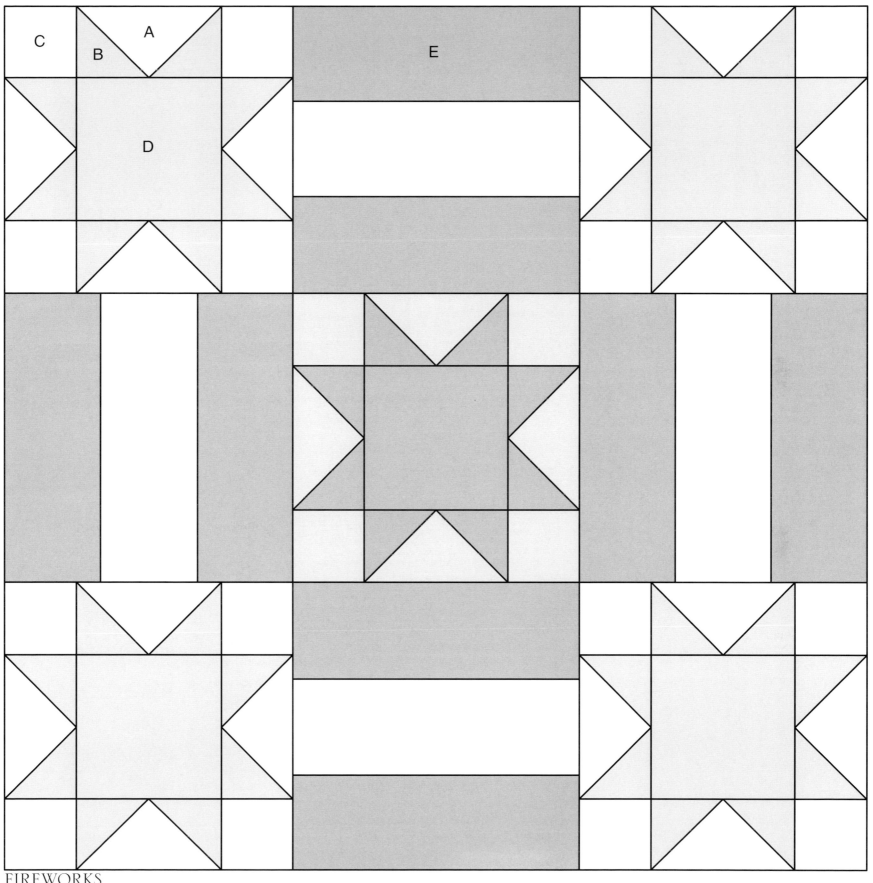

FIREWORKS
FULL-SIZE BLOCK

Americana ~ Two Star

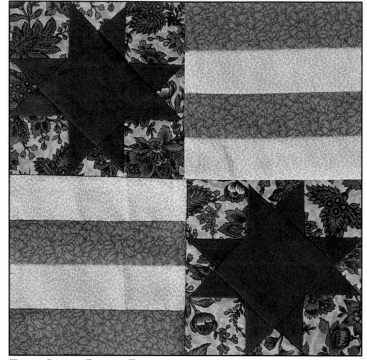

Two Star Quilt Block

Two Star Quilt Block

How To Construct This Block

Star unit: Sew A to B (4 times); add B to AB (4 times). Sew B to each side of BAB (2 times). Sew BAB to opposite sides of C (2 times). Sew BBABB to opposite sides of BABCBAB. Repeat these steps for a second star unit. Stripe unit: Sew four D's together (2 times). Sew star unit to stripe unit (2 times). Sew two sets together.

To Make A Bed Quilt

This quilt is designed to be a twin-size quilt measuring 63×90 inches. We have used the 4½-inch Sawtooth border, page 204, as shown.

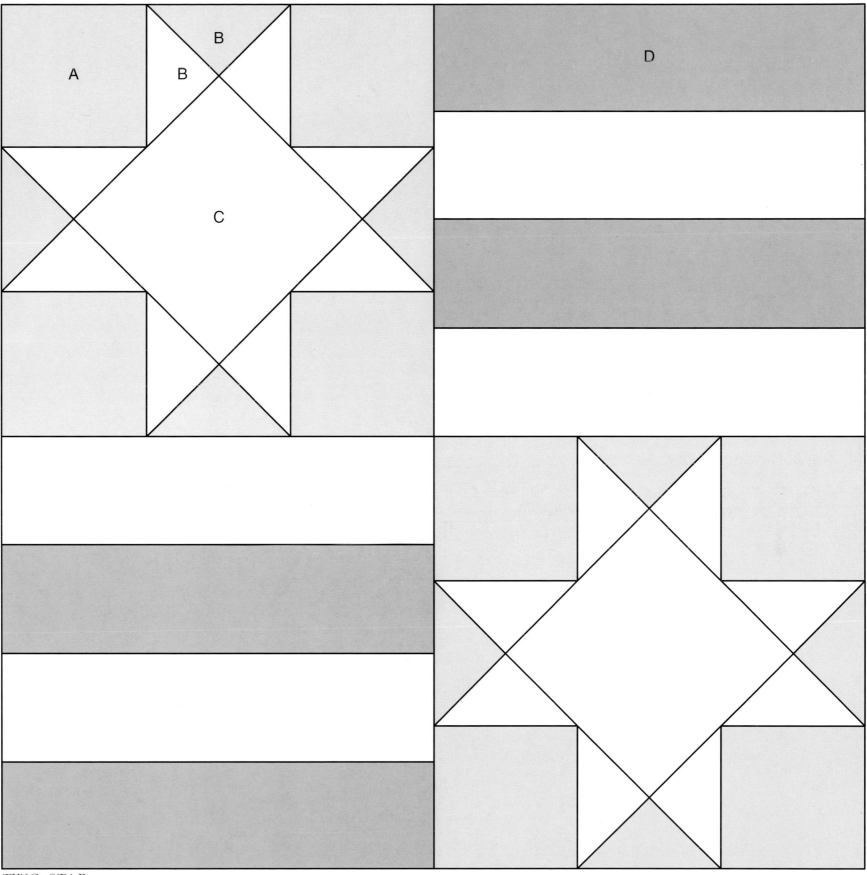

TWO STAR
FULL-SIZE BLOCK

COLOR TRIANGLES QUILT BLOCK

COLOR TRIANGLES QUILT BLOCK

How To Construct This Block

The pieces for this block could be constructed using a template, or you may cut a 3⅞" square in half diagonally to create two A triangles. Cut a total of 18 A triangles. Sew two A pieces together along long edges. Make a total of nine AA units. Join AA units together into three rows, then sew the three rows together to make block.

To Make A Bed Quilt

This quilt is designed to be a full-size quilt measuring 81×99 inches. We have used the 4½-inch Sawtooth border, page 204, as shown.

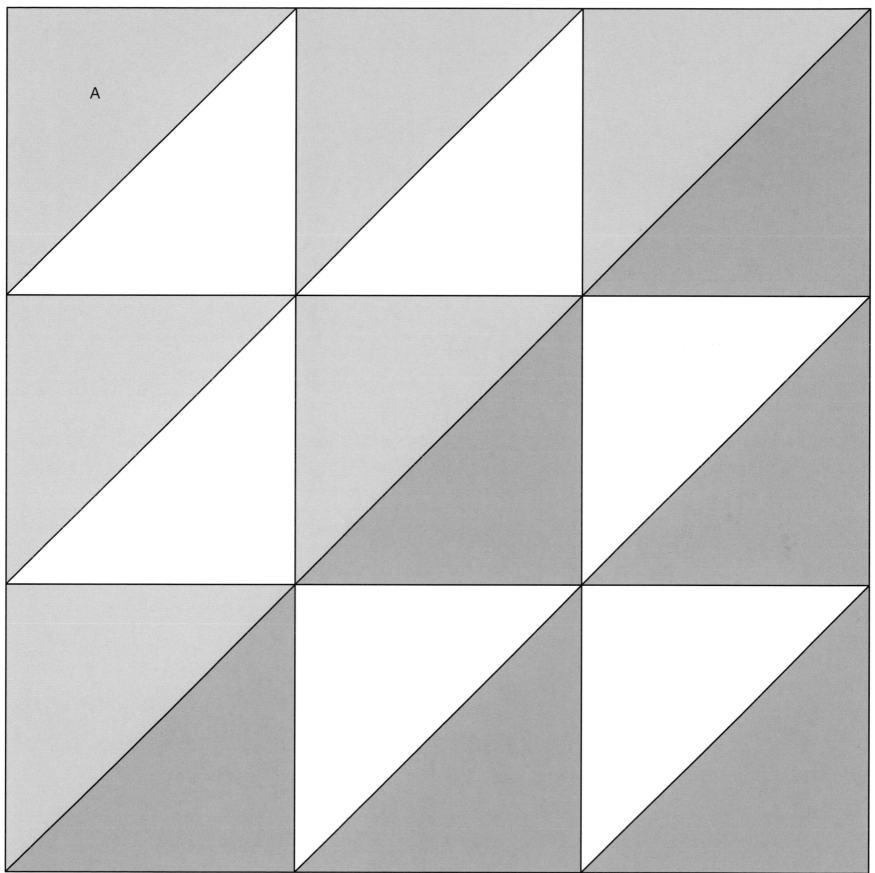

COLOR TRIANGLES
FULL-SIZE BLOCK

TICKING STRIPES QUILT BLOCK

TICKING STRIPES QUILT BLOCK

How To Construct This Block

Sew A piece to B piece to make a triangle (4 times). Sew AB to AB (2 times). Join the two units together.

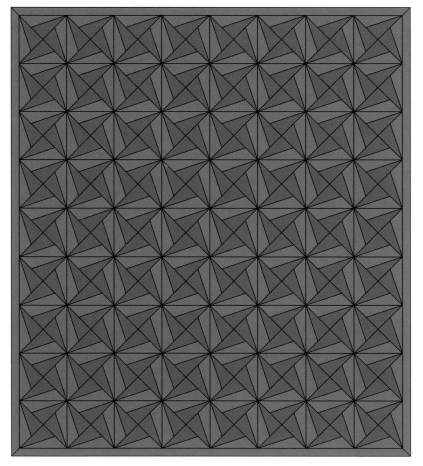

To Make A Bed Quilt

This quilt is designed to be a full-size quilt measuring 75×84 inches. We have used a 1½-inch plain border as shown.

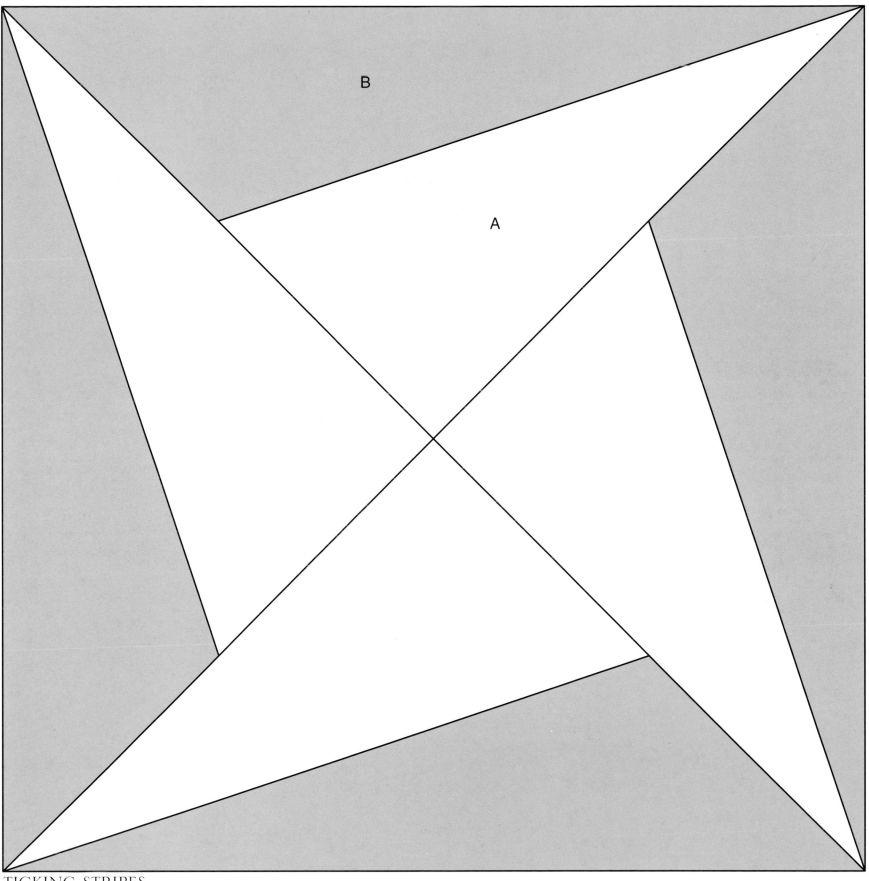

TICKING STRIPES
FULL-SIZE BLOCK

STARS AND STRIPES QUILT BLOCK

STARS AND STRIPES QUILT BLOCK

How To Construct This Block

Sew AA together (4 times). Sew B to each side of AA unit (2 times). Sew AA unit to each side of B. Stitch BAAB to AABAA, then add second BAAB. Sew to left side of C. Make three star and stripe units. Stitch three units together to complete the block.

To Make A Bed Quilt

This quilt is designed to be a full-size quilt measuring 78×96 inches. We have used the 3-inch Stars and Stripes border, page 197, as shown.

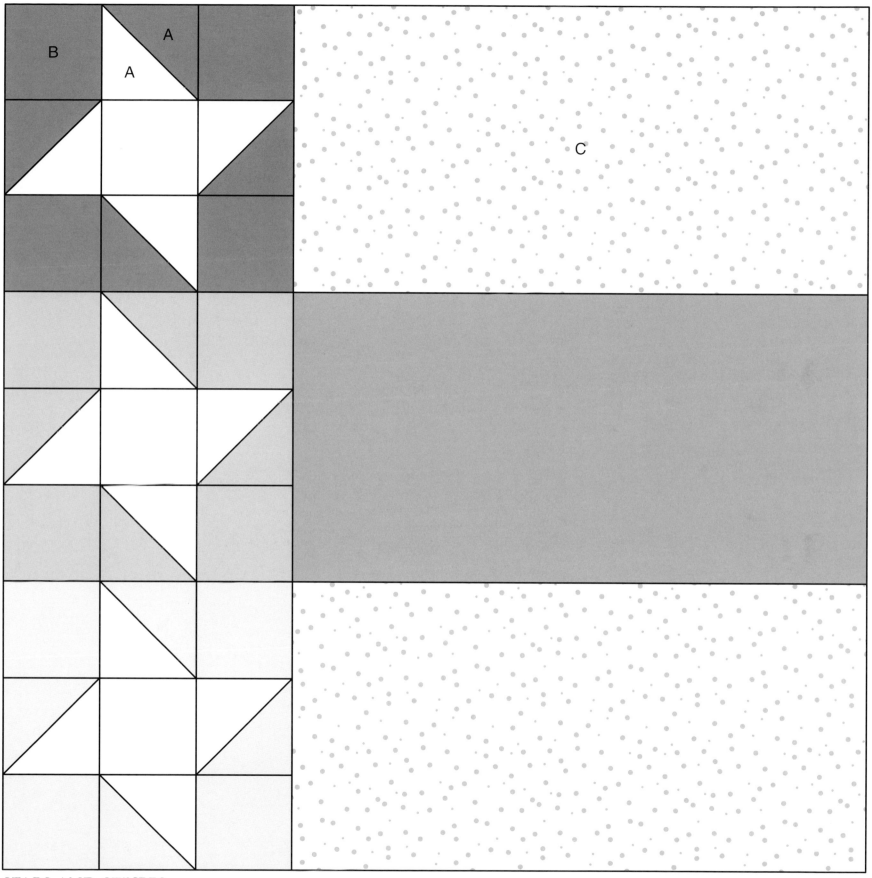

STARS AND STRIPES
Full-Size Block

AMERICANA ❦ WOVEN STAR

WOVEN STAR QUILT BLOCK

WOVEN STAR QUILT BLOCK

How To Construct This Block

Make BB unit (4 times). Sew BB to A (4 times). Join BBA to C (4 times). Sew two BBAC's together (2 times). Sew the two sets together.

To Make A Bed Quilt

This quilt is designed to be a twin-size quilt measuring 66×93 inches. We have used a 3-inch plain border and the 3-inch Diamond and Stripes border, page 199, as shown.

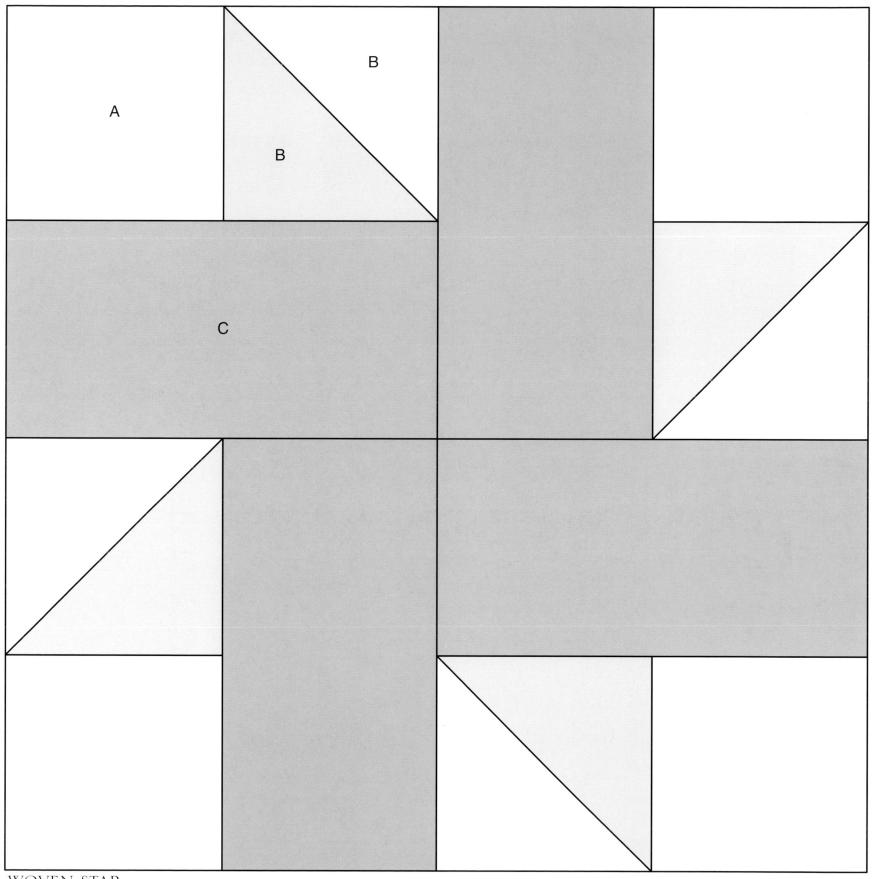

WOVEN STAR
FULL-SIZE BLOCK

JEWEL STAR QUILT BLOCK

JEWEL STAR QUILT BLOCK

How To Construct This Block

Sew A to B (2 times). Sew AB unit to C (2 times). Sew Ar to Br (2 times). Sew ArBr to C (2 times). Sew ABCBrAr unit to D (2 times). Join the two halves to complete the block.

To Make A Bed Quilt

This quilt is designed to be a queen-size square quilt measuring 90×90 inches. We have used two 2¼-inch plain borders and the 4½-inch Sawtooth border, page 204, as shown.

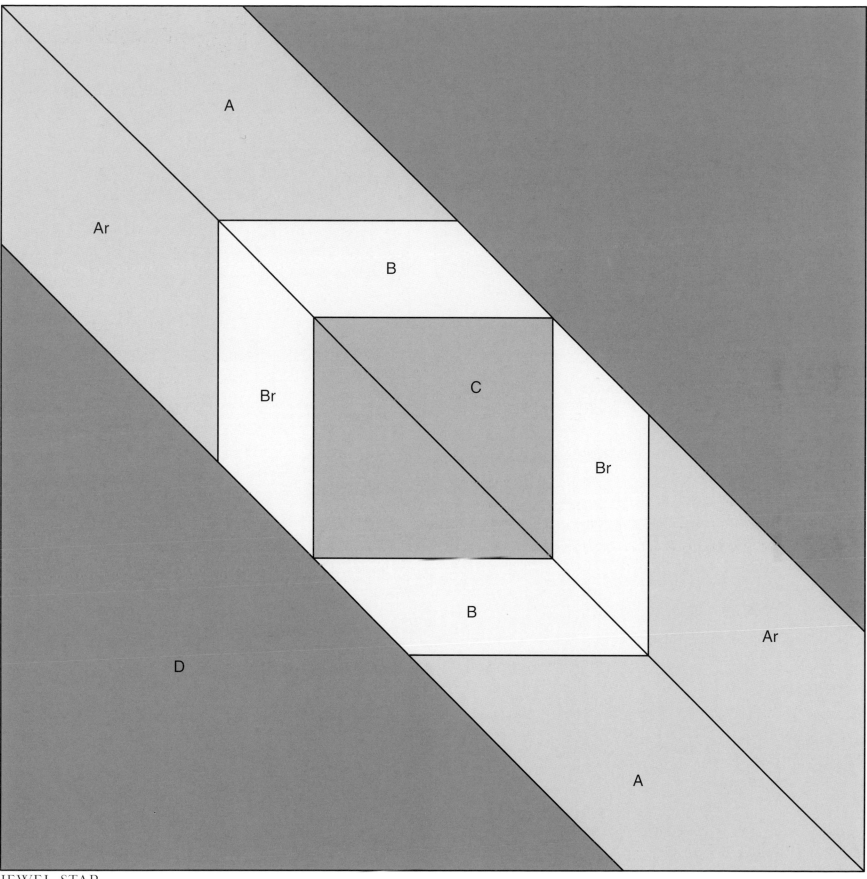

JEWEL STAR
FULL-SIZE BLOCK

119

AMERICANA ～ STARS AND BARS

STARS AND BARS QUILT BLOCK

STARS AND BARS QUILT BLOCK

How To Construct This Block

Sew three A's (4 times). Sew B to C; add D (2 times). Sew BCD to E (2 times). Sew Br to Cr; add D (2 times). Sew BrCrD to E (2 times). Sew F to F; add F (3 times). Sew three F units together to make a nine-patch. Sew AAA unit to BrCrDE; add AAA unit (2 times) for Rows 1 and 3. Sew BCDE to F unit (nine-patch); add BCDE for Row 2. Sew Rows 1, 2, and 3 together to complete the block.

To Make A Bed Quilt

This quilt is designed to be a queen-size quilt measuring 84×93 inches. We have used two 3-inch borders of 1-inch stripes with the checkered nine-patch unit of the block as setting squares at the border corners as shown.

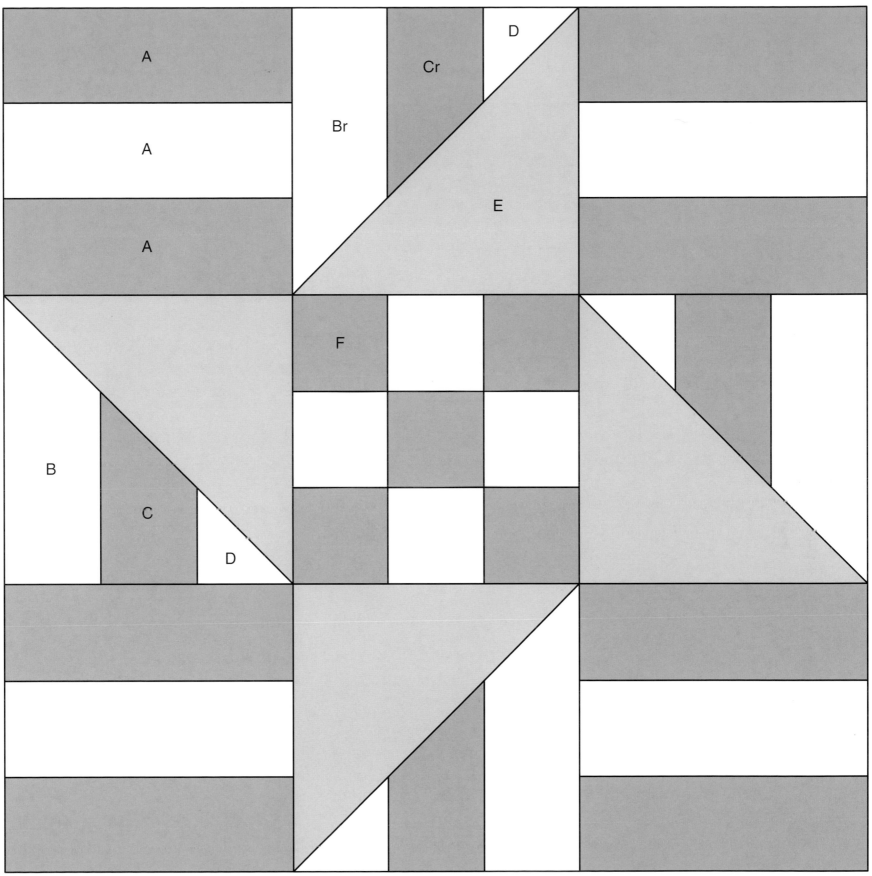

STARS AND BARS
FULL-SIZE BLOCK

RAINBOW STARS QUILT BLOCK

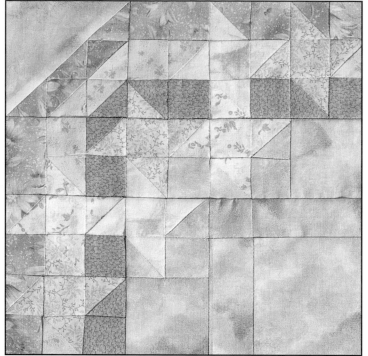

RAINBOW STARS QUILT BLOCK

How To Construct This Block

In chosen colors, lay out pieces in correct position. Be careful of placement. Sew A to A to make a half-square triangle (25 times). Row 1—Sew A to C; add AA. Sew B to ACAA. Sew ACAAB to AA; add B. Row 2—Sew A to AA; add B. Sew AAAB to AA; add B and AA. Sew AAABAABAA to B; add AA. Row 3—Sew A to (3)AA; add B. Sew A(3)AAB to AA; add B, AA, and another B. Sew Row 1 to Row 2. Add Row 3 to make Unit 1. Sew G to left side of Unit 1. Row 4—Sew B to AA; add B. Sew BAAB to AA; add B and another AA. Row 5—Sew AA to B; add AA. Sew AABAA to B; add AA and B. Sew Row 4 to Row 5 to make Unit 2. Sew C to left side of Unit 2. Sew E to right side of Unit 2. Row 6—Sew AA to B; add AA. Sew AABAA to B; add AA, B, and D to make Unit 3. Row 7—Sew B to AA; add B. Sew BAAB to AA; add B. Row 8—Sew AA to B; add AA. Row 9—Sew B to AA; add B. Sew Row 8 to Row 9. Add E. Sew Row 7 to Row 8 and 9. Add D and F to make Unit 4. Sew Units 1, 2, 3, and 4 together.

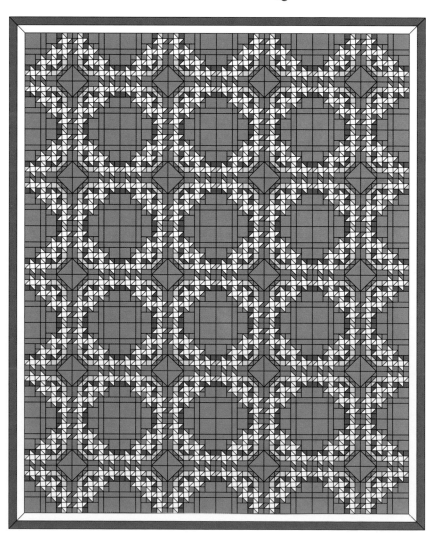

To Make A Bed Quilt

This quilt is designed to be a twin-size quilt measuring 78×96 inches. We have used two 1½-inch plain borders as shown.

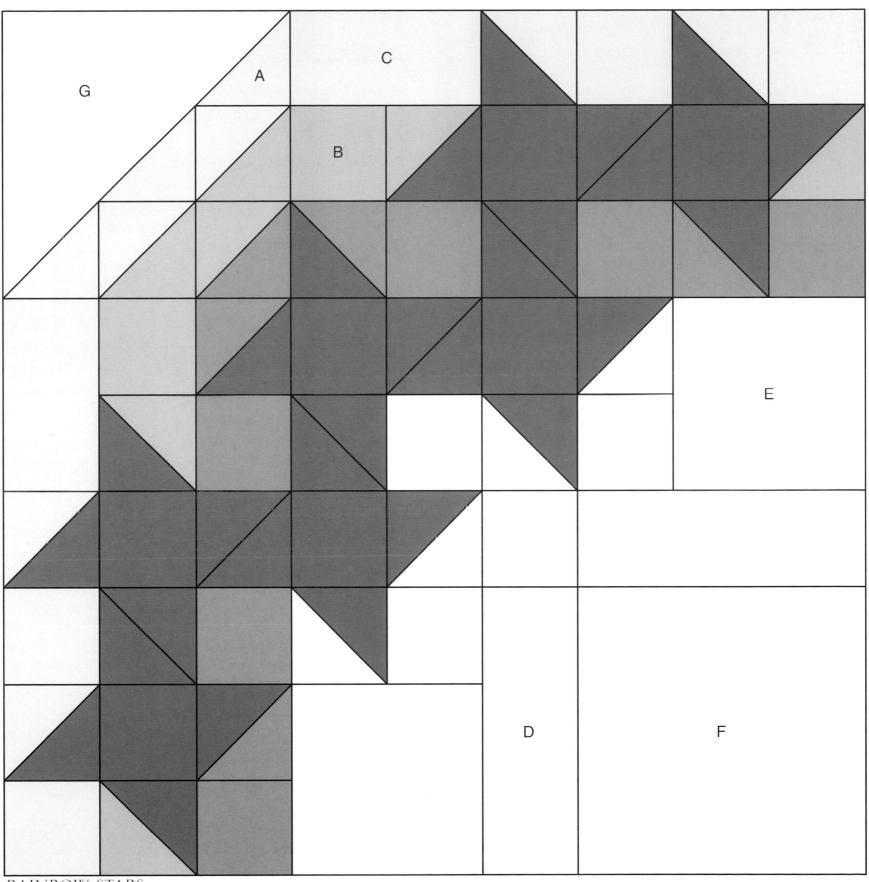

RAINBOW STARS
FULL-SIZE BLOCK

FOUR FLAGS QUILT BLOCK

FOUR FLAGS QUILT BLOCK

How To Construct This Block

Sew AAA unit (4 times). Sew BBB unit (4 times). Sew AAA unit to C piece (4 times). Sew BBB unit to AC unit (4 times). Sew bottom ABC unit to D piece, matching left edges. Working clockwise, sew ABC unit to ABCD (3 times). Appliqué E piece to center of D piece.

To Make A Bed Quilt

This quilt is designed to be a twin-size quilt measuring 69×93 inches. We have used a 3-inch plain border with setting squares made from the center of the block, the 3-inch Diamond and Stripes border, page 199, and 3-inch sashing strips with setting squares as shown.

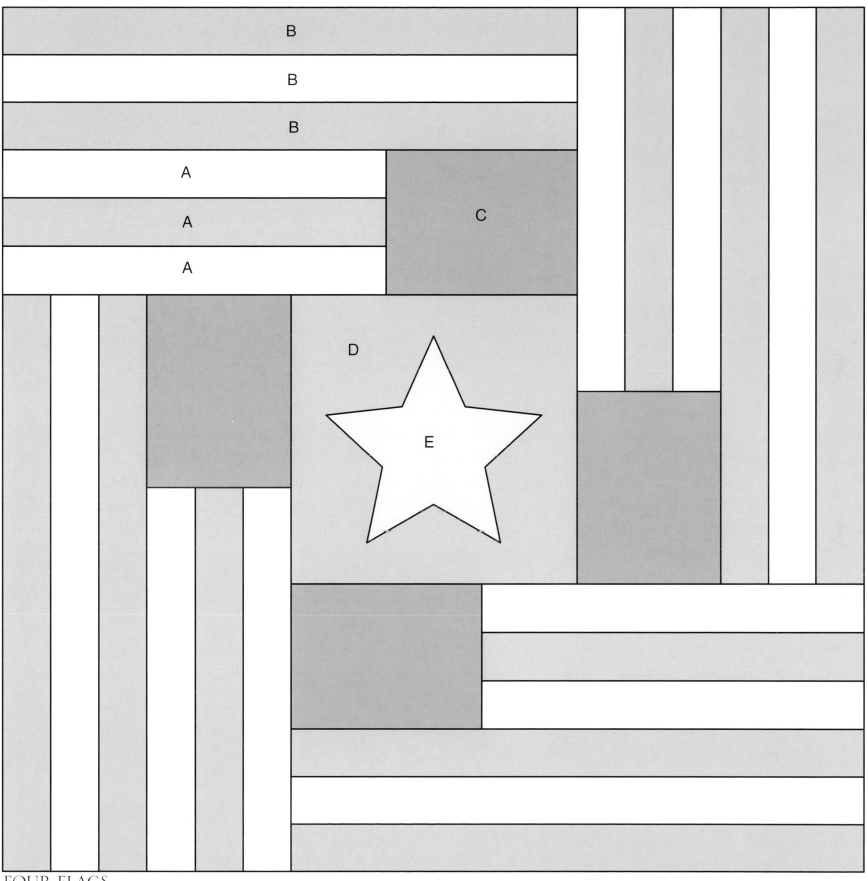

FOUR FLAGS
FULL-SIZE BLOCK

125

MEMORIAL FLAG QUILT BLOCK

MEMORIAL FLAG QUILT BLOCK

How To Construct This Block

Make BBB unit (4 times). Sew D to C; add E (6 times). Join two CDE units to make a square (3 times). For Rows 1 and 3, sew A to BBB unit; add CDE unit. For Row 2, sew BBB unit to CDE unit; add BBB unit. Sew the three rows together to complete the block.

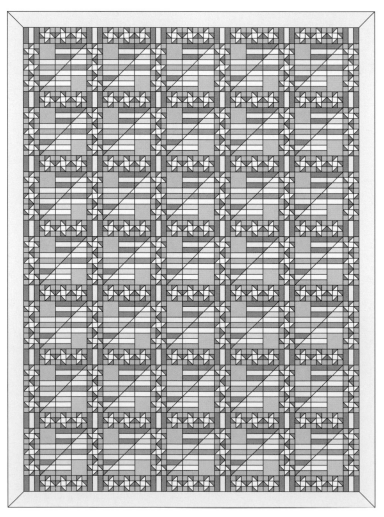

To Make A Bed Quilt

This quilt is designed to be a twin-size quilt measuring 69×93 inches. We have used a 3-inch plain border and the 3-inch Stars and Stripes border, page 197, as sashing strips as shown.

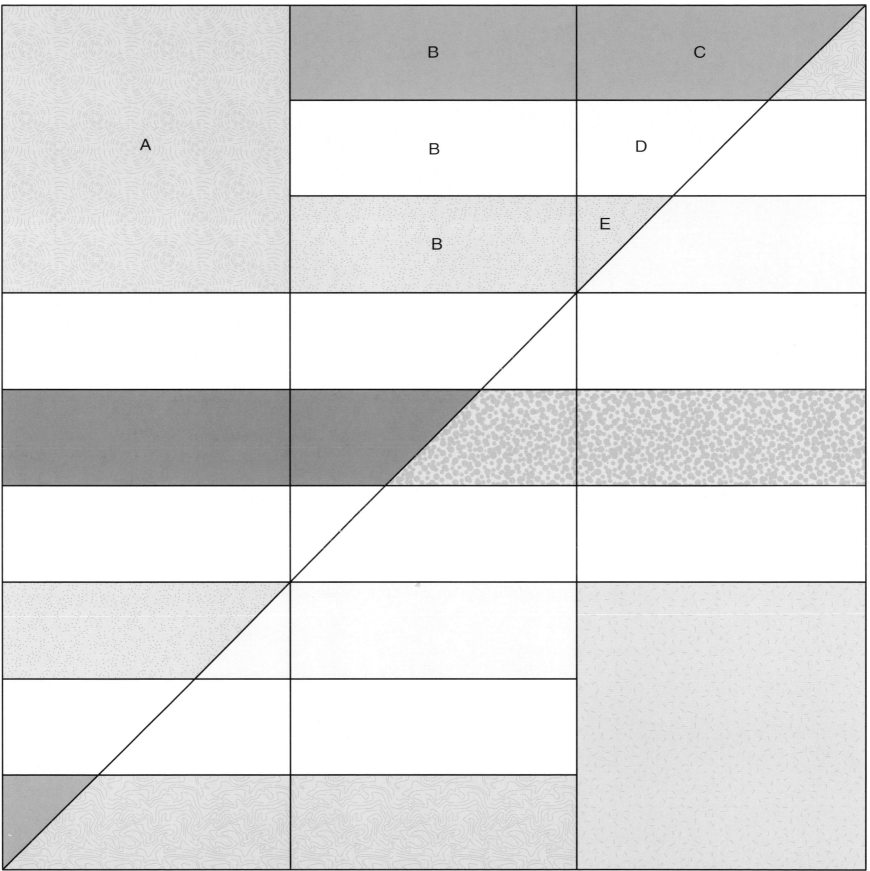

MEMORIAL FLAG
FULL-SIZE BLOCK

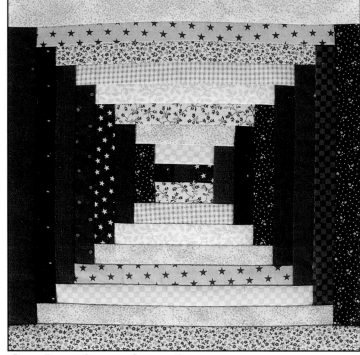

OLD LOG CABIN QUILT BLOCK

OLD LOG CABIN QUILT BLOCK

How To Construct This Block

Note: Antique log cabin quilt blocks were often sewn together with strips cut to approximate measure rather than using templates. The templates we have provided will yield a 9½" block if sewn perfectly. However, strips may also be cut and then sewn until the 9½" size is reached, trimming to fit. This is how the antique log cabin blocks with narrow strips were usually done.

Sew each strip in numerical order beginning with 1. Sew 2 and 3 to 1. Add 4 and 5 to 213. Continue until 33 strips have been added. Press seams away from center.

To Make A Bed Quilt

This quilt is designed to be a twin-size quilt measuring 63×99 inches. We have used three 1½-inch plain borders as shown.

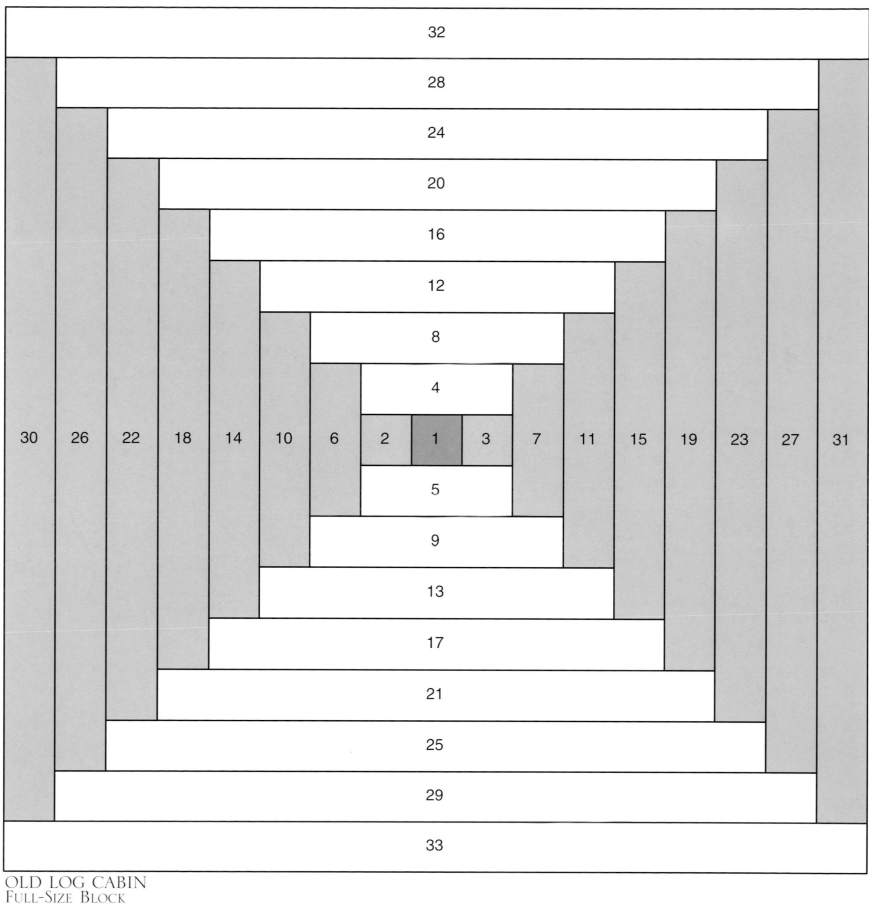

OLD LOG CABIN
FULL-SIZE BLOCK

STATUE OF LIBERTY FAN QUILT BLOCK

STATUE OF LIBERTY FAN QUILT BLOCK

How To Construct This Block

Fan spokes should be stitched in a progressive order, instead of sewing pieces together in groups and then stitching together. This will give a smoother round edge. Sew A to B, then sew on C. Sew on next B and repeat sewing on C and B pieces. End strip with Ar. Sew D to bottom edge of strip and E to top edge.

To Make A Bed Quilt

This quilt is designed to be a full-size square quilt measuring 87½×87½ inches. We have used the 3¼-inch Fan border, page 196, and 3-inch sashing strips as shown.

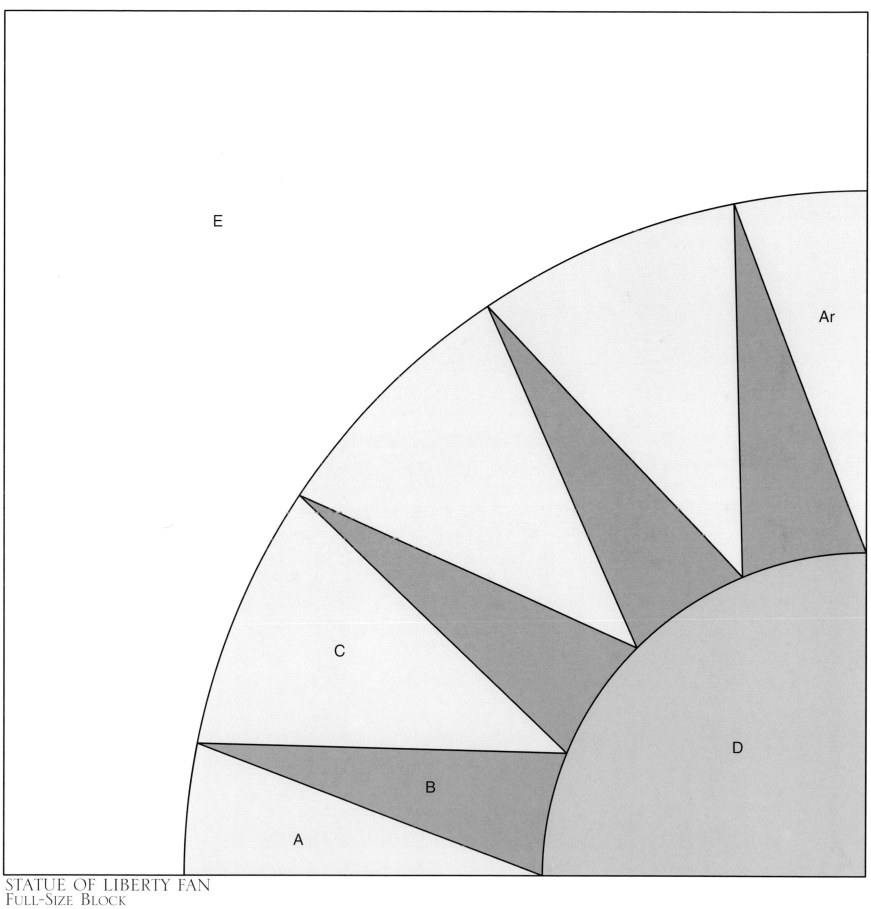

STATUE OF LIBERTY FAN
FULL-SIZE BLOCK

PATRIOTIC PINWHEEL QUILT BLOCK

PATRIOTIC PINWHEEL QUILT BLOCK

How To Construct This Block

Sew A to B (2 times). Sew AB unit to C (2 times). Sew ABC unit to opposite sides of D to complete block.

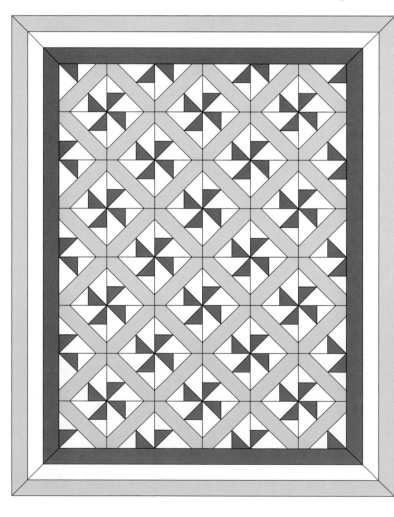

To Make A Bed Quilt

This quilt is designed to be a twin-size quilt measuring 72×90 inches. We have used three 3-inch plain borders as shown.

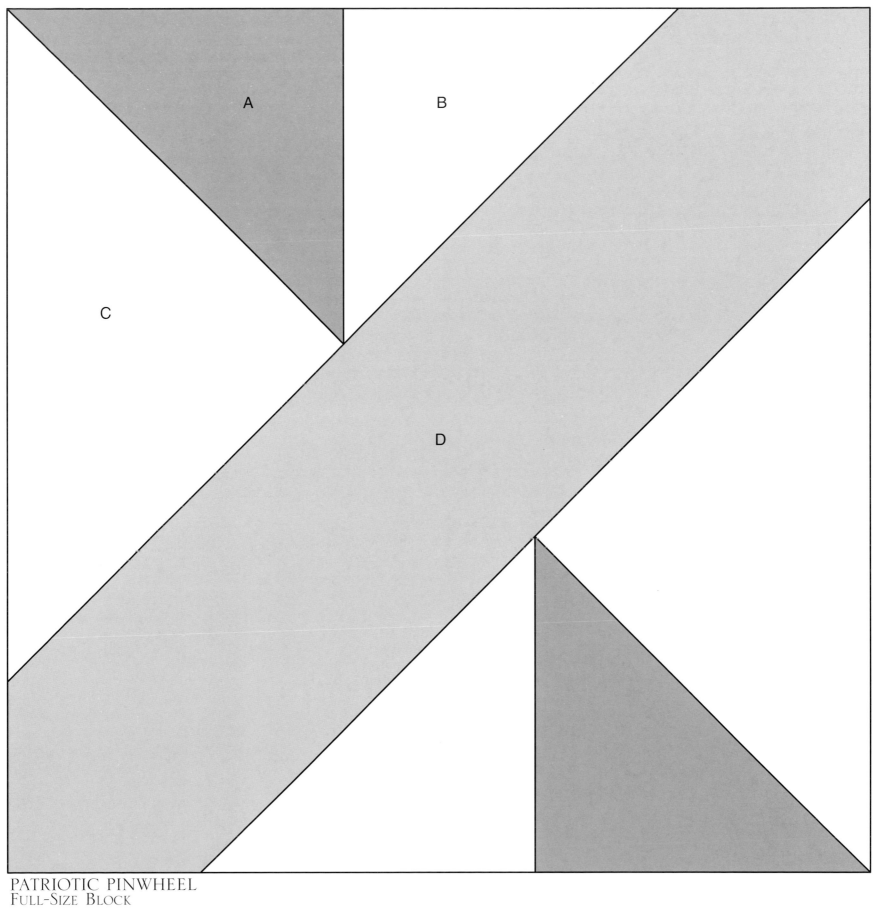

PATRIOTIC PINWHEEL
FULL-SIZE BLOCK

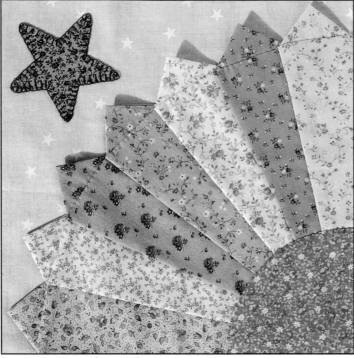

LIBERTY FAN QUILT BLOCK

LIBERTY FAN QUILT BLOCK

How To Construct This Block

Trace fan placement onto 9½"-square background fabric. Cut seven 2½" squares for prairie points. To make prairie points, press square in half diagonally with wrong sides facing to form a triangle. Press triangle in half matching raw edges. Baste prairie points to background fabric indicated by the dashed-and-dotted line on pattern, with ¼" seam. Press under seam allowance at top edge of all A's. Baste A to background fabric at bottom edge of block. With right sides facing, stitch A to basted A. Press to right side. Continue stitching and pressing A to A (5 times) to complete fan. Appliqué top edge of fan over prairie point raw edges. Machine baste block edges as needed. Appliqué B and C to background fabric. Detail fan and star with the blanket stitch if desired.

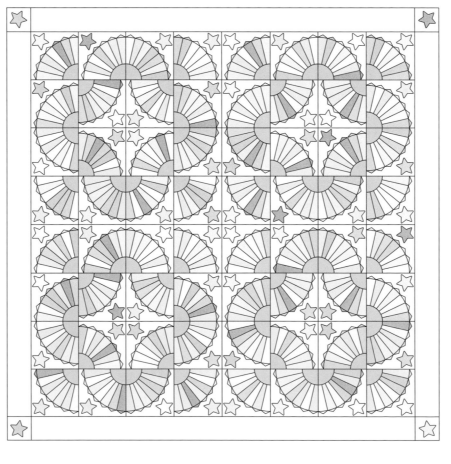

To Make A Bed Quilt

This quilt is designed to be a full-size square quilt measuring 81×81 inches. We have used a 4½-inch plain border with an appliquéd star in the corner blocks.

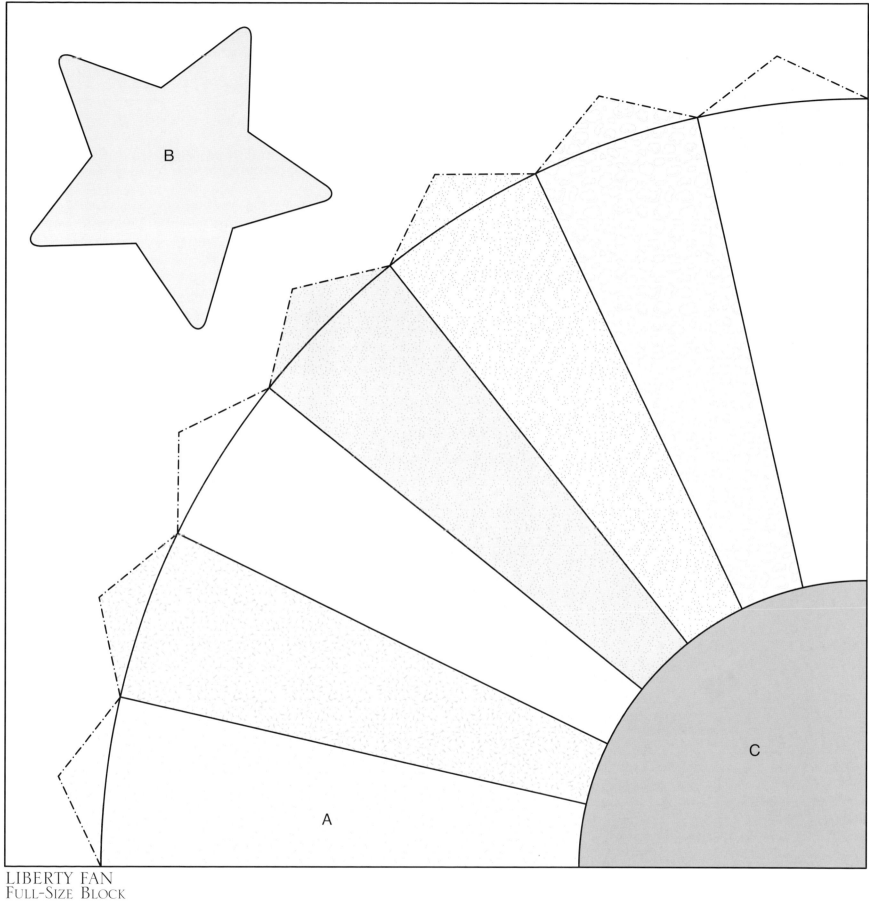

LIBERTY FAN
FULL-SIZE BLOCK

ST. CHARLES QUILT BLOCK

ST. CHARLES QUILT BLOCK

How To Construct This Block

Sew four A's into a large diamond (8 times). Join two B's (4 times). Sew four A units together (2 times). Join two sets with a center seam. Set in BB (4 times) to form corners of block. Set in triangle B (4 times) to complete the block.

To Make A Bed Quilt

This quilt is designed to be a twin-size quilt measuring 66×93 inches. We have used 2-, 1-, and 3-inch plain borders with setting triangles as shown.

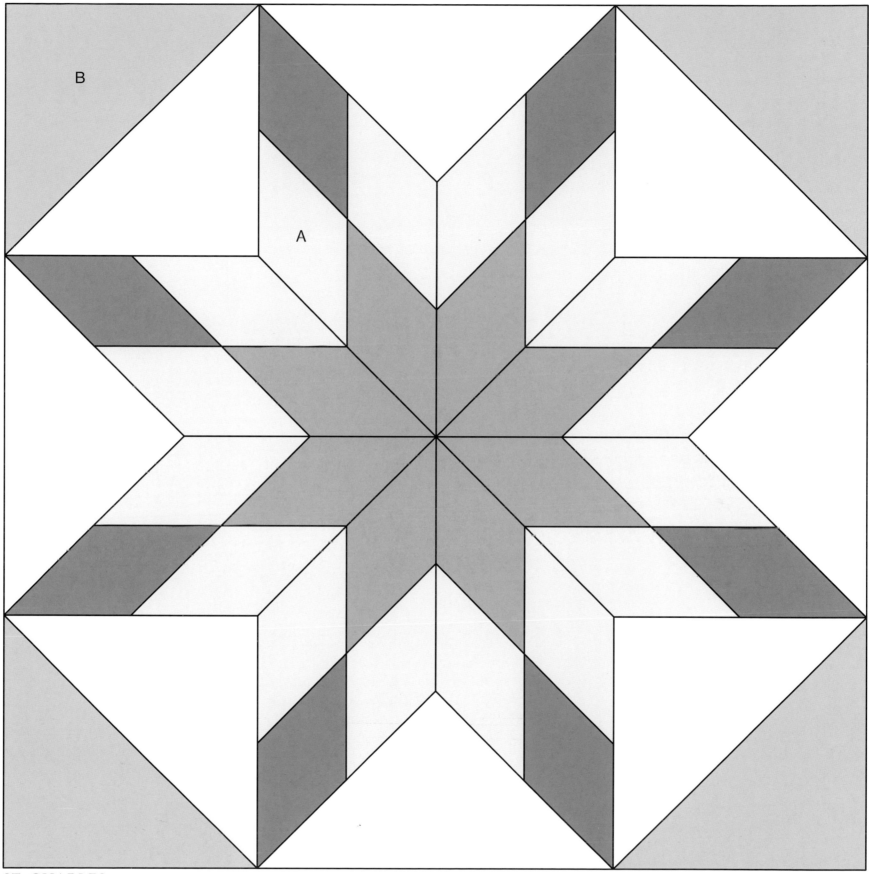

ST. CHARLES
Full-Size Block

AMERICANA ❧ TIPSY STAR

TIPSY STAR QUILT BLOCK

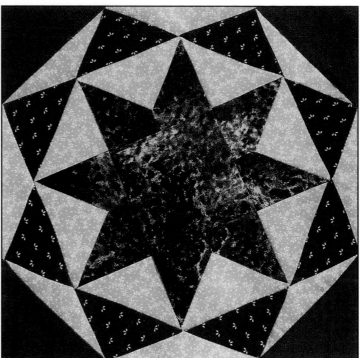

TIPSY STAR QUILT BLOCK

How To Construct This Block

Stitch B and Br (4 times). Set in C to BBr (4 times). Sew a BBrC unit to top and bottom of A. Join two C's (4 times). Add CC to each side of BBrC unit (2 times). Sew CCBBrCCC to each side of BBrCABBC. Sew D to E (4 times). Sew C to E (4 times). Join DE to CE (4 times). Add DECE to each side of center unit.

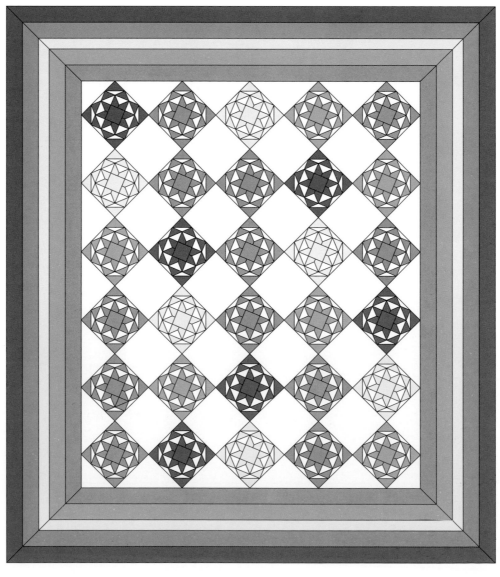

To Make A Bed Quilt

This quilt is designed to be a queen-size quilt measuring 91¾×104½ inches. We have used 3-, 3-, 2-, 3-, and 3-inch plain borders as shown. The block is set on point with 9-inch setting blocks between.

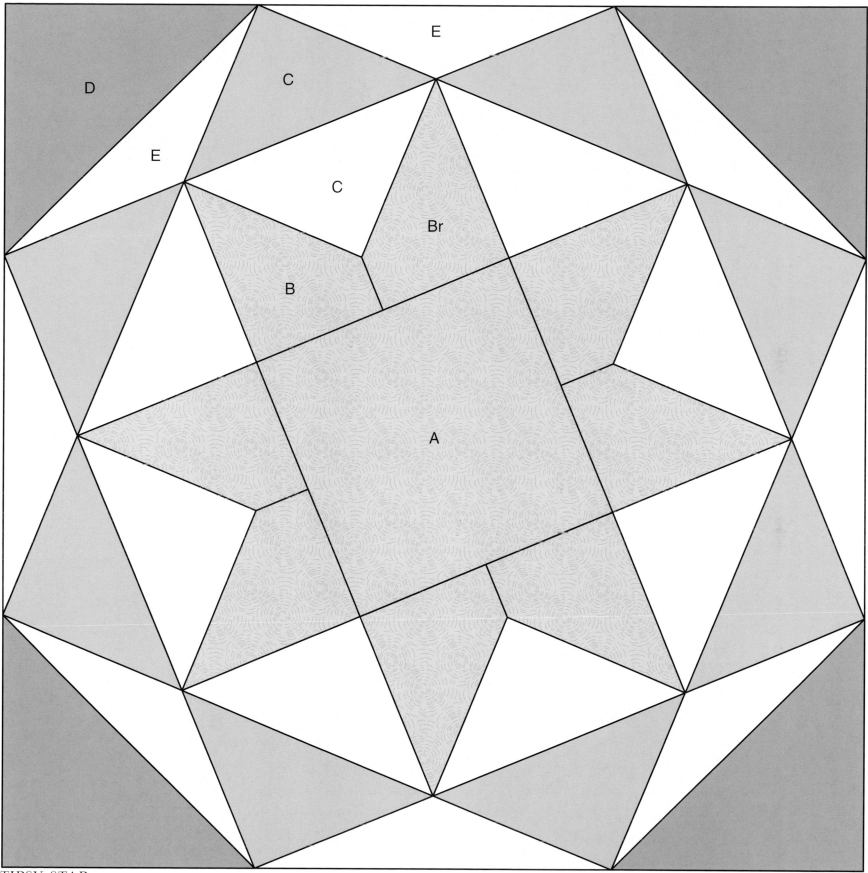

TIPSY STAR
FULL-SIZE BLOCK

CHECKERED STAR QUILT BLOCK

CHECKERED STAR QUILT BLOCK

How To Construct This Block

Sew BB units together along long edges to make eight squares. Sew A squares and BB units into five horizontal rows as shown. Join rows to complete the block.

To Make A Bed Quilt

This quilt is designed to be a full-size quilt measuring 81×90 inches. We have used the 4½-inch Sawtooth border, page 204, as shown.

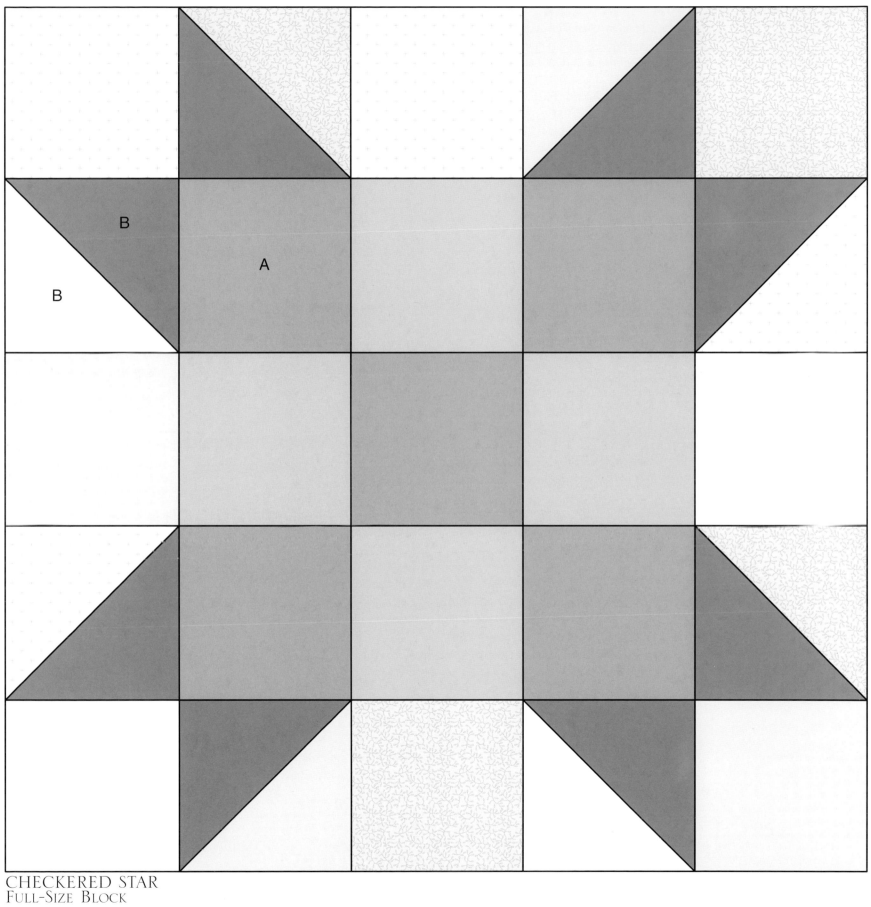

CHECKERED STAR
FULL-SIZE BLOCK

AMERICANA SAMPLER QUILT

As shown on page 99. Finished size: 63×75 inches.

MATERIALS

- 20—9½" completed unfinished quilt blocks in coordinating colors
- 1½ yards of navy blue print for sashing
- ⅓ yard of gold print
- 1¼ yards of dark red print for border
- 2 yards of white on white print for border
- 10" square of medium blue print for corner squares
- Gold embroidery floss; 4 yards fabric for backing; 69×81" quilt batting

Quantities specified for 44/45"-wide 100% cotton fabrics. All measurements include a ¼" seam allowance unless otherwise specified.

CUT THE FABRIC

To make best use of fabrics, cut pieces in order listed. These listings include mathematically correct border lengths. You may wish to add extra length to borders now to allow for any sewing differences later. Trim border strips to actual length before adding them to the quilt top. For this, cut white border strips lengthwise (parallel to selvage).

From navy blue print, cut:
49—3½×9½" sashing strips

From gold print, cut:
30—3½" squares
16—Pattern A—(Five-Pointed Star border, page 208)

From dark red print, cut:
7—2½×42" binding strips
7—2×42" strips—Piece to make:
    2—2×67" border strips
    2—2×55" border strips
4—Pattern C (Five-Pointed Star border)

From white print, cut:
2—5×66½" border strips
2—5×54½" border strips

From medium blue print, cut:
4—Pattern B (Five-Pointed Star border)
4—Pattern Br (Five-Pointed Star border)

ASSEMBLE THE QUILT TOP

1. Lay out 20 blocks in a pleasing arrangement, four blocks horizontally, five rows vertically.
2. Sew one navy blue 3½×9½" sashing strip to the right side of each block.
3. To the left side of each block that begins each horizontal row, sew one navy blue 3½×9½" sashing strip.
4. Sew together each horizontal block row. Press the seams toward sashing strips.
5. Sew one gold print 3½" square to the right side of 24 navy blue 3½×9½" sashing strips.
6. For each horizontal sashing row, you will need four sashing strips from Step 5. Join four strips horizontally (6 times). Sew a gold print 3½" square to left side of each row.
7. Sew each row together beginning and ending with a sashing row strip. At this point, the quilt top should measure 51½×63½" including the seam allowance.

MAKE THE BORDERS

1. Sew one dark red 2×67" border strip to each side of quilt top. Begin and end stitching ¼" from the top and bottom of border. Likewise, sew one dark red 2×55" border strip to the top and bottom of quilt top. Miter corners. Press seams toward the borders.
2. Referring to photograph, *page 99,* position two gold stars at the beginning and end of each white border strip. Appliqué in place with matching thread. The maker of this quilt also blanket-stitched around each appliquéd star with gold embroidery floss.
3. Sew one Pattern B to the left side of Pattern C. Sew a Pattern Br to the right side of Pattern C (4 times).

Your setting square blocks should each measure 5" including the seam allowance.

ADD THE BORDER

Sew one white print 5×66½" border strip to each side of quilt top. Sew one setting square block to each end of two white 5×54½" border strips. Sew one border to top of the quilt and one to bottom.

COMPLETE THE QUILT

Layer quilt top, batting, and backing. This quilt was quilted by outlining the pieces in blocks. Sashing was quilted in a diamond shape with stars quilted in setting squares. Stars are quilted randomly in white border; bind.

AMERICANA CHAIRBACK CUSHION

As shown on page 100. Finished size: 16×16 inches.

MATERIALS

- One 9½" completed unfinished Fireworks quilt block, page 106, in coordinating colors
- ¼ yard of solid red; ⅛ yard of navy print
- ⅛ yard of striped fabric
- 17" backing square; 17" batting square

All seam allowances are ¼" wide.

CUT THE FABRIC

From solid red, cut:
2—1×16½" outside border strip
2—1×15½" outside border strip
4—3½" corner squares

From striped print, cut:
4—3½×9½" border strips

From navy print, cut:
4—1×21½" tie strips

MAKE THE TOP

Sew a 3½×9½" striped border strip to each side of block. Sew a red 3½" square to each side of remaining

3½×9½" stripe border strips. Sew one strip to top and bottom of block. Add 1×15½" border strip to each side of block. Then sew a 1×16½" border strip to top and bottom of block. Press seams toward border.

ASSEMBLING THE CHAIRBACK CUSHION

Fold each 1×21½" navy tie strip in half lengthwise, right sides together. Sew lengthwise, sewing one end closed at an angle. Turn right side out; press. Stack together two tie strips at ¼" from each corner on top edge of block front. Raw edges together at edges of block, the ties hanging down toward center of right side of block. Stitch ties in place. Lay block on backing fabric, right sides together, then lay both pieces together on batting. Baste. Trim backing and batting to size of chairback block. Stitch together leaving a 4" opening at bottom edge. Turn and press. Stitch the opening closed. Quilt as desired. The maker quilted in the ditch around seams.

PICNIC BASKET COVER

Measure your picnic basket lid to determine what size to cut your fabrics. This cover is designed to fit a picnic basket lid that measures 13×20 inches. Make any necessary measurement changes for your own picnic basket cover before beginning the project.

As shown on page 100. Finished size: 13×20 inches.

MATERIALS

- Two 9½" completed unfinished Woven Star quilt blocks, page 116, in coordinating colors
- 1¾ yards of red check; ¼ yard of white print; 2 yards of piping cord; 15×22" piece of fleece; 2—2½" star appliqués

All seam allowances are ¼" wide.

CUT THE FABRIC

To make the best use of your fabrics, cut the pieces in the order that follows.

From red check, cut:
36×42" rectangle. Cut enough 5½"
    bias strips to piece:
        2—5½×55" strips for ties
        2—5½×45" ruffle strips
12×18" rectangle. Cut enough 1½"
    bias strips to piece:
        2—1½×40" cording strips
        2—10½×13½" backing pieces
        4—2½×9½" sashing strips
        2—1½×13½" sashing strips

From white print, cut:
2—3½×42" strips for ruffle

MAKE THE COVER TOP

Sew the two blocks together. Begin at outside edge of a quilt block, sew a 2½×9½" sashing strip to top of the cover. Stop stitching ¼" from inside edge of block. Repeat with three remaining sashing strips, adding to the top and bottoms of two blocks, again leaving a vent opening. Sew a 1½×13½" sashing strip to each side of basket cover top.

Layer cover top and fleece together; baste. Quilt as desired. Trim fleece to match the top. Cut a slit in the fleece 2½" long at center top and bottom for a vent.

ASSEMBLE THE BASKET LID COVER

Cut two pieces of piping cord, each 36" long. Cover the piping cord with the 1½" bias strips. Position one piping cord on the right side of the cover front, raw edges together, beginning and ending at the vent opening. Stitch the piping to one half of the cover top. Repeat with the second piping cord. Trim raw edges to match the cover edges. Right sides together, join one red check 5½×45" bias strip with one white print 3½×42" strip lengthwise

to make a ruffle strip 8½×42" long. Repeat for a second ruffle strip. With right sides together, fold ruffle in half lengthwise. Sew across the ends of ruffle. Turn to the right side; press. Position ruffle's finished edges ¼" from edge of vent. Gather raw edges, adjusting gathers around one half of the top. Stitch ruffle over piping, matching raw edges. Repeat for second half of basket top.

Measure 2½" from each top and bottom edge of backing squares. Sew together, beginning and ending at the 2½" mark.

Lay cover back on cover top, right sides together. Begin ¼" from a vent, sew to opposite side, stopping ¼" from vent. Repeat for a second side, this time, leave an opening for turning along the side seam. Stitch. Trim corners; turn right side out. Stitch opening closed at side seam.

Turn under seam allowances on sashing and back at vent and turn to back side of the cover. Hand stitch facing hem.

FINISHING THE BASKET LID COVER

With right sides together, sew each tie together lengthwise, tapering to a point on either end. Leave an opening for turning. Trim corners. Turn to right side. Stitch openings closed; press. Make a pleat at the center of each tie. Stitch each tie over a vent opening. Glue or sew an appliquéd star to center of each block. Place cover on basket lid. Secure by tieing in a bow around handles.

STARS AND STRIPES PLACE MAT

As shown on page 101. Finished size: 11½×18½ inches.

MATERIALS

**Two 9½" completed unfinished Stars
    and Stripes quilt blocks, page 114, in
    coordinating colors**

¼ yard of blue print
⅓ yard of red print for back
12×19" piece of quilt batting
6—½" gold star buttons

All seam allowances are ¼" wide.

CUT THE FABRIC

From blue print, cut:
2—1¾×18½" strips for borders
2—2×42" strips for binding

From red print, cut:
1—12×19" rectangle for back

MAKE THE PLACE MAT

Sew two blocks together with the stars on the outside edges. Sew one 1½×18½" strip to top of place mat and one to bottom of place mat.

Layer the top, batting and back together; baste. Quilt as desired. The maker outline quilted around the small star blocks and stripes. Finish place mat with binding. Sew a gold star button in center of each star.

JEWEL STAR TABLECLOTH

As shown on page 101. Finished size: 61¾×61¾ inches.

MATERIALS

**Four 9½" completed unfinished Jewel
    Star quilt blocks, page 118, in
    coordinating colors**
3¼ yards of solid blue
1¾ yards matching striped blue fabric
½ yard cream print for border
½ yard of blue print for border

Quantities specified are for 44/45"-wide,
    100% cotton fabrics. All measurements
    include ¼" seam allowances.

CUT THE FABRIC

To make the best use of your fabrics, cut the pieces in the order that follows. For this project, the border strips are cut the length of the fabric (parallel to the selvage).

Extra length has been added to the border strips to allow for mitering the corners.

From solid blue, cut:
4—17½×54" border strips
5—2×54" binding strips

From striped blue fabric, cut:
4—3×59" B border strips (Sawtooth
    border, page 204)

From cream print, cut:
12—6" squares, cutting each
    diagonally twice in an X for a
    total of 48 A triangles (Sawtooth
    border)

From blue print, cut:
2—7¾" squares, cutting each in
    half diagonally for a total of four
    C triangles (Sawtooth border)
11—6" squares, cutting each
    diagonally twice in an X for a
    total of 44 A triangles (Sawtooth
    border)
    *Note: The triangles cut in an
    X will have the long side cut on
    the straight of the grain for the
    outside border.*

ASSEMBLE THE CENTER

Referring to photograph, *page 101,* lay out four blocks. Sew together blocks in each row. Then join rows.

ADD THE BORDERS

Match the center of a solid blue 17½×54" border strip and the center of a 3×59" B border strip. Sew two strips together lengthwise. Extra fabric has been added to allow for mitering. Repeat for the remaining three border strips.

Matching the centers, join the border strips to each side of the center blocks, stopping ¼" from each corner. Miter border strips. Square the edges and press seams open. The top should measure 57½" including the seam allowance.

ASSEMBLE THE PIECED BORDER

1. For one pieced border, you will need 12 cream A triangles and 11 blue print A triangles. Sew the A triangles in a horizontal row.
2. Repeat for three more pieced borders. The pieced border should measure 2⅞×57½" including the seam allowance.
3. With the cream triangles closest to the tablecloth edge, sew each border to the the tablecloth. Press the seam allowances toward the triangle border.
4. Sew one blue print C triangle to each corner of tablecloth.
5. Add binding to finish your tablecloth.

LOG CABIN QUILT

Many early quilt makers made this pattern from silk and velvet scraps, old neckties, and soft wool pieces.

This quilt makes a very pleasing patriotic quilt using a navy with white stars print, red centers and accompanying white strips.

The maker must have first used all of her navy and stars print. She then used what blue she had on hand to finish the rows. Different shirting fabrics with tiny prints were used for the white strips.

There are several ways to set the blocks. The directions to make this quilt will use only four fabrics. If a scrappy look is desired, substitute a fat quarter (18×22") of a different blue for 11 blocks. The strip border shown contains only one strip of blue, the directions do not put the blue strip in the border. The strips vary in size from 1" to 2". The maker used the scraps in the size strip that she had. Nothing is larger than 2" finished.

As shown on page 101. Finished size: 62×71 inches.

MATERIALS

3¼ yards of white with tiny print
2¼ yards of navy blue with stars print
½ yard of red print
½ yard of white with stripe
3¾ yards of backing fabric
67×77" batting

Quantities specified are for 44/45"-wide, 100% cotton fabrics. All measurements include a ¼" seam allowance unless otherwise stated.

CUT THE FABRIC

The pattern on *page 129* can be used as a template pattern. However, we suggest cutting strips of fabrics and squaring up the block to fit the 9½" unfinished block as listed in this method. This method is much more efficient for a log cabin block. To make best use of your fabrics, cut pieces in the order that follows.

From white with tiny print, cut:
3—4½×42" strips for border
4—4½" border squares
94—1×42" strips for blocks

From blue with star print, cut:
76—1×42" strips for blocks—Cut 84—1" squares from two of these strips

From red, cut:
3—4½×42" strips for border
1—1×42" strips for blocks—Cut 42—1" squares from one of these strips

From white with stripe
3—4½×42" strips for border

ASSEMBLING THE BLOCKS

1. Sew one blue 1" square to the opposite sides of one red 1" square. Repeat for a total of 42 center units. *Note: Use the assembly line or strip piecing method to construct log cabin blocks.* Lay a random length of a white 1" strip, right side down on the center unit. Sew the strip to the center unit side. Without lifting the presser foot, place another sewn center unit under the 1" strip. Continue sewing. When at the end of a strip, stop sewing. Cut between each center block. Press the strip away from the center. Repeat until all of the center units are sewn to a strip.
2. Add each strip in numerical order, pressing the strip away from the center. Add strips until all 33 strips have been added.
3. Repeat Steps 1 and 2 for a total of 42 blocks. At this point, the block should measure 9½" including the seam allowance.

Note: After every two strips are added, use a ruler and square-up your block, also cutting off any excess fabric from the block.

ASSEMBLING THE QUILT TOP

Refer to the Quilt Assembly Diagram, *right*, for the correct placement of the blocks, sewing seven rows of six blocks each. Sew the rows together. At this point, the quilt top should measure 54½×63½" including the seam allowance.

CUTTING AND ADDING THE BORDERS

1. From the white print, red print, and white with stripe 4½×42"strips, cut the following: varying widths of a minimum width of 1½" to maximum width of 2½".
2. Join the assorted border strips, alternating colors, along the 4½" sides to make two 4½×63½" long side border strips and two 4½×54½" top and bottom border strips.

Note: These are mathematically correct border lengths. You may wish to add extra length to the border strips to allow for any sewing differences and then trim to fit your quilt top.

3. Sew each 4½×63½" border strip to each side of the quilt top. Sew one white with print 4½" square to each end of the two 4½×54½" border strips. Add one strip to the top of the quilt top and one to the bottom of the quilt top.

COMPLETE THE QUILT

This quilt is quilted in the ditch, or close to the seams. The maker did not bind the quilt. The edges were turned over to the back of the quilt and hemmed over the backing. If you choose to bind the quilt you will need seven 2×42" strips. Yardage has not been allowed for a binding.

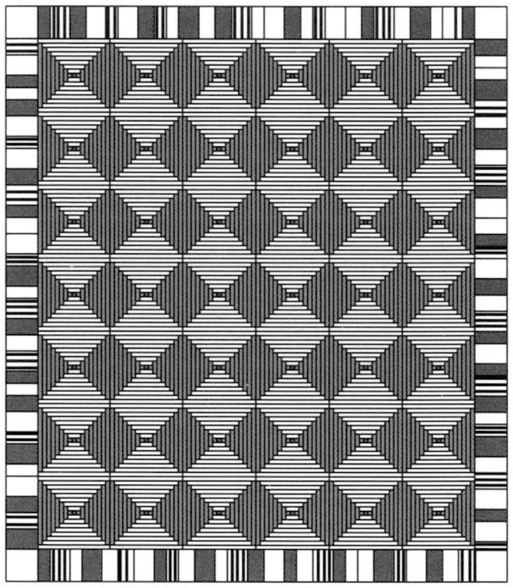

Quilt Assembly Diagram

JUST FOR FUN

We had so much fun with the blocks in this collection that we designed four miniature quilts using the twenty blocks in this chapter. Instructions for the quilts you see here begin on *page 188*. Turn the page for more fun-to-make project ideas.

Vintage Charm Sampler Quilt

Noah's Friends Child's Quilt

Merry Christmas Wall Quilt

Fleur de lis Wall Piece

PROJECTS YOU CAN MAKE

Using old and new quilt block ideas, we've chosen fanciful projects for you to make and treasure. From a colorful Antique Butterfly Quilt to a vintage Housedress Hot Pad, you're sure to find something you'll want to make just for fun! We've used a sampling of the borders as trims and sashings between the blocks for some of the projects. Sketch out your ideas first, then have fun mixing your favorite blocks from this chapter. Instructions for all of these whimsical and wonderful projects begin on *page 190*.

HOUSEDRESS HOT PAD WITH CHECKERBOARD BORDER TEA TOWEL

ANTIQUE BUTTERFLY QUILT

RECTANGLE MAKES THE SQUARE SCREEN PANELS

CHERRY PIE QUILT

HOUSEDRESS QUILT BLOCK

HOUSEDRESS QUILT BLOCK

How To Construct This Block

Sew A to B and B to C; set in F section. Repeat for other side of dress. Stitch halves together along center front. Stitch D and Dr pieces to E; stitch to dress. Add trims as desired.

To Make A Bed Quilt

This quilt is designed to be an extra-length twin-size quilt measuring 69×105 inches. We have used a 3-inch plain border, the 3-inch Diamond border, page 198, 3-inch sashing strips, and setting squares as shown.

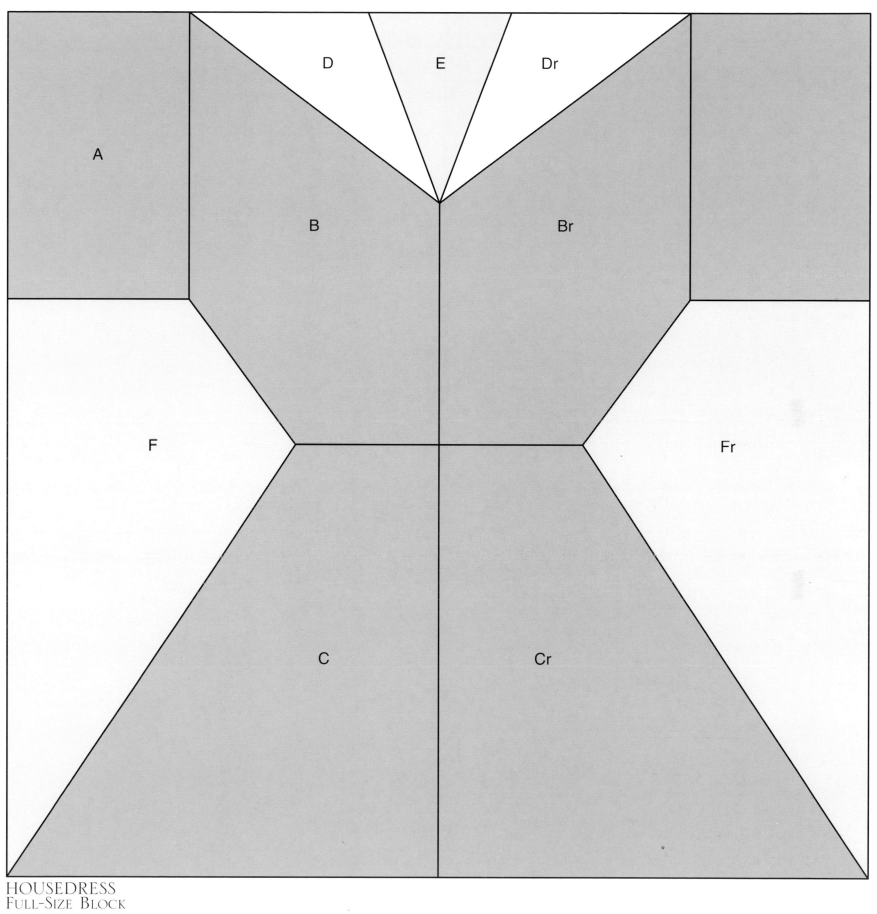

HOUSEDRESS
FULL-SIZE BLOCK

CHERRY PIE QUILT BLOCK

CHERRY PIE QUILT BLOCK

How To Construct This Block

Position pieces to be appliquéd onto a 9½" background square. Appliqué pieces A and B; add C (3 times). Appliqué piece D, overlap second D and appliqué. Satin-stitch around leaves; add veins. Buttonhole-stitch or satin-stitch around cherries.

For alternate fusing method of appliqué, see page 212.

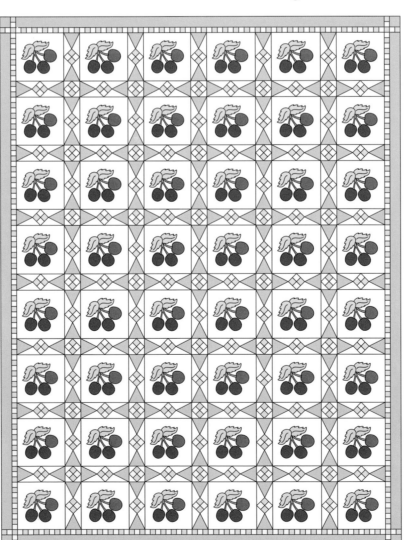

To Make A Bed Quilt

This quilt is designed to be a twin-size quilt measuring 75×99 inches. We have used the 3-inch Checkerboard border, page 195, and the 3-inch To the Point border, page 199, for sashing strips as shown.

CHERRY PIE
FULL-SIZE BLOCK

FLEUR DE LIS QUILT BLOCK

FLEUR DE LIS QUILT BLOCK

How To Construct This Block

Sew a piece B to each side of piece A. Stop and start stitching ¼" from each end, being careful not to stitch through the seam line. Match and sew together the edges of adjacent B pieces, starting the stitching ¼" from the end next to the A piece. Appliqué the D pieces on piece A, then appliqué the C pieces on the B pieces.

For alternate fusing method of appliqué, see page 212.

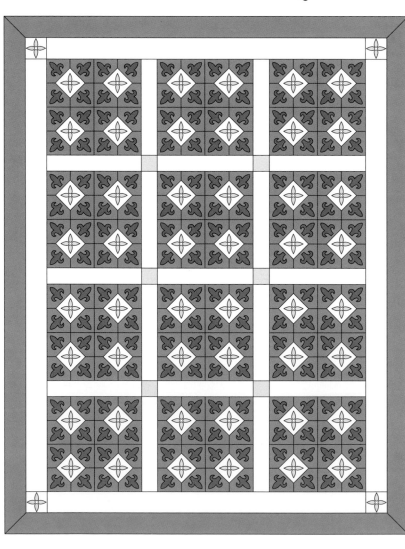

To Make A Bed Quilt

This quilt is designed to be a twin-size quilt measuring 74×95 inches. We have used a 3-inch plain border, a 4-inch plain border, 3-inch sashing strips, and setting squares as shown.

FLEUR DE LIS
FULL-SIZE BLOCK

NOAH'S ARK QUILT BLOCK

NOAH'S ARK QUILT BLOCK

How To Construct This Block

Sew A to B; add C. Sew D to E and Dr to Er. Sew F to G. Sew DE to FG; add DrEr. Appliqué O to F. Sew ABC to DEFGDrEr for Unit 1. Sew I to H; add I. Appliqué two M's to left I and two N's to right I. Sew K to J; add Kr. Sew IHI to KJKr; add L for Unit 2. Sew Unit 1 to Unit 2. Appliqué O to B.

For alternate fusing method of appliqué, see page 212.

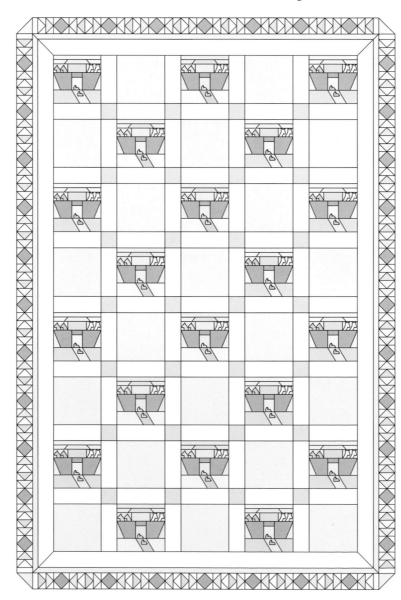

To Make A Bed Quilt

This quilt is designed to be an extra-length twin-size quilt measuring 71×107 inches. We have used a 3-inch plain border, the 4-inch Eclectic border, page 200, 3-inch sashing strips, and setting squares as shown. We have placed 9-inch setting blocks between the Noah's Ark blocks.

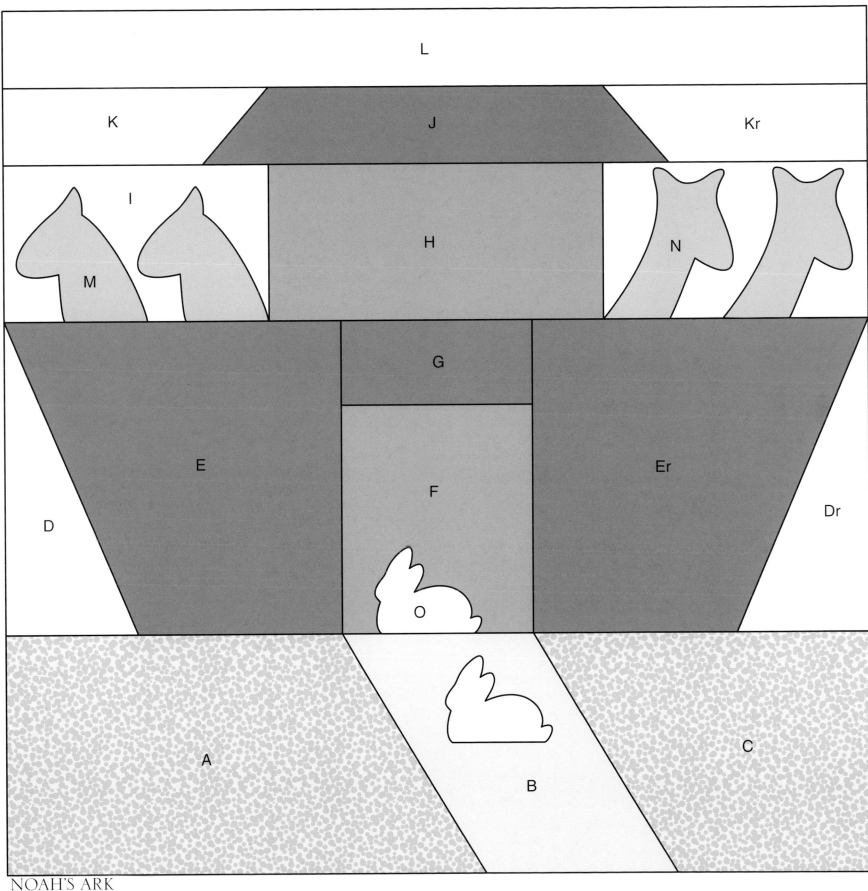

NOAH'S ARK
FULL-SIZE BLOCK

ROOSTER QUILT BLOCK

ROOSTER QUILT BLOCK

How To Construct This Block

Appliqué A, B, C, D, and E pieces onto a 9½" background square. Appliqué F, G, H, I, and J pieces. Sew a small button for the eye.

For alternate fusing method of appliqué, see page 212.

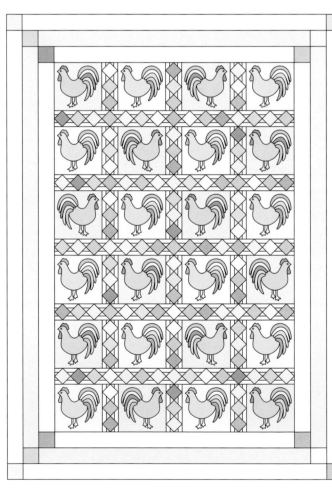

To Make A Bed Quilt

This quilt is designed to be a twin-size quilt measuring 63×87 inches. We have used three 3-inch plain borders with setting squares in the corners and the 3-inch Diamond and Stripes border, page 199, for sashing strips as shown. Reverse templates as needed to face rooster in the opposite direction.

ROOSTER
FULL-SIZE BLOCK

DUCK QUILT BLOCK

DUCK QUILT BLOCK

How To Construct This Block

Sew A to A, then sew to one end of G. Sew C to B, and sew D to E. Sew CB to DE; add F. Sew this unit to AAG unit, then sew H to top edge of this unit to form the head. Sew J to K; add L. Sew M to opposite edge of L. Sew O to P and Q to R. Sew OP and QR units together and sew this unit to N. Sew JKLM to top edge of this unit for body of duck. Sew J to T, then sew this unit to S. Sew STJ unit to top of duck body unit. Sew duck body unit to head unit, then sew I to bottom edge of duck to complete block.

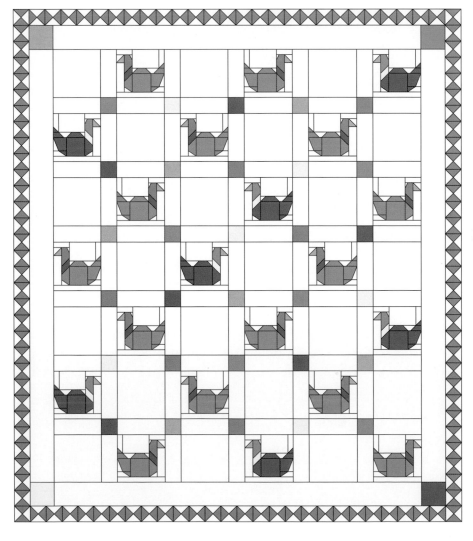

To Make A Bed Quilt

This quilt is designed to be a full-size quilt measuring 84×96 inches. We have used a 4½-inch plain border, the 3-inch Pie Crust border, page 195, 3-inch sashing strips, and setting squares as shown. Reverse the templates as needed to face duck in opposite direction. We have placed 9-inch setting blocks between the Duck blocks.

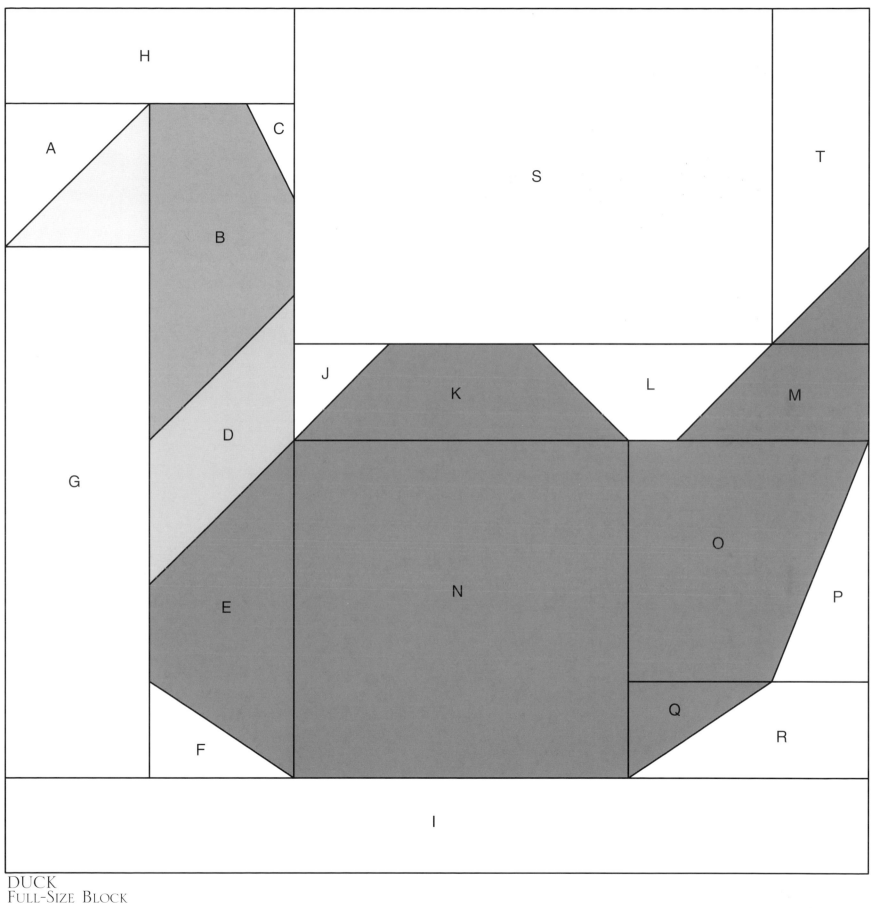

DUCK
FULL-SIZE BLOCK

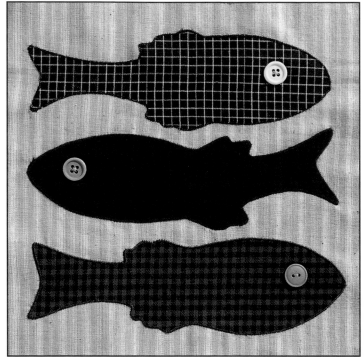

FISH QUILT BLOCK

FISH QUILT BLOCK

How To Construct This Block

Appliqué A, B, and C pieces onto 9½" background square. Sew buttons on for eyes if desired.

For alternate fusing method of appliqué, see page 212.

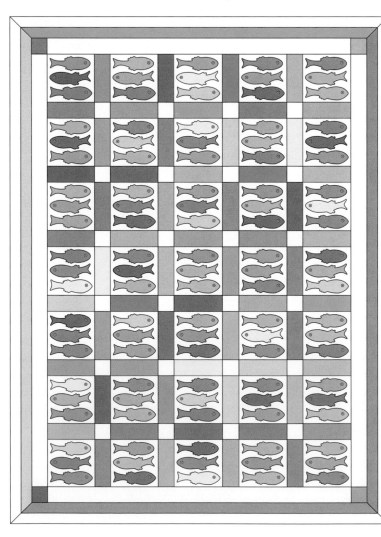

To Make A Bed Quilt

This quilt is designed to be a twin-size quilt measuring 71×95 inches. We have used a 3-inch plain border with setting squares in the corners, two 2-inch plain borders, 3-inch sashing strips, and setting squares as shown. We suggest using plaid, batik-like or flannel fabrics.

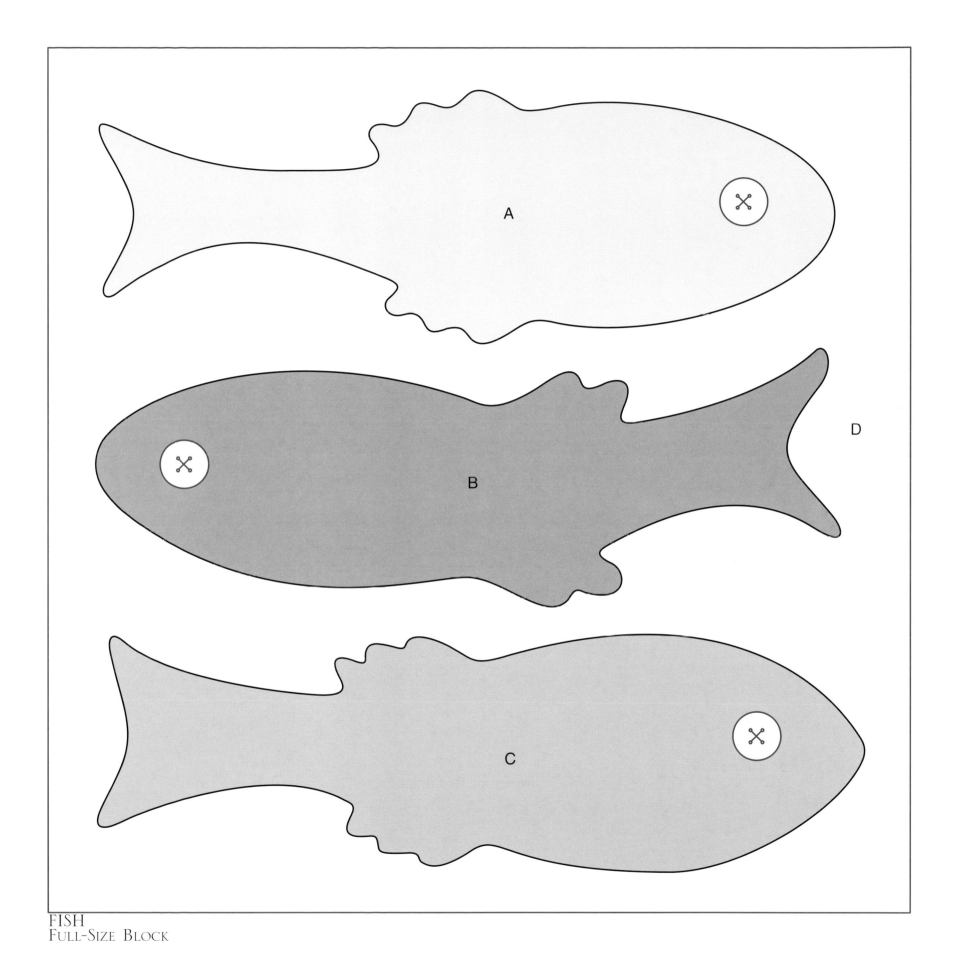

FISH
FULL-SIZE BLOCK

RIBBONS ALL AROUND QUILT BLOCK

RIBBONS ALL AROUND QUILT BLOCK

How To Construct This Block

This block could be made using a template, but we suggest speed strip sewing. Sew three $1\frac{1}{2}\times10\frac{1}{2}$" strips together, then cut into three $3\frac{1}{2}$" squares. Repeat with second group of three strips. Sew the blocks together into three rows, then sew three rows together to make the block.

Traditional piecing: Cut twenty-seven $1\frac{1}{2}\times3\frac{1}{2}$" A rectangles or use the A template piece. Sew three A rectangles together to make the AAA unit (9 times). Sew three units together into rows. Then, sew three rows together to make the block.

To Make A Bed Quilt

This quilt is designed to be a queen-size quilt measuring 84×102 inches. We have used a 3-inch plain border and the 3-inch Diamond and Stripes border, page 199, as shown.

A

RIBBONS ALL AROUND
FULL-SIZE BLOCK

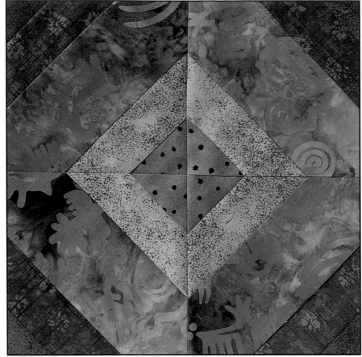

RECTANGLE MAKES THE SQUARE QUILT BLOCK

RECTANGLE MAKES THE SQUARE QUILT BLOCK

How To Construct This Block

Sew A to B along long edge of A. Then join AB to C along long edge. Join second A and B, and sew to center C piece. Make four units. Join four units together to complete the block.

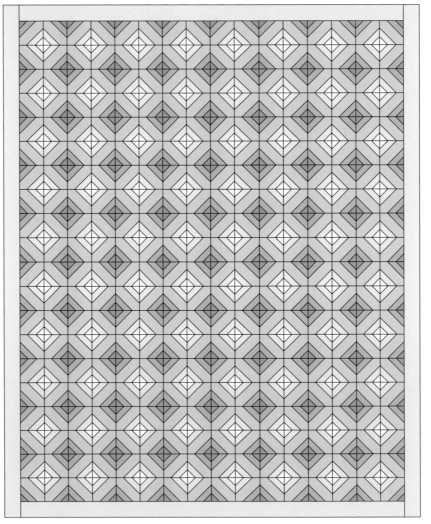

To Make A Bed Quilt

This quilt is designed to be a twin-size quilt measuring 78×96 inches. We have used a 3-inch plain border as shown.

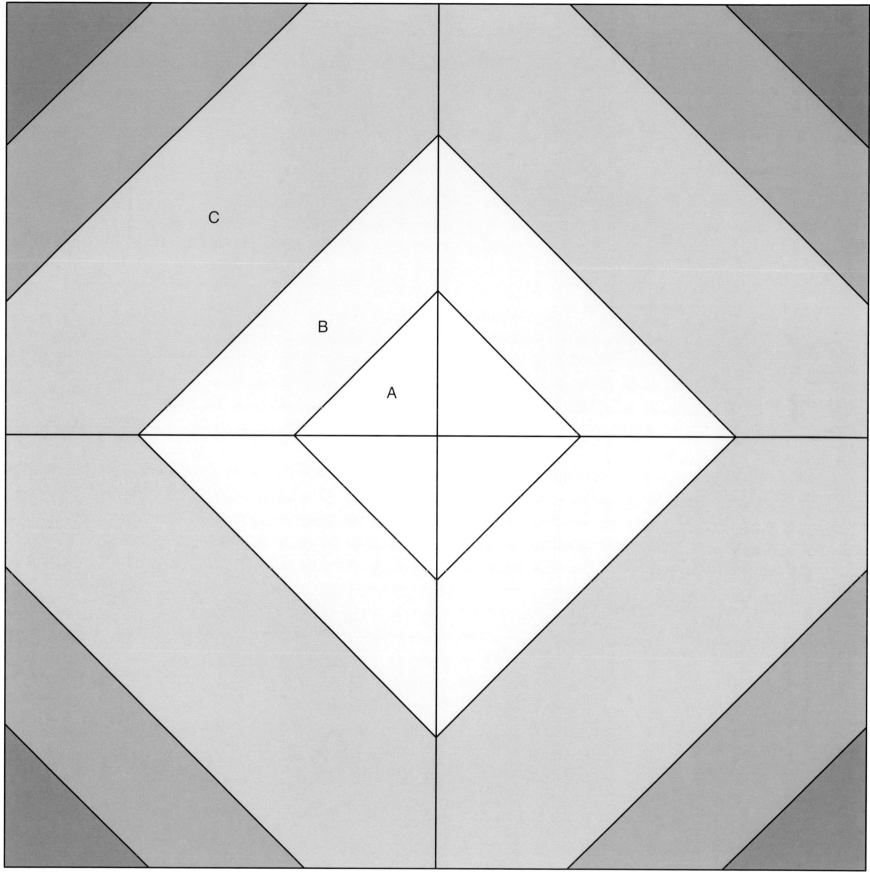

RECTANGLE MAKES THE SQUARE
Full-Size Block

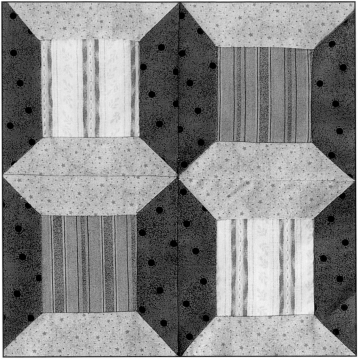

SPOOLS QUILT BLOCK

SPOOLS QUILT BLOCK

How To Construct This Block

Sew spool ends A to opposite edges of B, being careful not to stitch into end seam allowances. Join the background pieces A to the remaining edges of B. Miter AA seams. Make four units. Join four units together to complete the block.

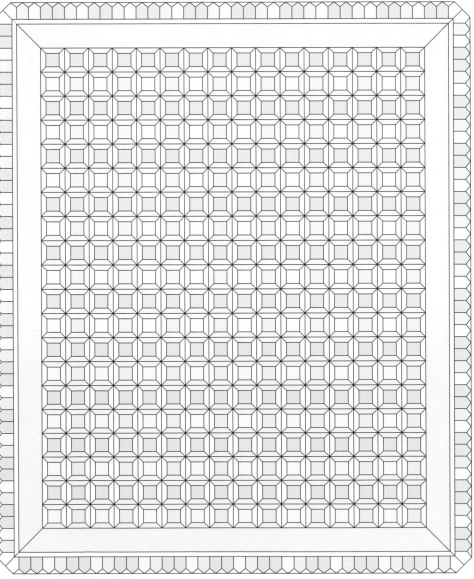

To Make A Bed Quilt

This quilt is designed to be a queen-size quilt measuring 89×107 inches. We have used a 4½-inch plain border and the 4-inch Stripes border, page 205, as shown.

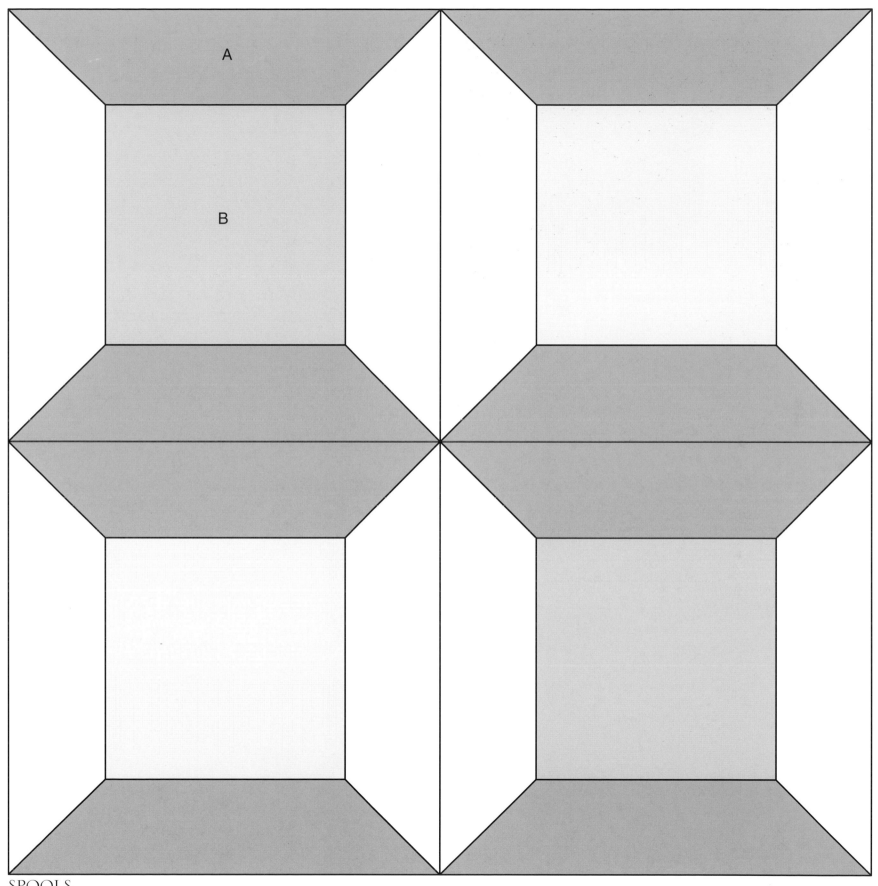

SPOOLS
FULL-SIZE BLOCK

FOLK BIRD QUILT BLOCK

FOLK BIRD QUILT BLOCK

How To Construct This Block

Sew A to B; add D. Set in C to ABD. Sew E to F; add B. Sew ABDC to FEB. Sew G to H; add I. Sew GHI to J. Sew ABDCFEB to GHIJ. Sew K pieces to each side of unit; miter corners. Appliqué L and M pieces. Satin-stitch beak and legs. Make a French knot for bird's eye.

For alternate fusing method of appliqué see page 212.

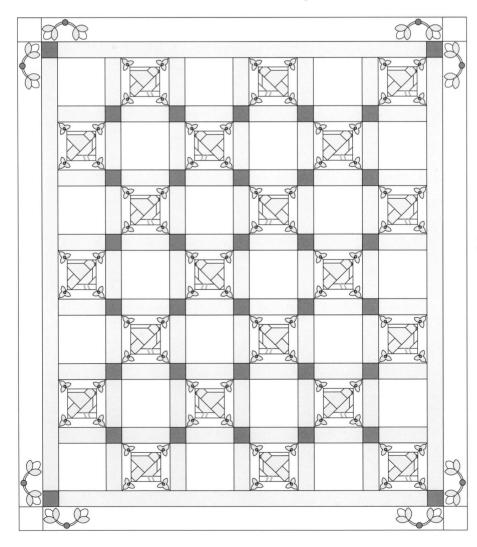

To Make A Bed Quilt

This quilt is designed to be a full-size quilt measuring 84×96 inches. We have used a 3-inch plain border with setting squares in the corners, the 4½-inch Leaf and Circle border, pages 196–197, 3-inch sashing strips, and setting squares as shown. Reverse templates as needed to face bird in opposite direction. We have placed 9-inch setting blocks between the Folk Bird blocks.

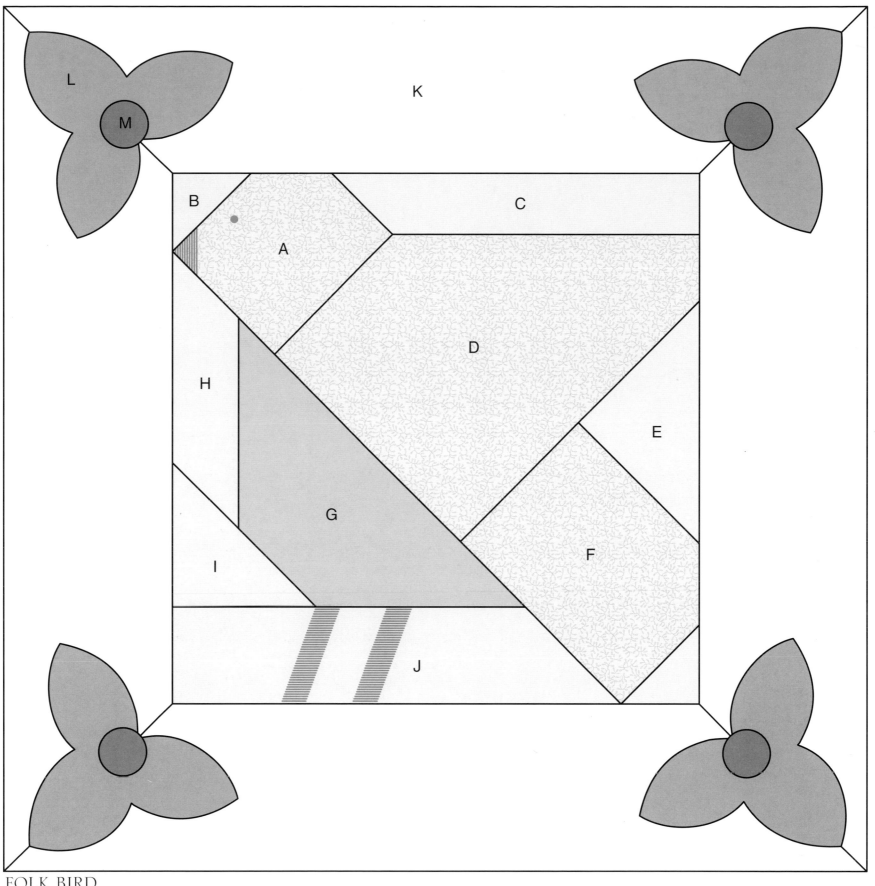

FOLK BIRD
FULL-SIZE BLOCK

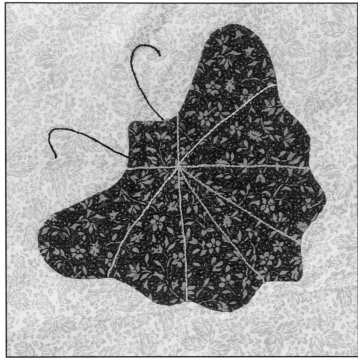

BUTTERFLY QUILT BLOCK

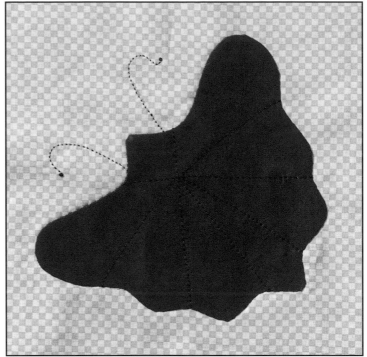

BUTTERFLY QUILT BLOCK

How To Construct This Block

Appliqué butterfly in place on a 10" foundation square. Add running stitches as indicated by the dashed lines on the pattern. Trim to 9½" square.

For alternate fusing method of appliqué, see page 212.

To Make A Bed Quilt

This quilt is designed to be a twin-size quilt measuring 69½×78½ inches. We have used a 4½-inch plain border, the 3¼-inch Fan border, page 196, and three 3-inch sashing strips around center butterfly motifs as shown.

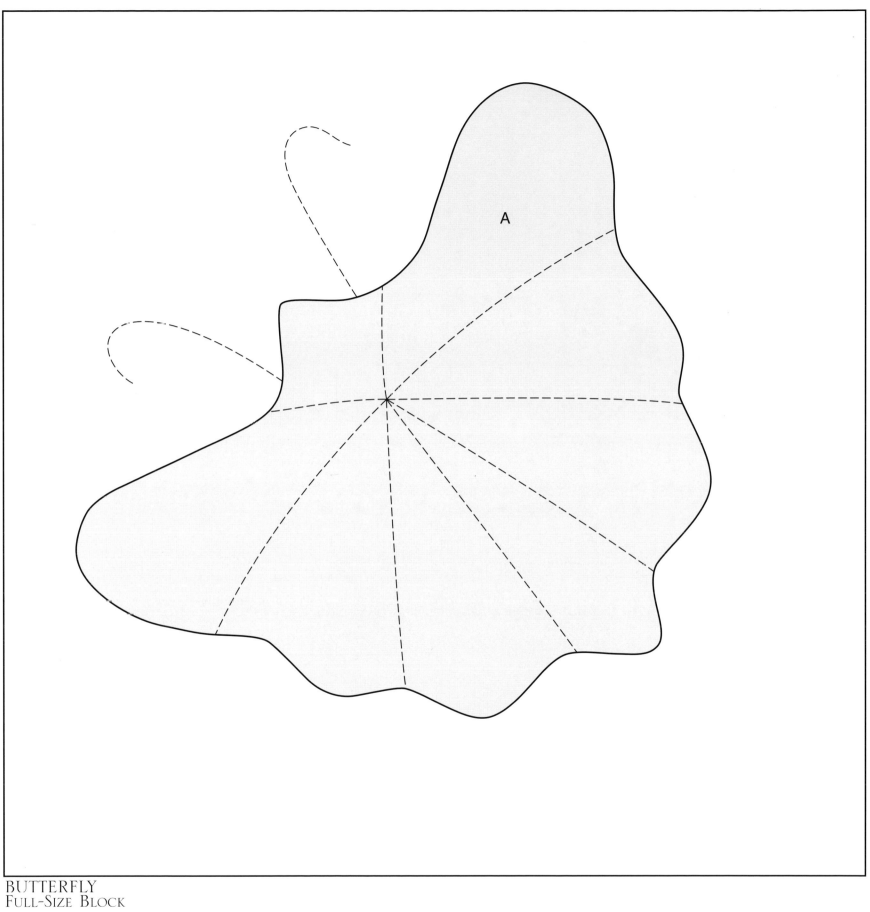

A

BUTTERFLY
FULL-SIZE BLOCK

FRIENDSHIP HEART QUILT BLOCK

FRIENDSHIP HEART QUILT BLOCK

How To Construct This Block

Appliqué A to B. Sew C to D (4 times). Sew CD to E (4 times). Sew CDE to F (4 times). Stitch two G pieces to one CDEF section (2 times). Stitch two CDEF sections to center diamond. Stitch remaining pieces together to complete block. Embroider a name in the center of the quilt block if desired.

For alternate fusing method of appliqué, see page 212.

To Make A Bed Quilt

This quilt is designed to be a full-size quilt measuring 78×96 inches. We have used the 3-inch Diamond and Stripes border, page 199, as shown.

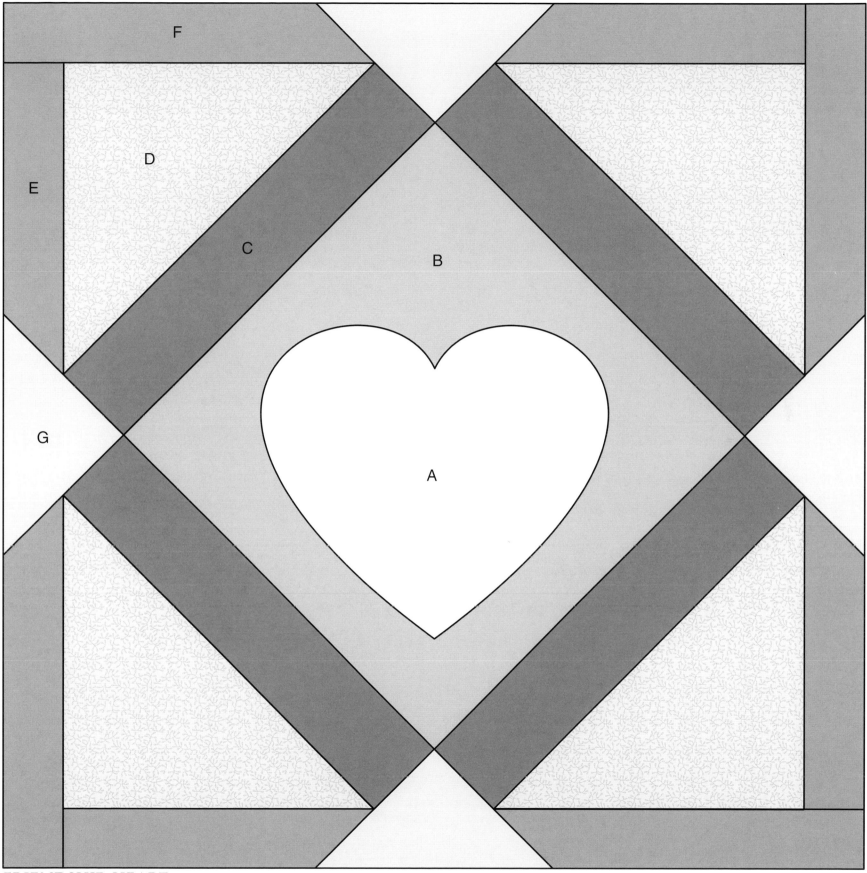

FRIENDSHIP HEART
FULL-SIZE BLOCK

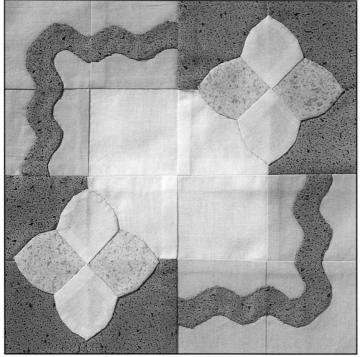

BUTTERFLIES IN THE CORNER QUILT BLOCK

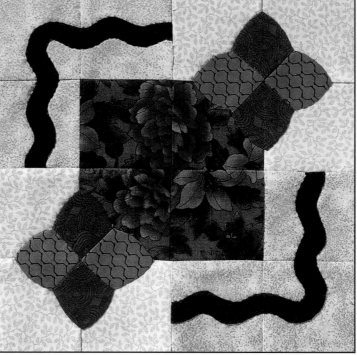

BUTTERFLIES IN THE CORNER QUILT BLOCK

How To Construct This Block

Sew A to B (4 times). Sew AB to AB (2 times). Sew C to C (8 times). Sew CC to CC (4 times). Appliqué D to two CCCC squares (2 times). Appliqué ABAB to two CCCC squares (2 times). Sew together to complete the block.

For alternate fusing method of appliqué, see page 212.

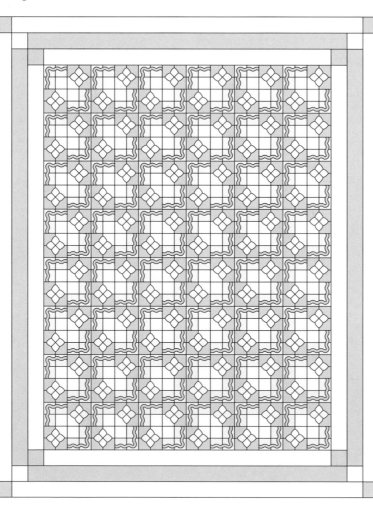

To Make A Bed Quilt

This quilt is designed to be a twin-size quilt measuring 72×90 inches. We have used three 3-inch plain borders with setting squares in the corners as shown.

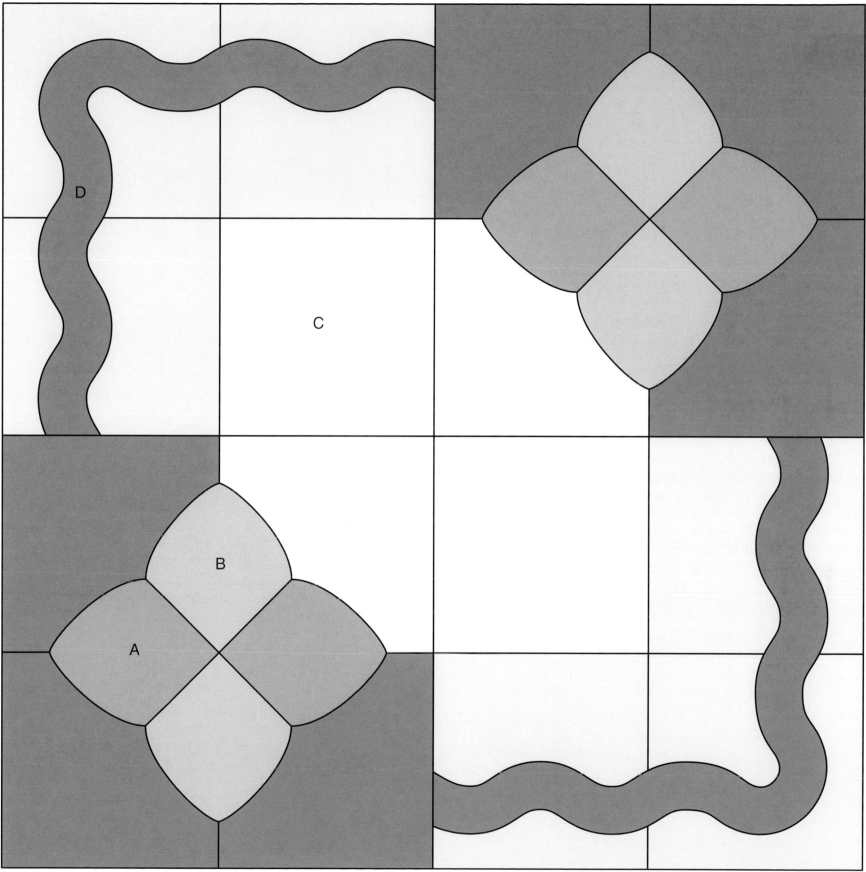

BUTTERFLIES IN THE CORNER
Full-Size Block

ALTPPLE BASKET QUILT BLOCK

APPLE BASKET QUILT BLOCK

How To Construct This Block

Basket unit: Row 1—Sew D to D (5 times). Sew DD units in a row; add D. To each end of Row 1, sew E. Row 2—Sew A to B (4 times). Sew AB units in a row. Row 3—Sew B to A (4 times). Sew BA units in a row. Row 4—Sew B to A (3 times). Sew BA units in a row; add B. Sew C to C (2 times). To each end of Row 4, sew CC. Sew the four rows together. Appliqué apples (H, I, J, and K) to F (2 times). Sew F to G; add F. Appliqué leaves (L, M, and N) to apples. Stems are embroidered using a satin and stem stitch. Sew FGF to basket unit to complete the block. Apples and leaves may be satin stitched, if desired.

For alternate fusing method of appliqué, see page 212.

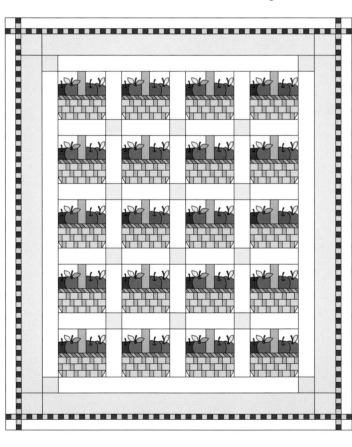

To Make A Bed Quilt

This quilt is designed to be a twin-size quilt measuring 65×77 inches. We have used 3- and 4-inch plain borders with setting squares in the corners, the 3-inch Checkerboard border, page 195, 3-inch sashing strips, and setting squares as shown.

APPLE BASKET
FULL-SIZE BLOCK

SUNBONNET SUE QUILT BLOCK

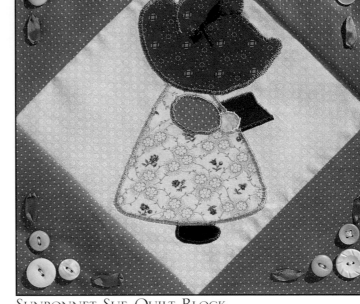

SUNBONNET SUE QUILT BLOCK

How To Construct This Block

Hand-appliqué C, D, E, F, G, and H to background square A, then use outline and running stitch on bonnet and book. Sew B pieces to opposite sides of A. Add B pieces to remaining sides of A. Sew buttons to corners of B. Add straight stitch in silk ribbons. Dress and bonnet may be outlined in satin stitch and a bow tied to the bonnet if desired.

For alternate fusing method of appliqué, see page 212.

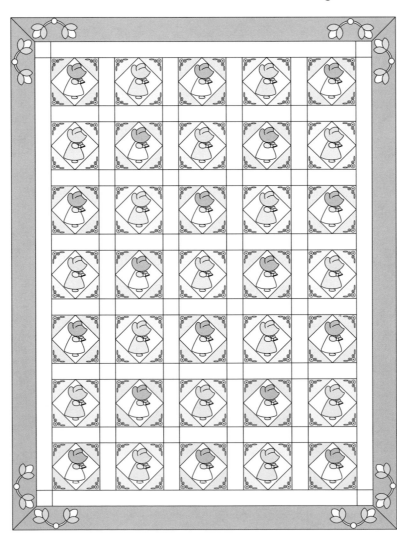

To Make A Bed Quilt

This quilt is designed to be a twin-size quilt measuring 72×96 inches. We have used a 3-inch plain border with setting squares in the corners, the 4½-inch Leaf and Circle border, pages 196–197, 3-inch sashing strips, and setting squares as shown.

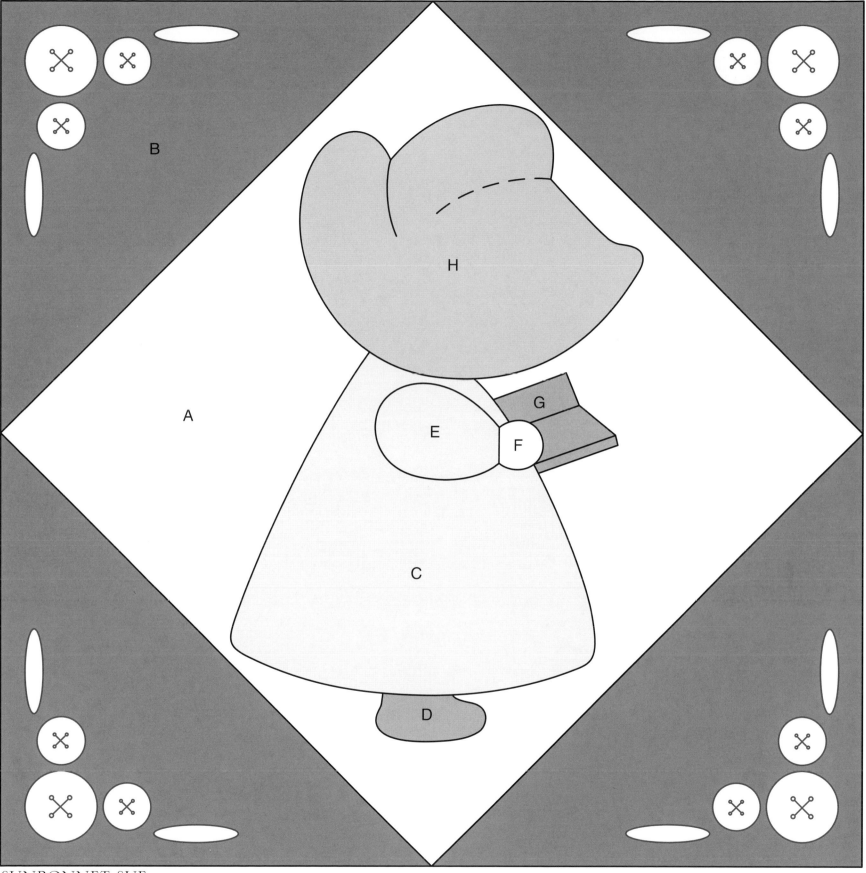

SUNBONNET SUE
FULL-SIZE BLOCK

179

CHRISTMAS WREATH QUILT BLOCK

CHRISTMAS WREATH QUILT BLOCK

How To Construct This Block

Sew G to F and G to Fr. Sew GF and GFr units together, matching F and Fr edges. Stop stitching ¼" from top end, where H will join. Sew H to GF and GFr units, sewing to one F edge, and stopping stitching ¼" from end where F and Fr pieces join. Reposition pieces and continue stitching H to other F edge to make bottom half of wreath. Make top half of wreath by sewing D to C and D to Cr. Sew A to B (2 times); add A to opposite edge of B (2 times). Sew two ABAr units together, matching B points. Sew E to top edge of double ABA unit, then sew a CD unit to each side of this unit. Sew top unit to bottom unit to complete the block.

To Make A Bed Quilt

This quilt is designed to be a full-size quilt measuring 81×93 inches. We have used a 3-inch plain border with setting squares, a second 3-inch plain border, 3-inch sashing strips, and setting squares as shown. We have placed 9-inch setting blocks between the Christmas Wreath blocks.

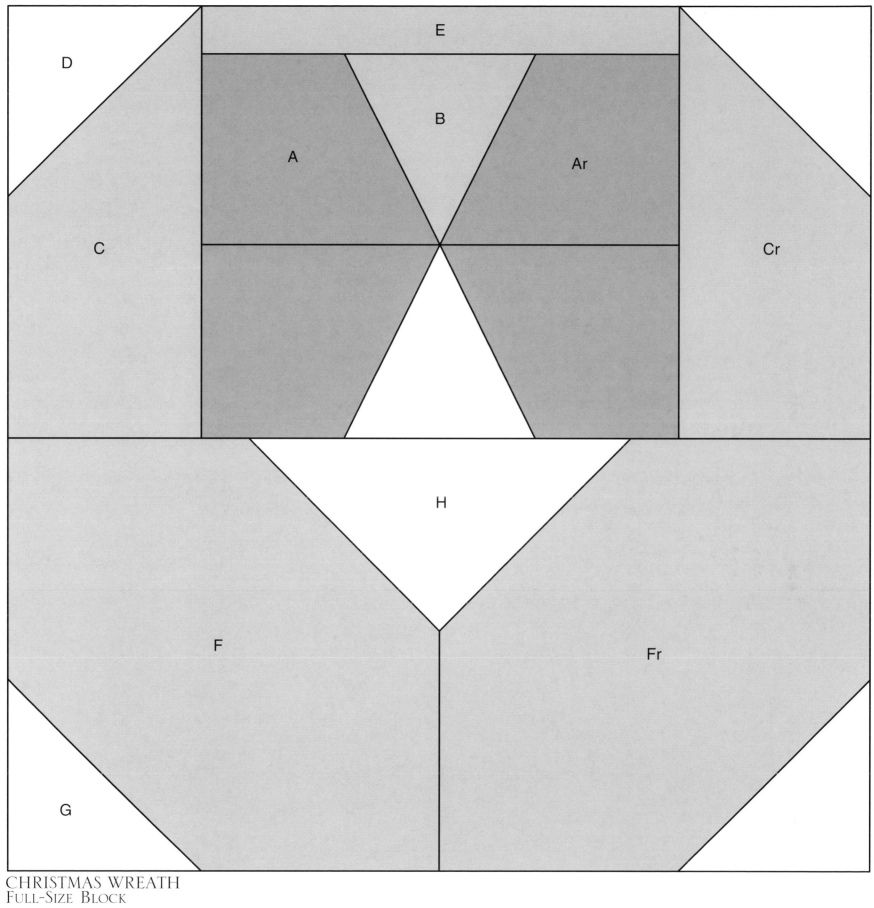

CHRISTMAS WREATH
FULL-SIZE BLOCK

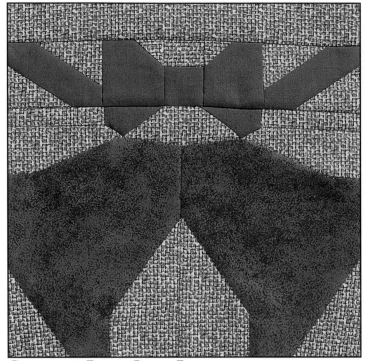

CHRISTMAS BELLS QUILT BLOCK

CHRISTMAS BELLS QUILT BLOCK

How To Construct This Block

Sew L to M and Lr to Mr; add L and Lr. Sew J to K add Jr to K. Sew LML to JK and LrMrLr to JrK. Sew H to I. Sew LMLJK to HI; add LrMrLrJrK for Unit 1. Sew N to Unit 1. Set in B to A and Br to Ar. Sew C to AB and Cr to ArBr. Sew ABC to ArBrCr for Unit 2. Sew G to F and G to Fr. Sew GF to E; add FrG. Set in D and Dr to GFEFrG (2 times). Set in DGFEFrGDr to Unit 2. Sew Unit 1 to Unit 2. Add jingle bell clappers if desired.

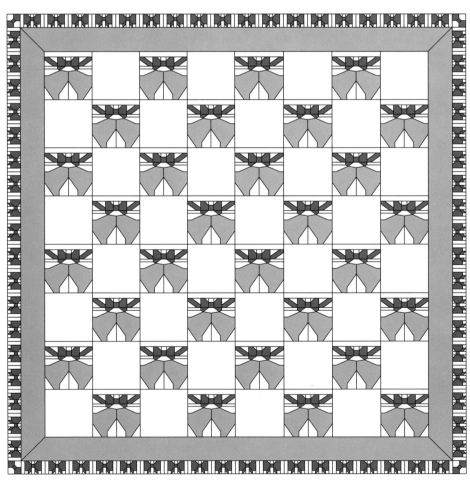

To Make A Bed Quilt

This quilt is designed to be a full-size square quilt measuring 86¼×86¼ inches. We have used a 4⅛-inch plain border and the 3-inch Bow border, page 209, as shown. We have placed 9-inch plain setting blocks between the Christmas Bells blocks.

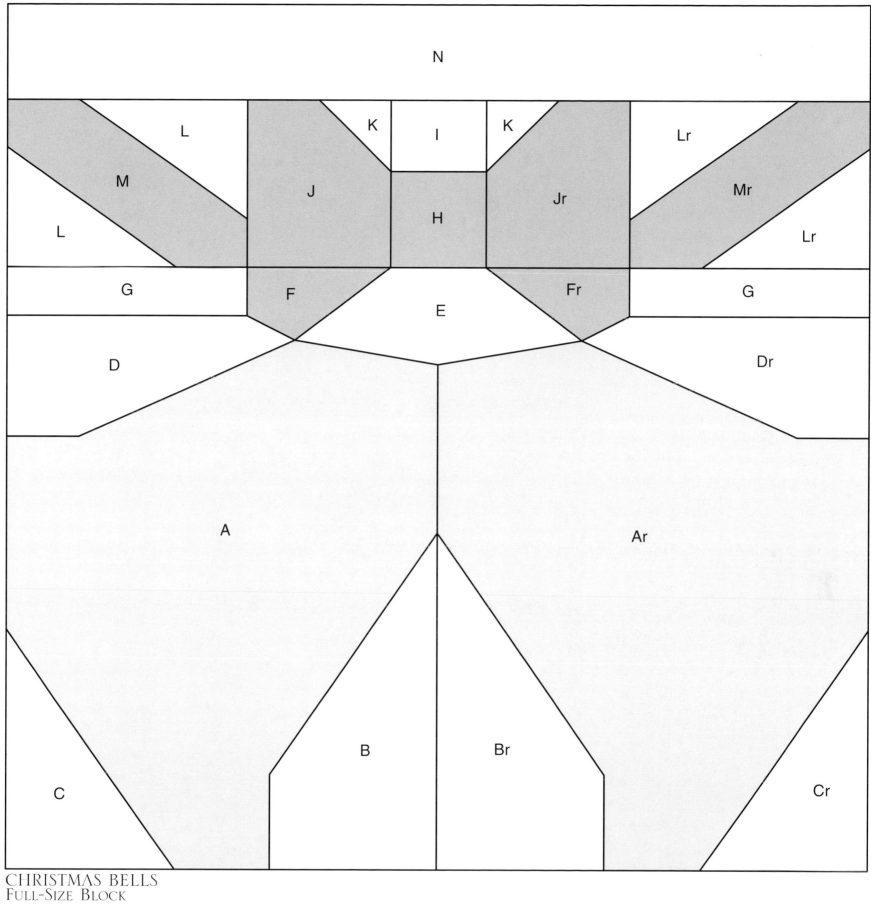

CHRISTMAS BELLS
FULL-SIZE BLOCK

SANTA AND TREE QUILT BLOCK

SANTA AND TREE QUILT BLOCK

How To Construct This Block

Tree unit: Sew A to B; add HH. Sew C to D; add JJ. Sew E to F; add KK. Sew ABHH to CDJJ; add EFKK.

Santa unit: Sew G to H; set in I. Sew GHI to J. Sew L to M; add K. Sew N to O; add P. Sew LMK to NOP. Sew GHIJ to LMKNOP for Row 1. Sew U to V; add W for Row 2. Sew Row 1 to Row 2. Sew R to S; add T. Sew RST to Q. Set in QRST to Rows 1 and 2. Sew X to Y; add Z. Sew AA to XYZ; add BB. Sew CC to DD; add EE. Sew CCDDEE to FF; add GG. Sew top of Santa to AAXYZBB; add CCDDEEFFGG. Sew Tree to Santa, add two buttons and embroider hanger to complete the block.

To Make A Bed Quilt

This quilt is designed to be a full-size quilt measuring 83×95 inches. We have used a 3-inch plain border with setting squares in the corners, the 4-inch Christmas Wreath border, page 207, 3-inch sashing strips, and setting squares as shown. Reverse templates as needed to face Santa in opposite direction. We have placed 9-inch setting blocks between Santa and Tree blocks.

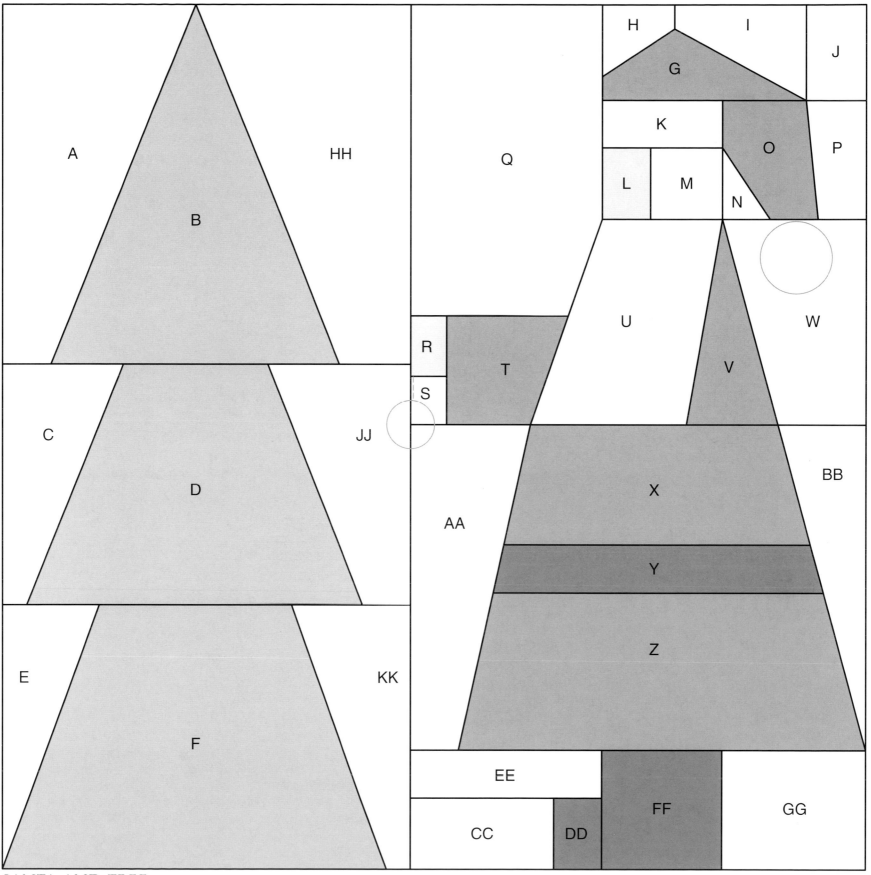

SANTA AND TREE
FULL-SIZE BLOCK

POINSETTIA QUILT BLOCK

POINSETTIA QUILT BLOCK

How To Construct This Block

Sew B to B (4 times). Sew BB unit to another BB unit (2 times), then sew these two units together. Center the B unit onto piece A. Place C units between B points, slipping edges of less slanted point under B pieces. Appliqué B unit, then C pieces. Center D on top of B unit and appliqué.

For alternate fusing method of appliqué, see page 212.

To Make A Bed Quilt

This quilt is designed to be a twin-size quilt measuring 64×73 inches. We have used a 4½-inch plain border, the 5-inch Ribbon border, page 203, and 4½-inch sashing strips around the center poinsettia motifs as shown.

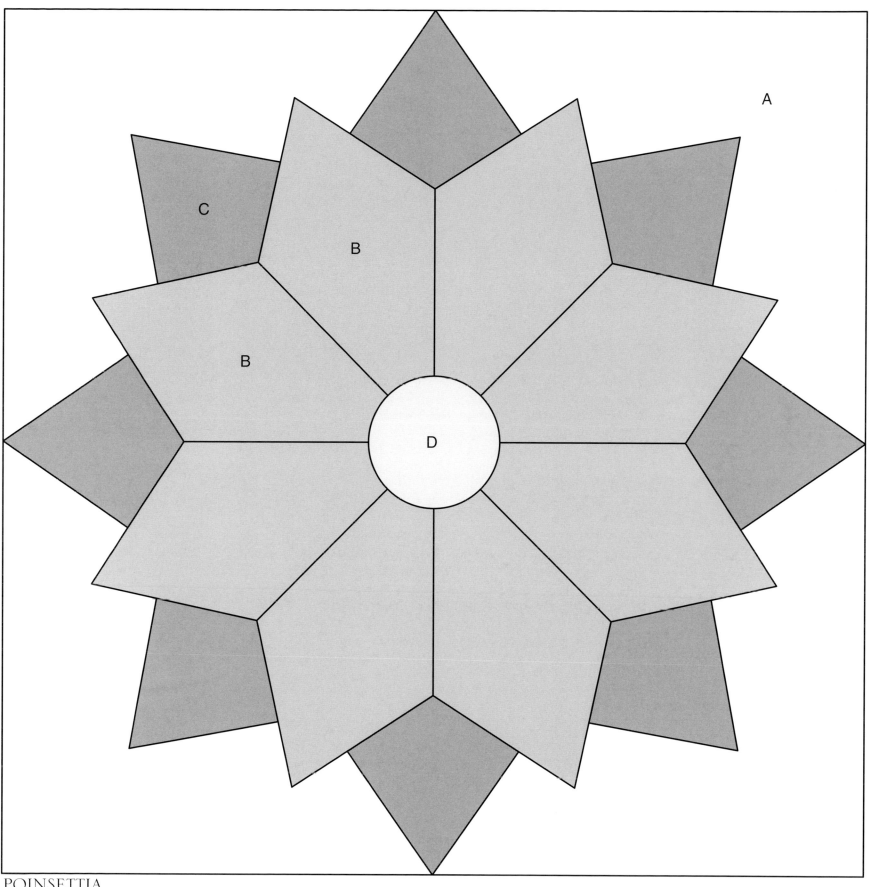

VINTAGE CHARM SAMPLER QUILT

As shown on page 145. Finished size: 46½×46½ inches.

MATERIALS

Eight 9½" completed unfinished quilt blocks in coordinating colors
⅝ yard of blue print
¼ yard of red and white print
1⅜ yards of yellow print
1⅓ yards of 30's reproduction fabric
47" square of fabric for backing
47" square of batting

Quantities specified are for 44/45"-wide 100% cotton fabrics. All measurements include a ¼" seam allowance unless otherwise specified.

CUT THE FABRIC

To make the best use of your fabrics, cut the pieces in the order listed. For this project, cut the yellow border strips lengthwise (parallel to the selvage).

From blue print, cut:
8—9½" squares

From red and white print, cut:
4—1¼×40" border strip

From yellow print:
4—5×49" border strips

From reproduction fabric, cut:
92—4¼" squares for prairie points

MAKE THE QUILT CENTER

Lay out all the blocks in four horizontal rows of four blocks each, alternating the blocks. Sew the blocks together in each row. Press seam allowance in one direction, aligning the direction with each row. Join the rows. Press the seam allowance in one direction. At this point, the pieced quilt center should measure 36½" square including seam allowance.

ADD THE BORDERS

1. Sew one red and white 1¼×40" border strip to one yellow 5×49" border strip, matching the centers of each strip, along the long edge. Repeat to make a total of four border strips.
2. Matching the center of border strip with the center of the quilt top, sew each border strip to the quilt top. Begin and end stitching ¼" from quilt top edges.
3. Miter border corners. The quilt top should measure 47" including seam allowance.

MAKE PRAIRIE POINTS

Fold each 4¼" square diagonally, wrong sides together to form a triangle and press. Fold a second time to make a smaller triangle; press. Align the raw edges of 23 triangles along each raw edge of the quilt top front. Slip the triangles inside each other, points facing toward the quilt center. Adjust to fit length of quilt top on each edge. Baste in place.

COMPLETE THE QUILT

Layer the quilt top and backing with the right sides together. Add the batting and baste. Stitch together leaving an opening for turning. Turn right side out and hand sew the opening closed. Quilt as desired. This quilt was hand-tied with yellow pearl cotton.

NOAH'S FRIENDS CHILD'S QUILT

As shown on page 145. Finished size: 36×36 inches.

MATERIALS

Five 9½" completed unfinished picture quilt blocks in coordinating colors
⅜ yard of solid burgundy
⅛ yard of solid dark red
⅛ yard of solid rose
¼ yard of solid teal
⅜ yard of solid dark blue
⅛ yard of medium blue
⅛ yard of solid green
½ yard of solid yellow
1⅜ yards of solid green flannel for binding and backing; 40" square of quilt batting; 16—½" buttons

Quantities specified are for 44/45"-wide 100% cotton fabrics. All measurements include a ¼" seam allowance unless otherwise specified.

Note—This quilt was created with five picture blocks made from flannel print and solids. Buttons were added for decoration; however, you may choose not to use buttons; French knots make a good alternative. Blanket stitches were used to highlight some areas of the blocks. The picture blocks are embellished before the quilt top is assembled.

CUT THE FABRIC

To make best use of your fabrics, cut pieces in order that follows.

From burgundy, cut:
20—Pattern A, or 2—1½×42" strips (Ribbons All Around block, page 162)
4—Pattern D (Chevron border, page 201)
24—Pattern B; 24—Pattern Br (Chevron border)

From dark red, cut:
20—Pattern A, or 2—1½×42" strips (Ribbons All Around block)

From rose, cut:
20—Pattern A, or 2—1½×42" strips (Ribbons All Around block)

From dark blue, cut:
16—Pattern A, or 2—1½×42" strips (Ribbons All Around block)
4—Pattern C (Chevron border)
48—Pattern J (Chevron border)

From medium blue, cut:
16—Pattern A, or 2—1½×42" strips (Ribbons All Around block)

From green, cut:
16—Pattern A, or 2—1½×42" strips (Ribbons All Around block)

From teal, cut:
4—1¾×27½" border strips
4—Pattern I (Chevron border)

From yellow, cut:
4—Pattern H (Chevron border)
48—Pattern F (Chevron border)
56—Pattern E (Chevron border)

From green flannel, cut:
40" backing square
4—2×42" binding strips

ASSEMBLE THE RIBBON SQUARES

Square 1:
For each of the strip sets, you will need one *each* of burgundy, dark red, and rose Pattern A or one 1½×42" strip of each color. Sew the strips together lengthwise. (If you are using the strip piecing method, repeat for two strip sets.) From the long strips cut 20—3½" squares.
Square 2:
For each of the strip sets, you will need one *each* of dark blue, medium blue, and green Pattern A or one 1½×42" strip of each color. Sew the strips together lengthwise. (If you are using the strip piecing method, repeat for a total of two strip sets.) From the long strips, cut 16—3½" squares.

MAKE THE RIBBON BLOCKS

Referring to photograph, *page 145*, lay out five Square 1's and four Square 2's in three rows of three squares each. Sew squares together in each row. Press seam allowance in each row in one direction, alternating direction with each row. Join rows to make a ribbon block. Block should measure 9½" square including seams. Repeat for a total of four ribbon square blocks.

ASSEMBLE THE QUILT CENTER

Lay out blocks in three horizontal rows of three blocks each, alternating the blocks. Sew together the blocks in each row. Press the seam allowance in one direction, alternating the direction with each row. Then join the rows. Press the seam allowance in one direction. The pieced quilt center should measure 27½" square, including the seam allowance.

MAKE THE CHEVRON BORDER

1. To make one corner setting square, you will need: One teal Pattern I, two yellow Pattern E, one dark blue Pattern C, one burgundy Pattern D, and one yellow Pattern H. To the two adjoining sides of a teal Pattern I, sew two yellow E's. To EIE add a dark blue Pattern C. Sew a burgundy Pattern D to Pattern C. Complete the square by sewing yellow Pattern H to Pattern D. Repeat to make four corner squares. Square should measure 5" including the seam allowance.
2. To make one border unit, you will need. One of *each* yellow Pattern E, dark blue Pattern J, burgundy Pattern B or Br, and yellow Pattern F. Sew dark blue J to yellow E. Sew a burgundy B to JE. Add yellow Pattern F to BJE. Make a total of 48 border units. Each unit should measure 2¾×3¾" including seam allowance.
3. To make one border strip, refer to photograph, *page 145* for correct placement, sew twelve border units from Step 2 together. Make a total of four border strips. Border strips should each measure 3¾×27½" including seam allowance.
4. To each border strip, sew a teal 1¾×27½" strip. See the photograph, *page 145*, for correct placement of strips. The border should measure 5×27½" including seam allowance.

ADD THE BORDERS

1. Aligning the long raw edges, sew one border to the top edge of the quilt center and one border to the bottom edge of the quilt center. Press the seam allowance toward the border strip.
2. Sew each short edge of border to one edge of a corner setting square. Repeat for two border units. Press seam allowance toward the border.
3. Aligning the long edges and matching the seams, join one border unit to each side of quilt center. Press seams toward the border units.

COMPLETE THE QUILT

Add four buttons at corners of center square in each ribbon block. Layer the quilt top, batting, and green flannel backing. Quilt as desired and bind.

MERRY CHRISTMAS WALL QUILT

As shown on page 145. Finished size: 39×39 inches.

MATERIALS

Five 9½" completed unfinished Rectangles Make The Square blocks, page 164, in coordinating colors
Four 9½" completed unfinished Christmas blocks in coordinating colors
Ribbon border pattern, page 203
⅓ yard of gold print for sashing
¼ yard of white on white print for border
½ yard of solid red for border and binding
1¼ yards of backing
44" square of quilt batting
4—1" buttons

Quantities specified are for 44/45"-wide 100% cotton fabrics. All measurements include a ¼" seam allowance unless otherwise specified.

Note: Each block is embellished before the quilt top is layered.

CUT THE FABRIC

From gold print, cut:
2—1½×31½" strips for sashing
4—1½×29½" strips for sashing
6—1½×9½" strips for sashing

From white on white print, cut:
4—3½×9½" strips for border
8 each—Pattern B, D, E, and Er
16 each—Pattern G and H
8 each—Pattern J, Jr, M, N, and Nr
4—Pattern P

From solid red, cut:
4—2½×42" for binding
4—1½×9½" border strips
8 each—Pattern A and B
16—Pattern C
8 each—Pattern F and Fr
16—Pattern I
12 each—Pattern K and Kr
4 each—Pattern O and Or

ASSEMBLE THE QUILT CENTER

1. Lay out the blocks in three horizontal rows of three blocks each, alternating the blocks.
2. Sew one gold print 1½×9½" sashing strip to each side of the center block in each row. Press the seam allowance toward the sashing strip.
3. Sew blocks together in each row. Press the seam allowance toward the sashing strips.
4. Sew one gold print 1½×29½" sashing strip to the top and bottom of the middle row. Press the seam allowance toward the sashing strips.
5. Join the three rows together. Press the seam allowance toward the sashing strips.
6. Sew one gold 1½×29½" sashing strip to the top of the quilt top and one to the bottom of the quilt top.
7. Sew one gold 1½×31½" sashing strip to each side of the quilt top. At this point the quilt top should measure 31½" square including the seam allowance.

MAKE THE RIBBON BORDER

1. Following the directions for the Ribbon border, *page 203*, sew eight bows.
2. Align the long edges together and sew one red 1½×9½" border strip to a white print 3½×9½" strip.
3. Sew Pattern J to K, add N to make JKN (4 times).
4. Sew Pattern Jr to Kr, add Nr to make JrKrNr (4 times).
5. To border strip from Step 2, sew one JKN to left side of border strip and one JrKrNr to right side of the border strip. Repeat with each of the three remaining border strips.
6. Sew a red bow onto each end of red and white border strips from Step 5. To right side of each border, sew a red Pattern O. To left side of each border, sew a red Pattern Or.
7. Referring to the photograph, *page 145*, sew a Ribbon border to each side of quilt top. Sew the Ribbon border to the top and the bottom of the quilt top.
8. At each corner of the border, set in one white print Pattern P.

COMPLETE THE QUILT

Layer quilt top, batting, and backing. Quilt as desired. Sew a button at the center of each of the four blocks. Bind your quilt.

FLEUR DE LIS WALL PIECE

As shown on page 145. Finished quilt size: 29×29 inches.

MATERIALS

Nine 9½" completed unfinished Fleur de lis quilt blocks, page 152, in coordinating colors
⅛ yard of yellow print for border
½ yard of purple print for binding
1 yard of backing
36" square of batting

Quantities specified for 44/45''-wide 100% cotton fabrics. All measurements include a ¼'' seam allowance unless otherwise specified.

CUT THE FABRIC
From yellow print, cut:
4—¾×29'' border strips

From purple print, cut:
3—3½×42'' binding strips

MAKE THE QUILT CENTER
1. Lay out blocks in three horizontal rows of three blocks each. Sew the blocks together in each row. Press seam allowance in one direction, alternating direction with each row.
2. Join rows. Press seam allowance in one direction. The pieced quilt center should measure 27½'' square including seam allowance.

ADD THE BORDER
1. Matching the center of a yellow ¾×29'' yellow border strip with the center of quilt top, sew each border strip to quilt top. Begin and end stitching ¼'' from quilt top edges.
2. Miter border corners. Quilt top should measure 28'' including seams.

COMPLETE THE QUILT
Layer the quilt top, batting, and backing. Quilt as desired. This quilt was machine quilted in the ditch around each block. The center square was also outlined. Bind your quilt. This binding is folded in half and added to the quilt with mitered corners to give the appearance of a second border.

ANTIQUE BUTTERFLY QUILT
As shown on page 146. Finished quilt top size: 90×102 inches.

This quilt is intended to be a charm quilt; all of the butterflies are of different fabrics. The quilt is a wonderful place to use the 1930's reproduction fabrics.

MATERIALS
48 *each* **of 8'' squares of various print scraps, or 2 yards total**
6 *each* **of 8'' squares of various solid scraps, or ½ yards total**
6¾ yards of muslin for blocks, borders, and binding
3¼ yards of solid yellow for borders
Black embroidery floss
7½ yards of backing
96×108'' batting

Quantities specified for 44/45''-wide, 100% cotton fabrics. All measurements include a ¼'' seam allowance unless otherwise specified.

CUT THE FABRIC
To make the best use of your fabrics, cut the pieces in the order that follows. For this quilt project, cut the border and the binding strips lengthwise (parallel to the selvage). The listing includes mathematically correct border lengths. You may need to add extra length to border strips now to allow for any sewing differences later. Add a ⅛'' seam allowance to the butterfly pattern to allow for the appliqué.

From *each* of 48 prints, cut:
1 butterfly piece A, page 171

From *each* of 6 solids, cut:
1 butterfly piece A

From muslin, cut:
54—10'' squares for foundation blocks
2—6½×90½'' border strips
2—5×90½'' border strips
5—2½×90'' binding strips

From solid yellow, cut:
4—5×27½'' border strips
4—5×54½'' border strips
4—5×81½'' border strips

APPLIQUÉ THE BUTTERFLY BORDER
1. For one butterfly block you'll need one muslin 10'' foundation square and one solid or print butterfly.
2. Fold the foundation square in half diagonally in both directions and lightly finger-crease to create positioning guides for appliqué piece.
3. Prepare the appliqué piece by basting the seam allowances under. Pin or hand-baste the butterfly onto the foundation. Refer to the photograph on *page 146* for the correct placement. The 48 print butterflies in this quilt have been placed facing one corner of the foundation block. The six solid butterflies are all facing the straight edge of the foundation block.
4. Using small slip stitches and threads in colors that match the fabric, appliqué the pieces in place.
5. Using black embroidery floss, make a blanket stitch around the edges of the butterfly. Add embroidery stitches, following lines on the pattern for the body of the butterfly and antenna.
6. Repeat Steps 1 through 5 to make a total of 54 blocks. Trim each block to measure 9½'' square, including the seam allowance.

ASSEMBLE THE QUILT CENTER
Refer to the photograph on *page 146* to lay out the six solid butterfly blocks in three horizontal rows of two blocks each. Sew together the blocks in each row. Then join rows. The pieced quilt center should measure 18½×27½'', including the required-seam allowance.

ADD A BORDER
Add one 5×27½'' yellow border strip to each side of the quilt center. Then sew a 5×27½'' yellow strip to top edge of the quilt center and one to the bottom edge. Press all seam allowances toward the border strips. The pieced quilt center should measure 27½×36½''.

ASSEMBLE A BUTTERFLY BORDER
Arrange 18 butterfly blocks surrounding the quilt center. Refer to photograph, *page 146,* for careful placement of butterflies. Sew four butterflies in two vertical rows. Add one row to each side of the quilt center. Sew five butterflies in two horizontal rows. Add one row to the top of quilt center and one to the bottom. The pieced quilt center should now measure 45½×54½'' including seam allowance.

ADD A BORDER
Sew one 5×54½'' yellow strip to each side of quilt center. Add one 5×54½'' yellow strip to top of the quilt and one to the bottom. Press all seam allowances toward border strips. Quilt center should measure 54½×63½'' including seams.

ASSEMBLE A BUTTERFLY BORDER
Arrange 30 butterfly blocks surrounding the quilt center. Again refer to the photograph for careful placement. Sew seven butterfly blocks in two vertical rows. Add one row to each side of quilt center. Sew eight butterfly blocks in two horizontal rows. Add one row to top of quilt and one to bottom. The pieced quilt center should measure 72½×81½'' including seams.

ADD THE BORDER
Sew one 5×81½'' yellow border strip to each side of the quilt center. Sew one 5×81½'' yellow strip to the top of the quilt center and one to the bottom of quilt center. Press the seam allowance toward the border strips. At this point, the top should measure 81½×90½'' including the seam allowance.

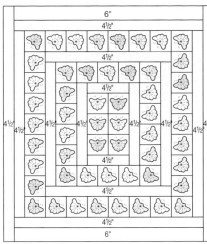

Quilt Assembly Diagram

Sew one 5×90½" muslin strip to each side of quilt top. Sew one 6½×90½" muslin strip to top of quilt and one to bottom of quilt. Press seams toward outside of quilt top.

COMPLETE THE QUILT

Layer the quilt top, batting, and backing. This quilt was quilted in a cable design inside yellow borders and diagonal 1" lines on outside muslin border. Each block was outlined around butterfly and then quilted ¼" inside outside edges of block. Bind quilt.

CHERRY PIE QUILT

As shown on page 146. Finished size: 49×49 inches.

This is a new quilt; however, the fabrics that are used are reproduction fabrics of old flour sacks. The cherries are edged with a buttonhole embroidery stitch, which really adds to the over-all "antique look" of the quilt.

MATERIALS
1 yard of light pink for cherry blocks
4—⅛ yard pieces of reds to pink for cherries
4—⅛ yard pieces of green for leaves
2—⅛ yard pieces of brown for stems
¾ yard total of assorted prints for sashing blocks
¾ yard of white for sashing blocks
1¼ yards of green for borders

1½ yards of blue for borders
6 yards of extra jumbo rick-rack
½ yard of fusing-adhesive material
Red and pink embroidery floss
1½ yards of 60"-wide fabric for backing
54" square of quilt batting

Quantities specified are for 44/45"-wide 100% cotton fabrics. All measurements include a ¼" seam allowance unless otherwise stated.

CUT THE FABRIC
To make the best use of your fabrics, cut the pieces as listed *below*. The border strips are cut the length (parallel to the selvage) of the fabric. Extra length has been added to allow for mitered corners.

From light pink, cut:
9—10" squares

From assorted prints, cut:
44—4¼" squares, cut each square with an X for a total of 176 quarter square triangles for Pattern B (Pie Crust border, page 195)

From white fabric, cut:
44—4¼" squares, cut each square with an X for a total of 176 quarter square triangles for Pattern A (Pie Crust border)

From green fabric, cut:
4—1½×44" border strips

From blue fabric, cut:
4—4½×54" border strips

MAKE THE APPLIQUÉ BLOCKS
1. Lay the fusing-adhesive material, paper side up, over the cherry pattern. Using a pencil, trace each of the pattern pieces nine times, leaving ½" between each tracing. Cut out the pieces ¼" outside traced lines.
2. Following the instructions from the manufacturer, press the

fusing-adhesive material pieces onto the back of the appropriate fabrics. Let the fabrics cool. Cut out the shapes on the drawn lines. Peel off the paper from the fabrics.
3. Fold a 10" pink square in half diagonally in both directions and lightly finger crease. Refer to the pattern for placement and arrange the cut-out shapes on the square.
4. Fuse the shapes in place with a hot, dry iron. Let all of the fabrics cool.
5. Repeat Steps 1 through 4 to make a total of nine blocks.
6. Machine satin stitch or close zig-zag around the leaves and stems in matching threads. With three strands of embroidery floss, work a buttonhole stitch around each cherry. Trim the blocks to measure 9½". This measurement includes the seam allowance.

MAKE THE SASHING BLOCKS
1. With right sides together, sew one print triangle B to one white triangle A on a short edge. Continue sewing a total of 176 triangle B's to triangle A's. Press the seam toward print triangle.
2. Lay out two units from Step 1. Sew the units together along the long side. Chain piece all 88 sets. Cut the sets apart. Each pieced triangle square should measure 3½" including the seam allowance.

MAKE THE SASHING STRIPS
1. Referring to Quilt Assembly Diagram for placement, sew three sashing blocks together in a horizontal strip with white triangles on the top and the bottom of each block. Repeat for twelve strips.
2. Sew thirteen sashing blocks together in a vertical row with the print triangles on the top and bottom of each block. Repeat for a total of four strips.

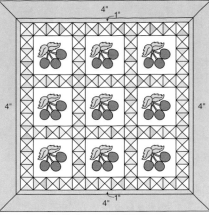

Quilt Assembly Diagram

ASSEMBLE THE QUILT INTERIOR
Referring to Quilt Assembly Diagram, *above*, for placement, lay out the appliqué blocks in three vertical rows. Following diagram, lay out sashing strips. Join small sashing strips and appliqué blocks in each of the vertical rows. Then join long vertical sashing strips to each vertical row. The pieced top should measure 39½" including seam allowance.

ADD THE BORDERS
1. Mark the center of one 1½×44" green border strip and one 4½×54" blue border strip. Matching centers, join the strips together. Repeat for a total of four border strips.
2. Add the border strips to the quilt top with mitered corners. The quilt top should measure 49½" square.

COMPLETE THE QUILT
Baste batting to the wrong side of the quilt top. Trim the batting to the same size as the quilt top. Stitch extra jumbo rick-rack in the seam line at the outer edge of the quilt top. Layer the quilt back and the quilt top, right sides together, and secure together with basting or pins. Sew the layers together, leaving an opening for turning. Trim the sides and corners; turn right side out. Slip stitch the opening closed. Baste the layers together. The quilt was machine quilted in the seam lines of the borders and sashing.

HOUSEDRESS HOT PAD

As shown on page 146. Finished size: 9½×9½ inches.

MATERIALS

One 9½" completed unfinished
   Housedress block, page 148
⅜ yard of print for back, binding, and loop
9½" square of extra loft fleece
2 buttons; small amount of lace,
   rick-rack, and ribbon

CUT THE FABRIC

From print cut:
1—9½" square for back
1—2×4½" strip for loop
1—2½×42" strip for binding

CONSTRUCT THE HOT PAD

Sew two buttons onto quilt block.
Layer the quilt block, fleece, and
backing; baste. Quilt by outlining
dress. Sew lace, rick-rack, and bow
onto dress through all layers. Press
2×4½" strip in half lengthwise, wrong
sides together. Press raw edges to
inside along long side and stitch
length of loop. Fold loop in half. Pin
loop, raw ends together at hot pad
edge, at center of back of hot pad.
   Bind hot pad. Bring loop up over
the finished binding and tack in
place at the top edge of the hot pad.

CHECKERBOARD TEA TOWEL

As shown on page 146. Finished size: 15×27 inches.

MATERIALS

Completed Checkerboard border,
   page 195:
   2—3½×21½" strips; 2—3½×9½" strips
   4—3½" setting squares (Note: For
   this project the setting squares are
   sewn to each end of the 3½×9½"
   border strips, resulting in two side
   border strips 3½×15½".)

15½×27½" rectangle of yellow
   pique fabric

All measurements include ¼" seams.

ADD THE BORDERS

1. Measure and draw a stitching line
3¼" inside the four outside edges of
15½×27½" yellow fabric on right
side of fabric. See Diagram 1, *below.*
2. On wrong side of each border
strip, on the inside edge, measure
and draw a ¼" sewing line. See
Diagram 2, *right.*
3. Right sides together, matching
stitching lines, sew one 3½×21½"
strip to long side of towel. Border
will begin and end 3¼" inside each
side of towel. Repeat with second
3½×21½" border. Press border,
right side up, toward outside edge
of tea towel. See Diagram 3, *right.*
4. Following the directions in
Step 3, sew a 3½×15½" border to
each short side of the towel. See
Diagram 4, *right.*

COMPLETE THE TEA TOWEL

Clean finish, by over-casting, the
outside edges of tea towel. Press
under ¼" hem. Fold to back side of
tea towel and top stitch hem. To
finish tea towel using binding in
place of this method, 3—2×42"
strips will be needed to make binding.
   Towel measurement can be
adjusted to become a different size.
The measurement however, must
be devisable by three. Adjust border
length measurements accordingly
and add ¼" seam allowances. The
setting squares will always be 3½"
square including seam allowance.

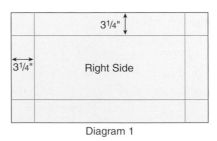

Diagram 1

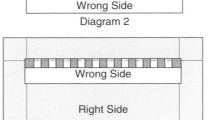

Wrong Side
Diagram 2

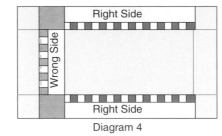

Wrong Side

Right Side

Diagram 3

Right Side

Wrong Side

Right Side

Diagram 4

SCREEN PANELS

As shown on page 147. Finished panel size: 18×54 inches.

*To recreate this screen panel you will
need five colors. You may wish to add
more colors to your panel. A secondary
pattern is created by using different
colors in Position A and B in one unit
of the block and repeating the
placement for four units to complete
one block. To determine the length of
panel that you will need, measure the
distance between top and bottom rods
that hold the panel and add 1". You
will need to add strips at the top and
bottom of your quilt blocks if the
measurement is less than 4½". Each
unit in a block measures 4½" or a
block measures 9" when completed.
Example: You need a panel 56" long,
add a 1½" strip at the top and bottom
of the block panel. When completed
our 54" panel would then measure
56". Likewise, a strip could be added
to each side of the panel to increase
the width for your panel.*

MATERIALS

¼ yard of light blue print
¼ yard of navy blue print
⅝ yard of green print; ¼ yard of teal print

¼ yard of brown print
1⅝ yards of backing fabric
20×56" piece of batting

All measurements include ¼" seams.

CUT THE FABRIC

From light blue print, cut:
48—Pattern A (Rectangle Make The
   Square block, page 164)

From navy blue print, cut:
48—Pattern A (Rectangle Make The
   Square block)

From green print, cut:
4—2×42" binding strips
2—3½×19½" sleeve strips
48—Pattern C (Rectangle Make The
   Square block)

From teal print, cut:
48—Pattern B (Rectangle Make The
   Square block)

From brown print, cut:
48—Pattern B (Rectangle Make The
   Square block)

MAKE THE BLOCKS

Sew twelve 9½" blocks.

MAKE THE PANEL

Lay out six blocks in two vertical
rows. Sew blocks together. Panel
should measure 18½×54½" with
seams. Now add or subtract from
panel to fit measurements. Layer
panel, batting, and backing. Baste
and quilt. This panel was machine
quilted in seam lines. Bind panel.

COMPLETE THE PANEL

Right sides together, sew lengthwise
each green 3½×19½" strip. Turn
right side out, fold in raw edges ¼"
on each side; press. Hand sew the
sleeve to the back of panel at top
and bottom edges. Sew both long
edges down so that the rod sleeve
will not show from the front when it
is put into place in the screen.

ALL THE BORDERS

What better way to frame your works of art
than to add an extraordinary pieced or appliquéd border.
We've chosen twenty-one borders that we think will
showcase your fine quilting skills in great style. From a simple
Checkerboard border to a multi-pieced Bow border, you can
adjust and combine these borders with your favorite blocks
to fit your personal quilting style. Instructions for each of
the borders and full-size border patterns (all you need to do
is add the ¼" seam allowance) start on the next page.

Pansy Bow Border

This border is 3" wide and has a 9" repeat.

For each repeat, make AAA unit. Sew BB unit (2 times). Sew a BB unit to each side of the AAA unit.

For each bow, sew two $1\frac{1}{2} \times 18\frac{1}{2}$" strips, right sides together, on one short $1\frac{1}{2}$" end. Make a diagonal cut on each end. Sew lengthwise, right sides facing, leaving an opening in the center of one long side for turning. Clip corners, turn to right side, and press. Slip-stitch the opening closed.

For each bow knot, sew two $1\frac{1}{2} \times 2\frac{1}{2}$" strips together with right sides facing along the long edges. Turn right side out and press.

Form two bow loops and streamers with the long strip, gathering in the center. Wrap center with bow knot strip and secure. Tack bow to center of B piece intersections at corners or as desired.

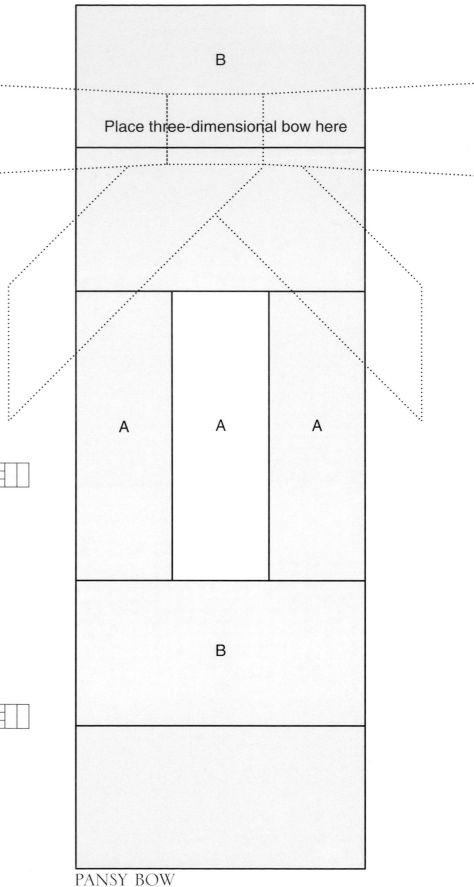

PANSY BOW
FULL-SIZE BORDER

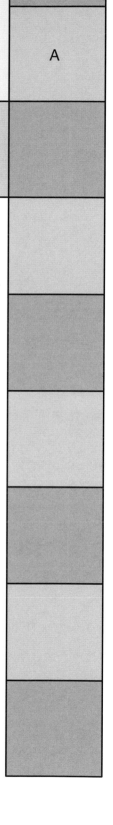

PIE CRUST
FULL-SIZE BORDER

Pie Crust Border

This border is 3" wide and has a 3" repeat.
Sew A to B (2 times). Sew AB unit to AB unit to make a square. Sew squares together for border.

Checkerboard Border

This border is 3" wide and has a 6" repeat.
For one 6-inch unit, sew six A pieces together to form a row. Sew a 6-inch B piece (or desired length to fit quilt) to A unit.

For the corner, sew two A pieces together. Join AA unit to C piece. Sew three A pieces together. Join AAA unit to the AAC unit for form a square. Sew the square corner unit to AAAAAB unit.

Note: B piece may extend to desired length of quilt.

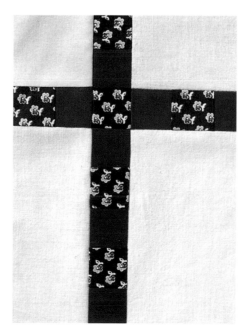

CHECKERBOARD
FULL-SIZE BORDER

Fan Border

This border in 3¼" wide and has a 9" repeat.

Sew E to the top, bottom, and each side of the quilt top. Sew three A's together. Appliqué B on the inside curve of AAA unit. Sew C on each side of AAAB unit. The completed border strip should begin and end with C. To make the corner block, sew six A's together. Appliqué D on the inside curve. Sew to the corner diagonal edge.

Leaf and Circle Border

This border is 4½" wide and has a random repeat. Appliqué B and Br (buds) and E and Er (stems) on background fabric. Appliqué C, Cr, D, Dr, and F.

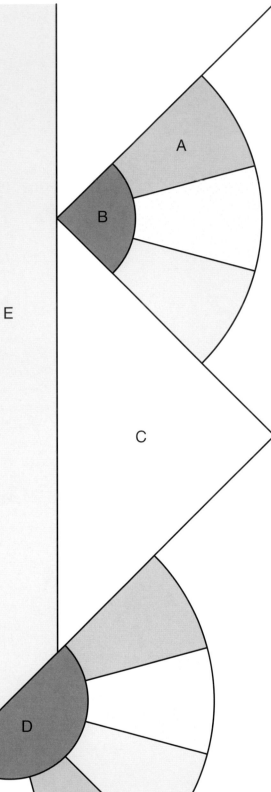

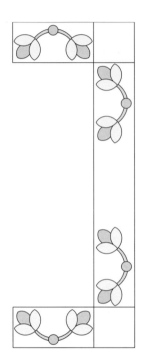

Stars and Stripes Border

This border is 3" wide and has a 3" repeat. For each star unit, sew A to A (4 times). Rows 1 and 3—Sew B to AA; add B (2 times). Row 2—Sew AA to B; add AA. Sew Rows 1, 2, and 3 together to make one star unit. Make star units for the desired length of the quilt. Add a CCC unit to each corner.

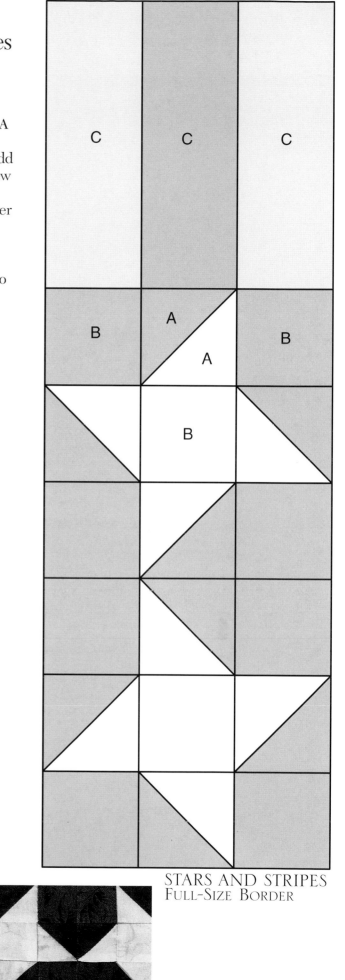

STARS AND STRIPES
FULL-SIZE BORDER

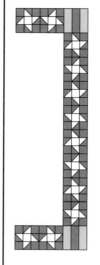

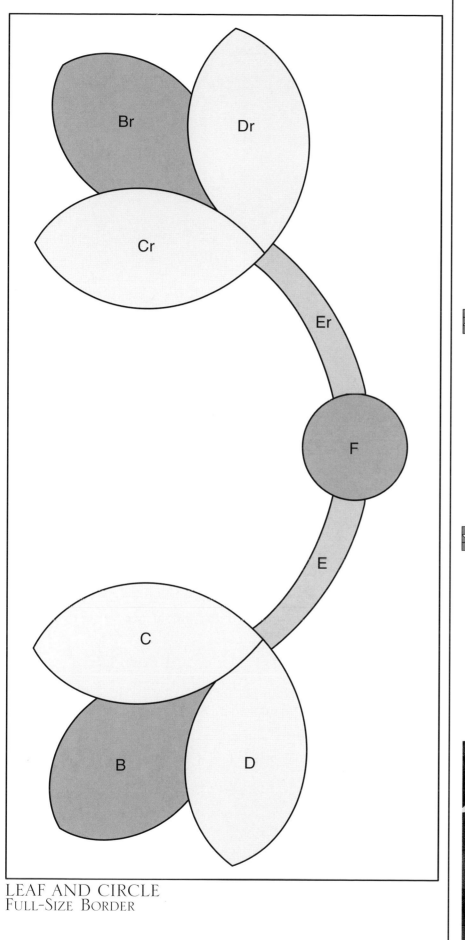

LEAF AND CIRCLE
FULL-SIZE BORDER

197

Diamond Border

This border is 3" wide and has a 4½" repeat.

Sew A to B. Sew A to AB. Sew AAB units together to form a border strip unit. To each end of each AAB border strip unit; add C. Sew F to a border strip unit (2 times). Sew F border strip to the top and bottom of the quilt top. Sew D to each end of a border strip unit (2 times). Sew F to a border strip unit (2 times). Sew D to E (4 times). Sew DE to each end of F border strip (2 times). Sew F border strip to each side of the quilt top.

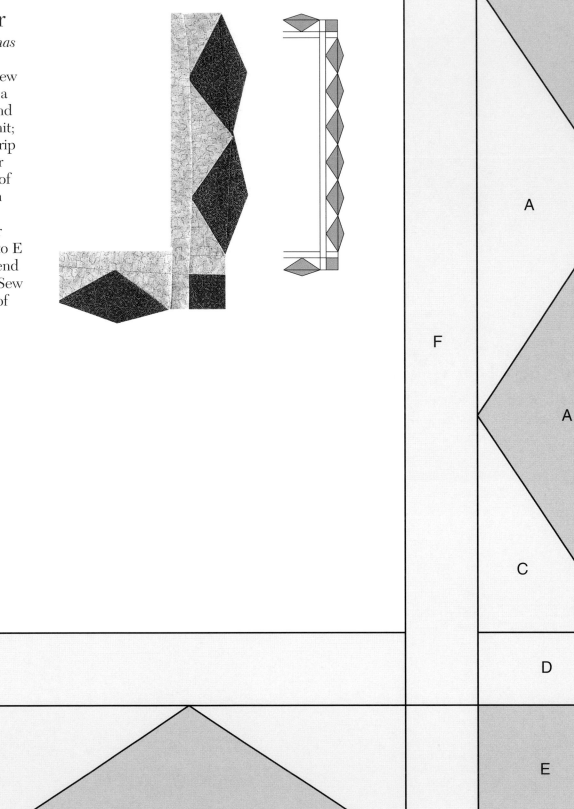

DIAMOND
FULL-SIZE BORDER

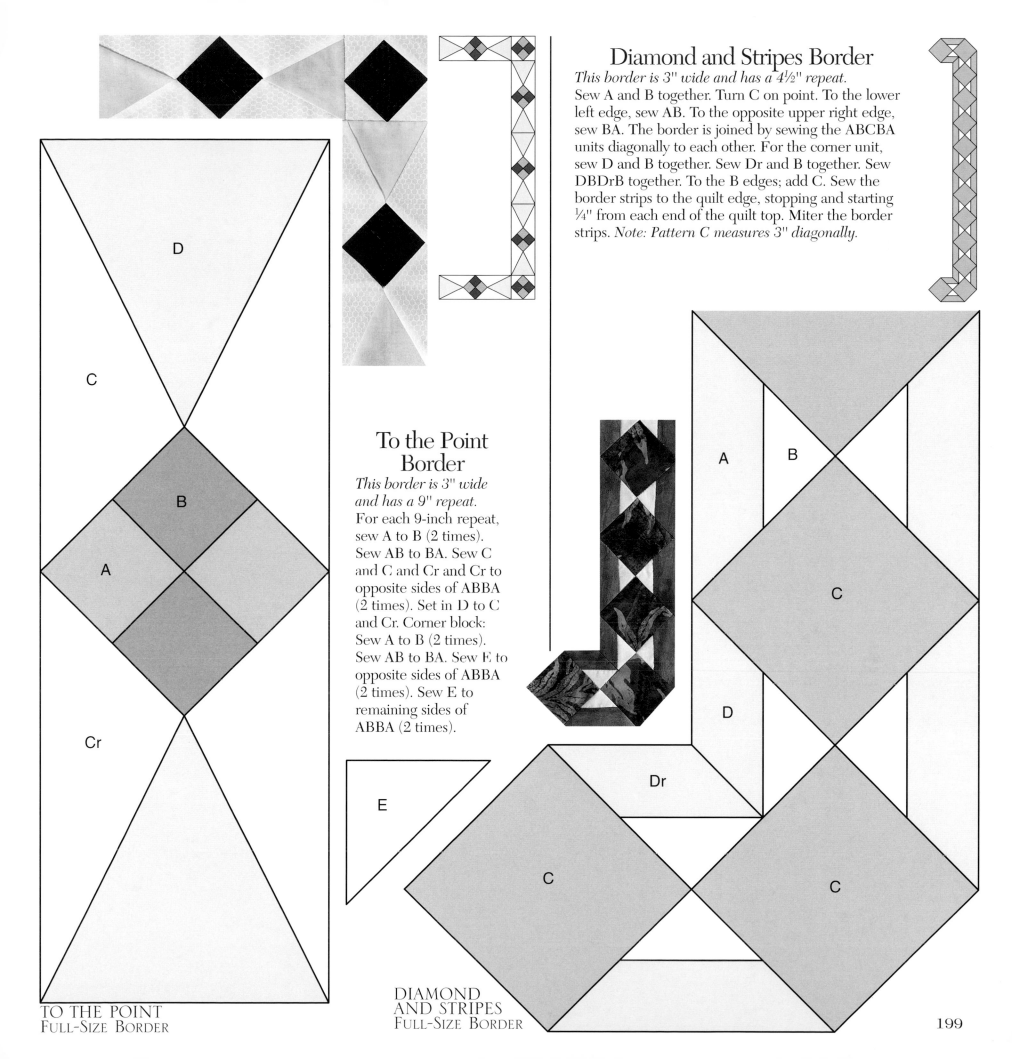

Diamond and Stripes Border

This border is 3" wide and has a 4½" repeat.
Sew A and B together. Turn C on point. To the lower left edge, sew AB. To the opposite upper right edge, sew BA. The border is joined by sewing the ABCBA units diagonally to each other. For the corner unit, sew D and B together. Sew Dr and B together. Sew DBDrB together. To the B edges; add C. Sew the border strips to the quilt edge, stopping and starting ¼" from each end of the quilt top. Miter the border strips. *Note: Pattern C measures 3" diagonally.*

To the Point Border

This border is 3" wide and has a 9" repeat.
For each 9-inch repeat, sew A to B (2 times). Sew AB to BA. Sew C and C and Cr and Cr to opposite sides of ABBA (2 times). Set in D to C and Cr. Corner block: Sew A to B (2 times). Sew AB to BA. Sew E to opposite sides of ABBA (2 times). Sew E to remaining sides of ABBA (2 times).

TO THE POINT
FULL-SIZE BORDER

DIAMOND
AND STRIPES
FULL-SIZE BORDER

Eclectic Border

This border is 4" wide and has a 6" repeat.

Sew F border strip to each side of the quilt top; miter corners. Sew B to opposite sides of A (2 times). Sew B to remaining sides of A (2 times). Sew B to C (2 times); add B. Sew BCB to BCB. Sew the required number of units together, referring to diagram, *below left,* for placement, to make four border strips. Sew D to each end of two border strips. Sew one border to the top and one to the bottom of the quilt top. Press the seams toward the outside border strip. Sew E to D (4 times). Press the seam toward D. Sew DE to each end of the two remaining border strips. Sew one DE border to each side of quilt top to complete border and quilt top.

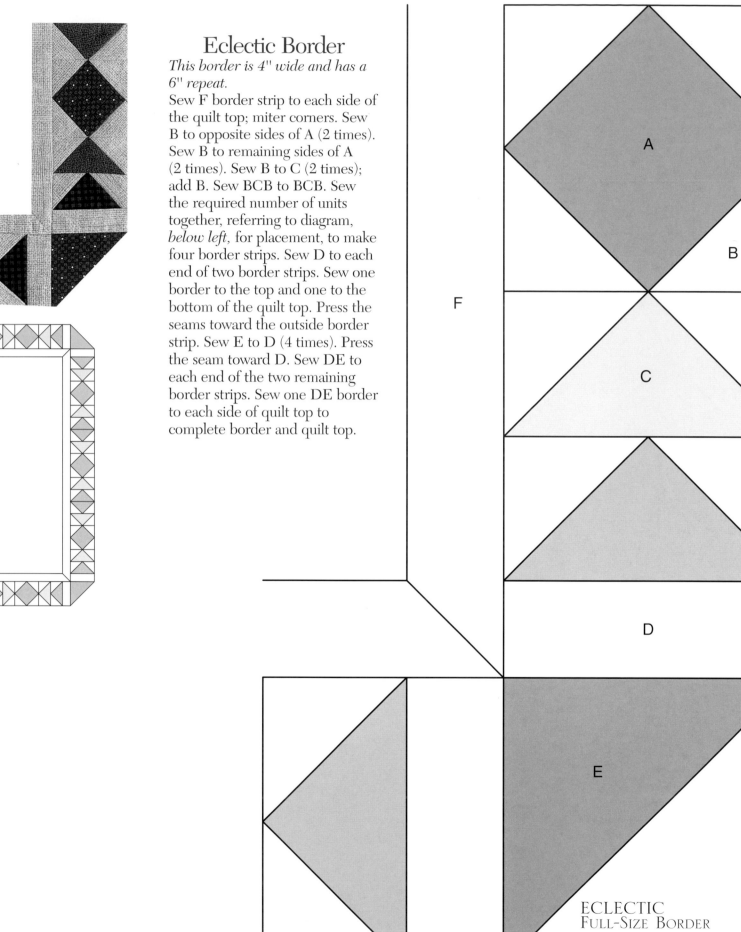

ECLECTIC
FULL-SIZE BORDER

Chevron Border

This border is 4½" wide and has a 4½" repeat.

Sew J to B; add F. Sew J to Br; add F. Sew E to JBF (2 times). Sew EJBF to EJBrF to make one Unit. Sew the required number of units together to make four border strips. Sew G to the inside length of a border strip (4 times). Sew one border to the top and one to the bottom of the quilt top. Press the seams toward the outside border strip. Sew E to I (4 times); add E. Sew C to D (4 times); add H (optional). Sew CD to EIE (4 times) to make the corner setting square. Sew a setting square to each end of the two remaining border strips. Press the seam allowance toward the chevron units. Sew one border to each side of quilt top to complete the border and quilt top.

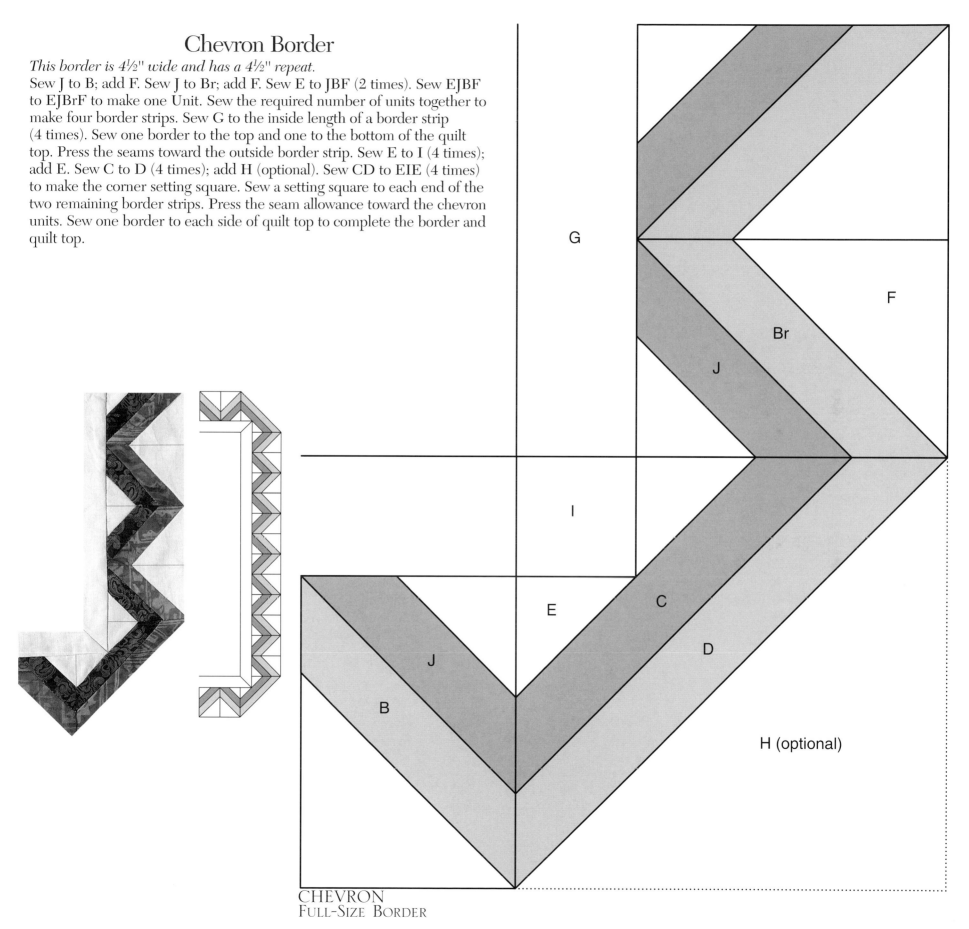

CHEVRON
FULL-SIZE BORDER

Ivy Border

This border is 5" wide and has a random repeat.

For a 9-inch repeat, appliqué B onto background fabric (A), then appliqué D and C pieces. For the corner, sew F to each end of the border strip, then sew E to the inside edge of the border. Sew the border strips to the quilt edge then miter corners.

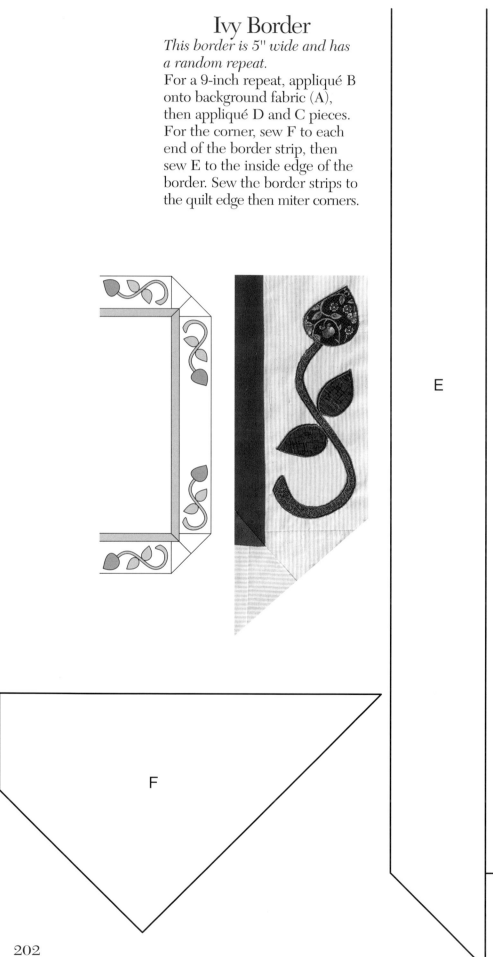

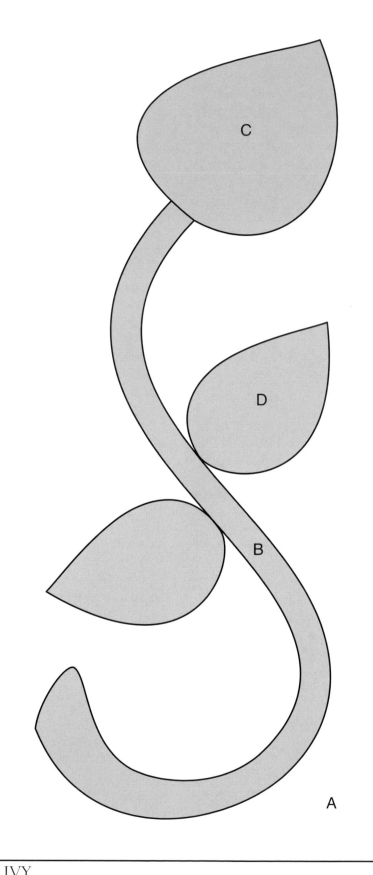

E

C

D

B

A

F

IVY
FULL-SIZE BORDER

Ribbon Border

This border is 5" wide and has a 9" repeat.
Sew B to opposite sides of A; set in B. Sew E to F and
Er to Fr. Sew EF to D; add ErFr, set in M (optional).
Set in EFDErFr to ABBB for Unit 1. Sew G to C
(2 times); add H. Sew I to GCH for Unit 2. Sew J to
K; add N (optional) for Unit 3. Sew Jr to Kr;
add Nr (optional) for Unit 4. Sew Unit 3 to
Unit 2; add Unit 1. Sew Unit 2 to 321; add
Unit 4 to complete one bow. Sew the
required number of units together to make
four border strips. Sew L to the inside
length of a border strip (4 times). Sew one
border to the top and one to the bottom of
the quilt top. Press the seams toward the
outside border strip. Sew O to P (4 times).
Sew Or to Q (4 times). Sew OP to OrQ
(4 times). Sew OPQ to each end of the two
remaining border strips. Press the seam
toward the ribbon unit. Sew one OPQ
border to each side of the quilt top to
complete the border and quilt top. *Note: Refer
to the set-in seam directions on page 213.*

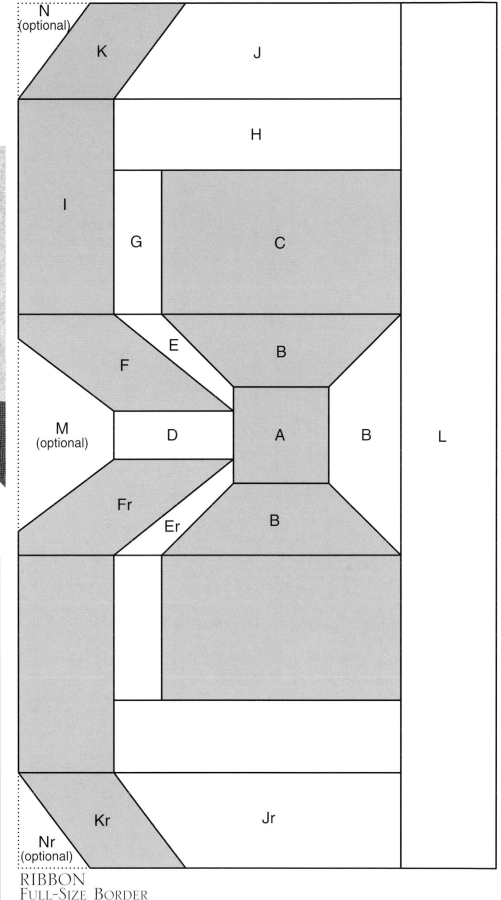

RIBBON
FULL-SIZE BORDER

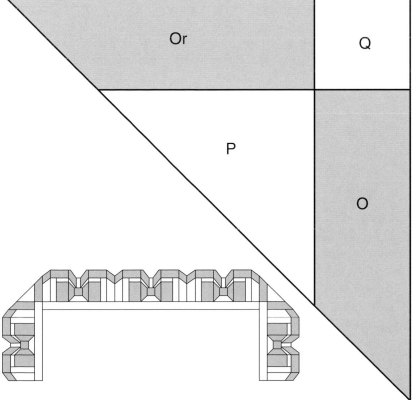

Sawtooth Border

This border is 4½" wide and has a 4½" repeat.

Sew B pieces to quilt edge, mitering the corners. (The B pieces should be cut in one continuous length to match each outside edge of the quilt.) Sew A pieces together to complete desired length of quilt. Sew the AA strip to the outside edges of B. Sew C, the corner triangle, on each corner.

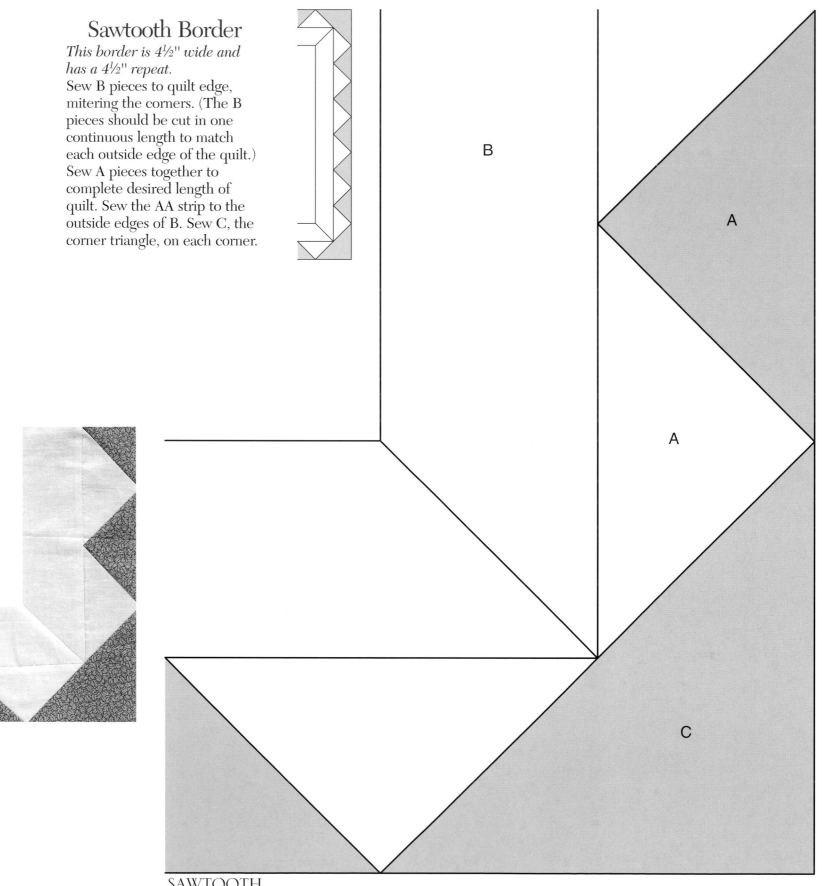

SAWTOOTH
FULL-SIZE BORDER

Stripes Border

This border is 4" wide and has a 4½" repeat.

Sew piece A to piece A, stopping the stitching ¼" from the end of the seam at the pointed ends. Sew piece C to the AA unit. Sew a slanted edge of C to the slanted edge of A, stopping ¼" from the end of the seam line (this should be at the point that you stopped stitching the AA pieces). Turn to reposition, matching C edge to the second A piece and start the stitching at the point ¼" from the edge. Repeat sewing AAC units for the desired length of the quilt border. Sew AAC units together. Once you have reached desired length, sew BBr corner block to AC edge. Sew on D strip. Sew the border units onto quilt edges, matching edges and seams of B and D pieces at the corners.

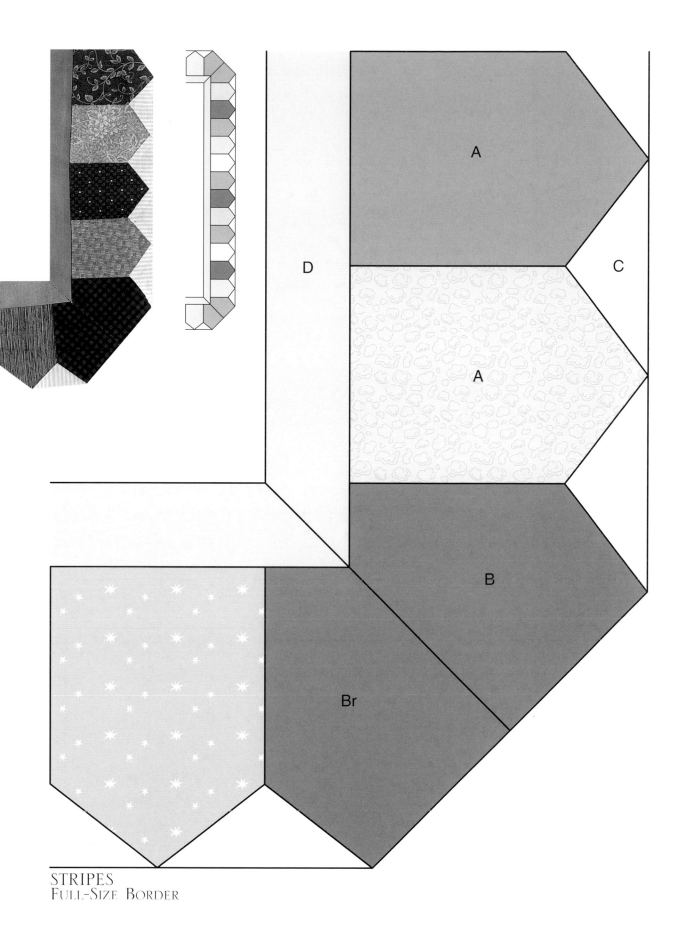

STRIPES
FULL-SIZE BORDER

Tulip Border

This border is 4" wide and has a 9" repeat.

This border has "set in seams". Start and stop the stitching ¼" from the ends that will have a piece set into it. Refer to the directions for setting in seams on *page 213*. Sew A to B and Ar to Br. Sew E to AB (2 times). Set in D to ABE (2 times). Sew ABED to ArBrED. Set in C. Sew the required number of units together, alternating the direction of the tulip to make four border strips. Sew F to the inside length of two borders. Sew F border to the top of the quilt and to the bottom of the quilt. Press seams toward the border strip. Sew G to each end of two remaining border strips. Add F to the inside length of each strip. Sew G to H (4 times). Sew GH to each end of F border. Press seams toward F strip. Sew one F border to each side of the quilt top to complete the border of the quilt top.

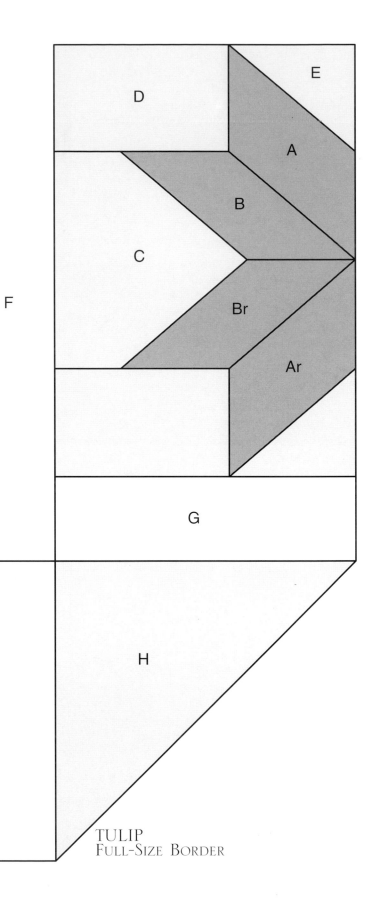

TULIP
FULL-SIZE BORDER

Christmas Wreath Border

This border is 4" wide and has a 6" repeat.
Sew B to C; add D. Sew E to BCD. Sew Br to Cr. Set in BrCr to BCDE. Sew A to A; set in AA to BCDEBrCr to make a wreath Unit. Sew F to the wreath Unit (4 times). Sew I to I (2 times). Set in H to II and II. Sew II to II to make a spacer Unit. Sew the required number of units together to make four border strips. Sew L to the inside length of a border strip (2 times). Sew one L border to the top of the quilt top and one L border to the bottom of the quilt top. Press the seam allowance toward the border unit. Sew K to one end of the remaining two border strips and Kr to the opposite end of the same two border strips. Sew L to the inside length of a border strip (2 times). Press the seam allowance toward the border unit. Sew J to K (2 times). Sew J to Kr (2 times). Sew one JK to one end of each L border strip and JKr to the opposite end of each L border strip. Sew one L border strip to each side of the quilt top to complete the border and quilt top. *Note: Refer to page 213 for setting in seam directions.*

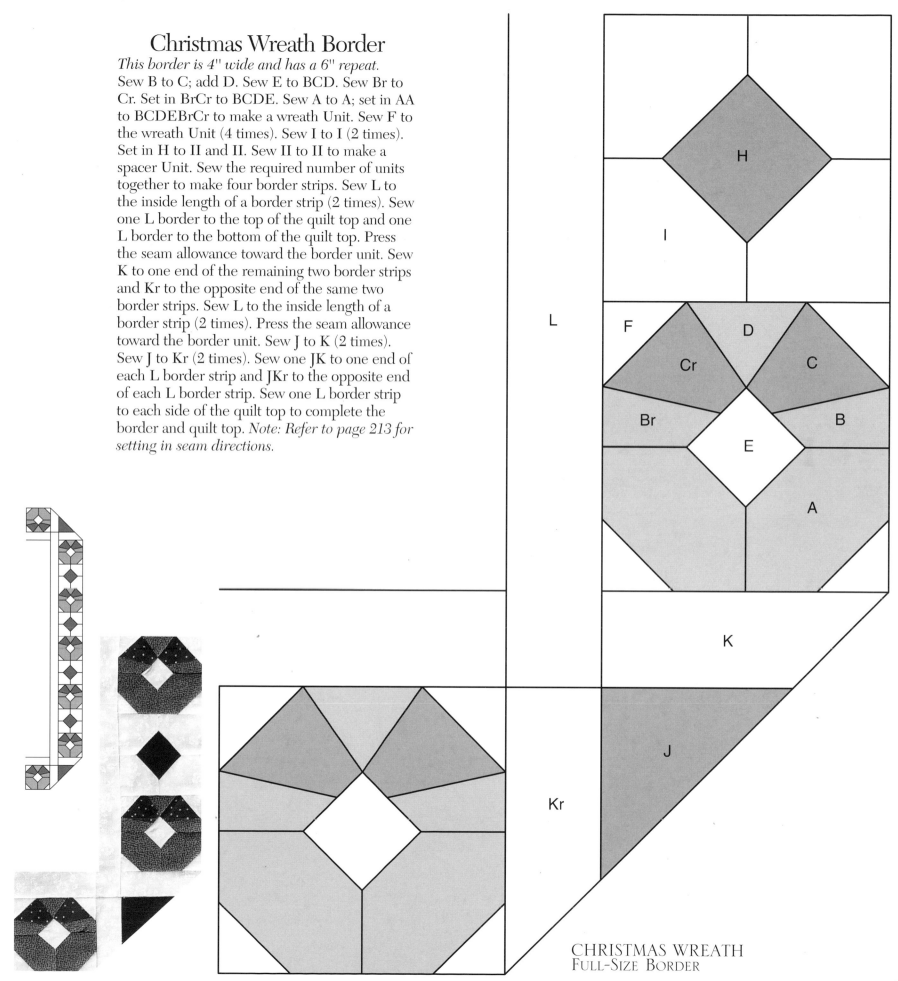

CHRISTMAS WREATH
FULL-SIZE BORDER

Five-Pointed Star Border

This border is 4½" wide and has a random repeat. The star may be placed evenly as well. Hand or machine appliqué star (piece A) to background fabric. Note: If hand appliqué is used, add the seam allowance to outer edge. To make corner block, sew C between B and Br pieces.

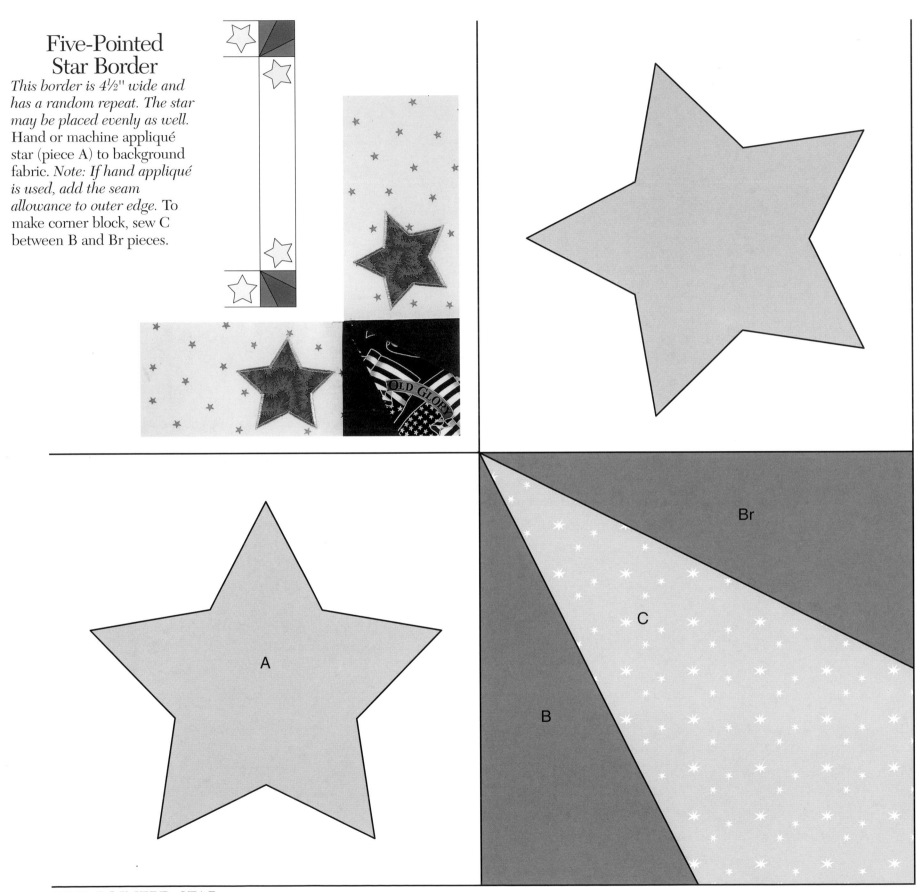

FIVE-POINTED STAR
FULL-SIZE BORDER

Bow Border

This border is 2½" wide and has a 4½" repeat.

Sew B to D; add C. Sew B to Dr; add C. Sew BDC to A (2 times); add B. Sew C to C; add E. Sew BDCAB to CCE; add BDrCAB for Unit 1. Sew F to each side of Unit 1 to complete the bow. Sew G to G (2 times). Set in C to GG; add GG. Sew GG to GG to complete corner setting square.

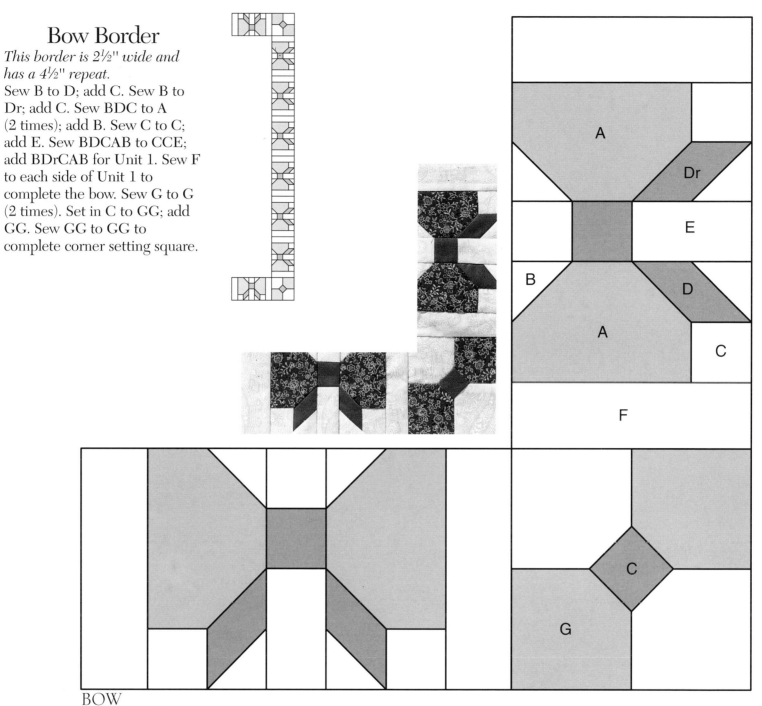

BOW
FULL-SIZE BORDER

Bud Border

This border is 4½" wide and has a 4½" repeat. Sew four A pieces together to form a square. Sew AAAA unit to C. Sew four B pieces together to form a square. Sew BBBB unit to another C piece. Sew the two units together to create a 4½" repeat. For the corner, sew four A pieces together. Sew D to two sides of AAAA unit. Sew border to each side of corner.

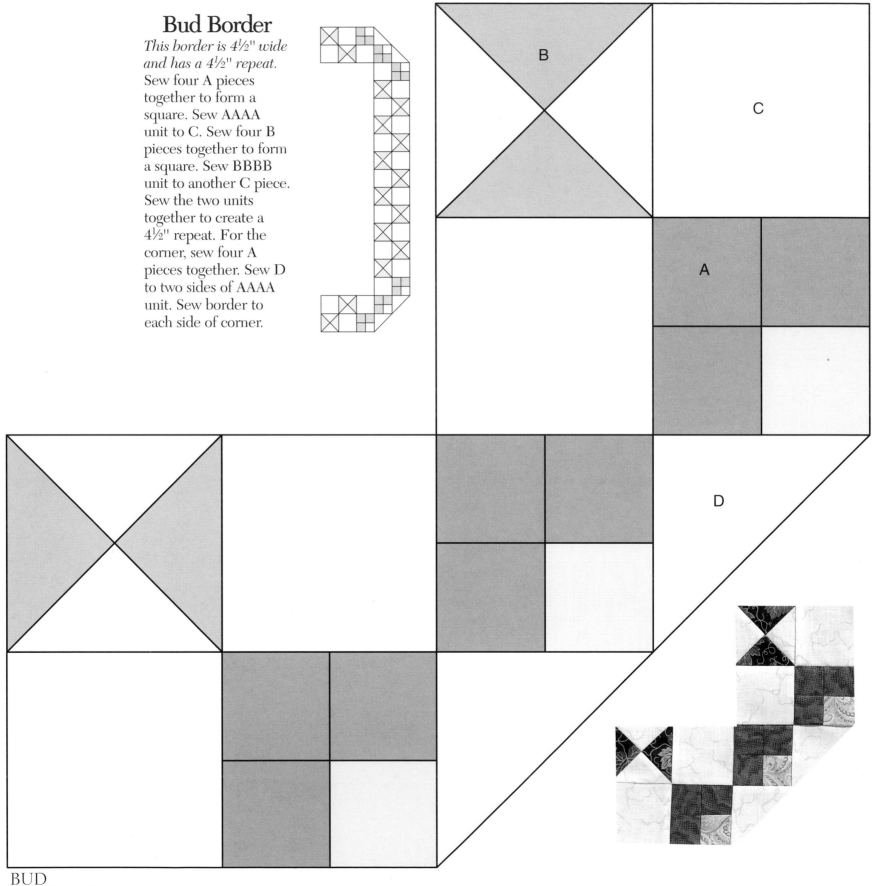

BUD
FULL-SIZE BORDER

Sawtooth and Diamond Border

This border is 5" wide and has a 6" repeat. Sew A to B in multiples for the length of the border. Sew the AB units together. At the end of the border strips, add a corner block C/Cr. Sew on the D strip. Sew the border units onto quilt edge, matching edges and seams of pieces C/Cr and D at the corners.

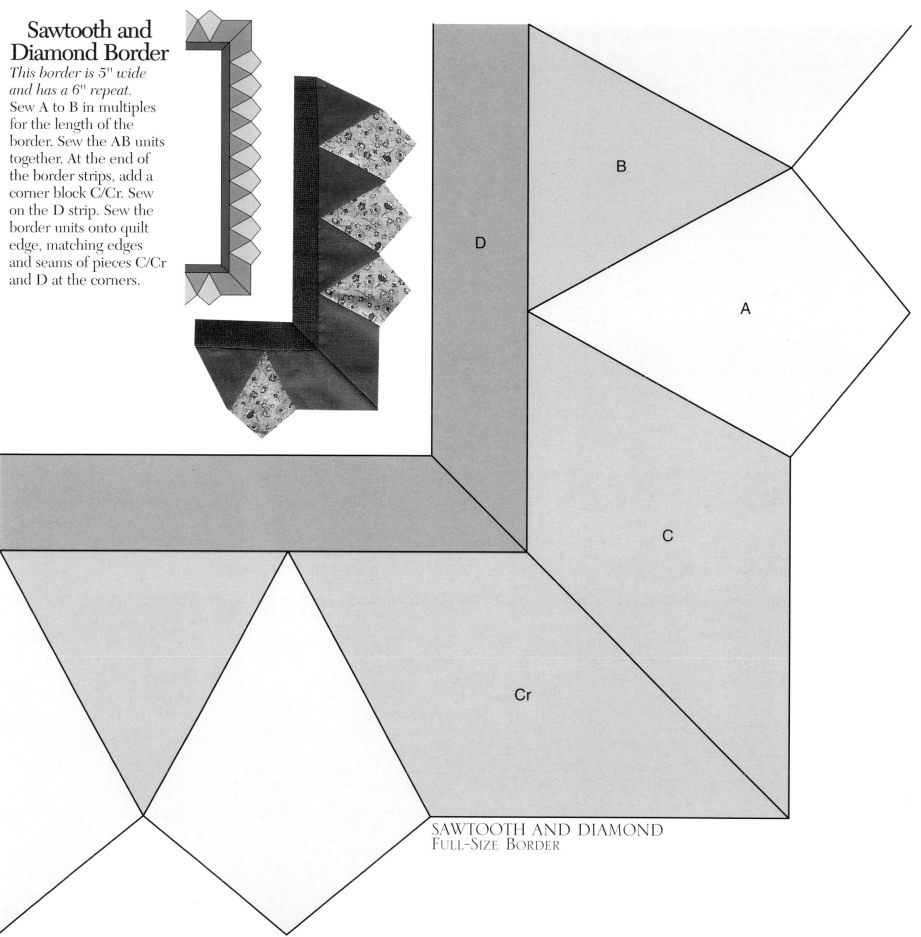

SAWTOOTH AND DIAMOND
FULL-SIZE BORDER

HOW TO MAKE PIECED-BLOCK TEMPLATES

All of our patterns are finished-size to make creating your templates easy and frustration-free. When selecting your template plastic, choose the kind of plastic that is slightly frosted. You can still see through it, spot it easily, and can mark on it without smearing or smudging. For the blocks in this book, steer away from template plastic with a grid printed on it. And avoid using cardboard for templates; it doesn't hold its shape well with continuous use.

Using a ruler and a fine-line permanent marker, trace the block pattern pieces onto your plastic. You'll add the ¼-inch seam allowance when you cut out the pieces. (See information at right for making appliqué templates.) Then cut out using scissors. (Be sure you're not using your fabric scissors to cut the plastic!)

It is not necessary to move the template plastic when tracing each template. If several pieces are grouped together, draw them that way, then cut them apart.

Note that we have labeled our block patterns using letters of the alphabet. Label your templates with these same letters using your permanent marker. Remember, the letters in each block are for that block only; piece B in one block isn't the same as B used in another block.

In some of the block patterns you will see pieces marked with a letter followed by a lower-case "r" (as in B and Br). This means that you must reverse (flip over) the B template to trace and cut this piece. You don't need two templates to cut B and Br: you simply use the other side of your B template.

Instructions for making the blocks will often include a direction such as "(4 times)". This means that you create the unit described a total of four times.

As you draw the templates, note any edge that will be on the outside of the block. Mark the template with an arrow along this edge to remind you to cut the fabric with the arrow on the straight of the grain. This will help keep your block from stretching. Also mark which edges are to be sewn together.

To store your blocks, small, clear plastic bags help keep each of your block templates separate and easy to find. These easy-to-label zipper-lock bags are available at quilting and craft stores.

HOW TO MAKE APPLIQUÉ-BLOCK TEMPLATES

Trace the entire design onto template plastic, as described at left. Letter the pieces in the design, and also letter the corresponding pieces on the template plastic. Then, cut out the individual template pieces.

Trace around the template pieces on the right side of the fabric with the template face up. Make a dotted line on the template to indicate areas that will be lying under another shape.

TRANSFERRING THE PATTERN FROM TEMPLATE TO FABRIC

Before you do any tracing and cutting of the fabric, you must decide if your quilting project will ever need to be washed. If so, you must prewash the fabric. If the fabric is going to shrink, or the dyes are going to run, you want it to happen before you stitch.

Lay your fabric out smoothly, wrong side up. Try using elements of the fabric print to enhance the design of the block, centering a flower or stripe for instance.

Position the template, face down on the wrong side of the fabric. It is a good practice to always place the template face down on the fabric, even when it doesn't seem to matter. There are times when it is very important, and this habit will help you avoid redrawing.

For appliquéd blocks, mark fabric on the right side. The seam allowance (between ⅛ and ¼ inch) is added when you cut out each piece.

Trace around the template onto the fabric using a number 2 pencil. This is the line on which you will sew. Mechanical pencils are excellent, because they stay sharp. Don't choose one with lead that is too thin—the 0.7mm size is large enough. If using dark fabrics, choose colored leads.

For pieced blocks, add a ¼-inch seam allowance to all sides using a ruler. You'll need a clear ruler printed with a fine-line ⅛-inch grid. Many of these rulers are not 100 percent accurate—the ¼-inch mark may be different on opposite sides of the ruler. If you own one of these, choose one edge and use only that edge.

You can also use the red ruler which is exactly ¼-inch thick. This useful alternative to the clear ruler is about 1 inch high, so it lifts your fingers up, keeping them out of the way as you trace. Its bright red color makes it easy to spot on your sewing table.

Transfer the template marks indicating which edges are to be sewn together to the seam allowances of the fabric. This is especially helpful when, for instance, a triangle has two sides of similar length.

HOW TO MAKE THE PIECED BLOCKS

Use your fabric scissors to cut out your fabric pieces along the seam allowance lines. When the pieces are all cut out, refer to our easy-to-follow instructions for the sequence in putting your block together.

As you begin to feed the pieces into your sewing machine, it is not necessary to backstitch; you will be sewing over the ends of the seams, so they aren't in danger of coming unsewn. Also, if you make a mistake, it is easier to rip out a seam that is not backstitched.

As each seam is pieced, you may want to trim away some of the points that protrude beyond the end of the seam allowance. Some of the seams may also need to be trimmed if they will be caught in the next seam you will sew.

THE FOUR- AND NINE-PATCH

A four-patch and a nine-patch are two common types of pieced blocks.

A four-patch is a square made of four smaller squares. To assemble, sew two together two times (making two pairs of squares); then join the two pairs into a square.

A nine-patch is a square made up of nine smaller squares—three rows of three squares each. To make a nine-patch, sew three squares together in a row three times, making three rows; then sew the rows together to make the larger square.

HOW TO MAKE THE APPLIQUÉD BLOCKS

There are several ways to do appliqué. We turn the edges of our pieces under with the needle as we sew. Basting beforehand is another option. Be sure to never use a colored thread if using the basting method. A contrasting thread can leave little, unsightly dots of color on the fabric.

Concave (inward) curves should be clipped before basting. Clip around the curve only up to 1/16 inch from the seam line. (If you clip right up to the line, you will get points along the curve.)

To baste each piece, roll the seam edge under along the marked line. Do not turn under seams that will lie under another shape, as this produces bulky ridges on the finished surface.

The actual application of one fabric piece to another is done with blind stitching. Using thread to match the piece being applied, bring your needle from the back to the front, catching a few threads of the rolled edge. Pull thread through. Re-enter the base fabric at the exact spot and slightly under the rolled edge. Make a linear stitch on the back, following the outline of the shape, coming up again through all layers. The linear stitches should be not more than ⅛ inch in length, less for very small or intricately shaped pieces.

When all application is finished, remove all basting threads. Any embroidery can then be added.

HOW TO MAKE FUSED-APPLIQUÉ BLOCKS

As an alternate method of appliqué, trace each pattern piece onto fusing adhesive material. Cut out the pieces and fuse to the wrong side of the chosen fabrics. Cut out and remove the paper. On a 10-inch background square, arrange each piece as the instructions specify and press in place. Use a machine satin stitch or hand embroider the edges of the fused pieces. Trim the block to measure 9½ inches square.

ACCENT STITCHES

For detail accents, specialty stitches are often added to a completed quilt block. You'll see these stitches are represented by dashed lines on the block patterns. The following illustrations will help you master the common stitches which we have also used in this book.

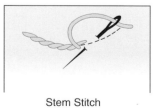

Stem Stitch

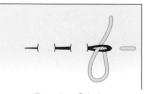

Running Stitch

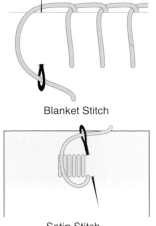

Blanket Stitch

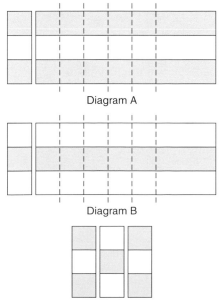

Satin Stitch

STRIP PIECING

In traditional patchwork, pieces are marked, cut, and sewn together one piece at a time. But when squares and rectangles are combined in a repeated pattern, you can simplify assembly by using strip-piecing techniques.

CUTTING STRIPS

With strip piecing, you sew together a specified sequence of horizontal strips into a strip set. The strip set is then cut into vertical units, each of which represents a row or unit of a quilt block.

Strips are cut on the crosswise grain, ½ inch wider than the desired finished size of the patch to allow for ¼-inch seam allowances. For example, for a 2-inch finished square, cut a strip 2½ inches wide.

STRIP SETS

By cutting units different widths or turning them upside down, a strip set is often used for more than one block row.

Diagram A

Diagram B

Diagram C

HOW TO SET IN SEAMS

When two patchwork pieces come together and form an angled opening, a third piece must be set into this angle. (Some blocks must have pieces set in, such as the "F" piece on the Housedress quilt block, on pages 148–149.) This happens frequently when making projects with diamond-shape pieces.

For a design that requires setting in, use either a window or pinhole template to mark each shape's sewing and cutting lines on the fabric. You must mark the exact point of each corner on the sewing line. By matching the corners of adjacent pieces, you'll be able to sew them together easily and accurately.

MAKE SET-IN PIECE TEMPLATES

To make a pinhole template, lay template plastic over the pattern. Trace the sewing lines onto the template plastic. Add a ¼-inch seam allowance around each sewing line; this will be the cutting line. Carefully cut out the template along the cutting line. Using a sewing-machine needle or any large needle, make a hole in the template at each corner of the sewing line (matching points). The holes need to be large enough to allow the point of a pencil or other fabric marker to poke through.

To mark the fabric, lay the template face-down on the wrong side of the fabric. Draw around the template. Then, using a pencil, mark dots on the fabric through the holes in the template to create matching points. Cut out the fabric pieces along the drawn lines. Check to be sure all pieces have matching points marked.

To make a window template, lay the template plastic over the pattern piece. Trace the sewing lines onto the template plastic. Add a ¼-inch seam allowance around each sewing line; this will be the cutting line. Carefully cut out the template along the cutting line. Then use a crafts knife to cut on the sewing line, and remove the center of the template.

To mark your fabric, lay the template face-down on the wrong side of the fabric. With a marking tool, mark the cutting line, sewing line, and each corner on the sewing line (matching points). Cut out the fabric pieces along the cutting lines. Check to be sure all pieces have sewing lines and matching points marked on them.

STITCH THE SET-IN PIECES

Join the two diamond-shape pieces, aligning the matching points carefully. Whether you're stitching by machine or hand, be careful to start and stop sewing precisely at the matching points (see Diagram 1). Backstitch to secure the ends of the seams. This prepares the angle created by the diamonds for the next piece to be set in. Follow the specific instructions for either machine- or hand-piecing.

MACHINE-PIECING SET-IN PIECES

Pin one piece of the angled unit to one edge of the square with right sides together (see Diagram 2). Match the corners of the seam, or the matching points, by pushing a pin through both fabric layers to check the alignment. Machine-stitch the seam from matching point to matching point. Backstitch to secure the ends of the seam. Do not stitch into the ¼ inch seam allowance. Then remove the unit from the sewing machine.

Bring the adjacent edge of the angled unit up and align it with the next edge of the square (see Diagram 3). Insert a pin in each corner to align the matching points, then pin the remainder of the seam. Machine-stitch between the matching points. Do not stitch into the seam allowance.

HAND-PIECING SET-IN PIECES

Pin one piece of the angled unit to one edge of the square with right sides together (see Diagram 4). Use pins to align the matching points at the corners of the pieces.

Sew the seam from the open end of the angle into the corner. Remove the pins as you sew between the matching points. Backstitch at the corner to secure stitches. Do not cut your thread.

Bring the adjacent edge of the square up and align it with the other edge of the angled unit. Insert a pin in each corner to align the matching points, then pin the remainder of the seam (see Diagram 5). Continue hand-stitching the seam from the corner to the open end of the angle, removing the pins as you sew.

PRESS THE UNITS

Press both seam allowances of the set-in square toward the diamonds; press the diamonds' joining seam to one side.

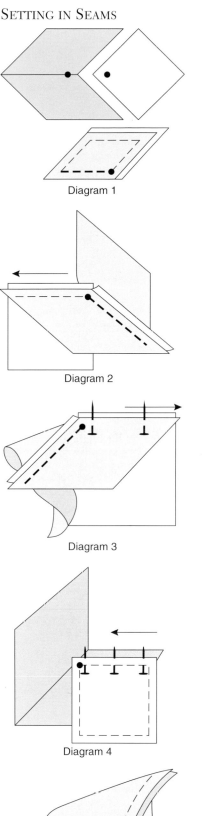

Diagram 1

Diagram 2

Diagram 3

Diagram 4

Diagram 5

DESIGNING THE QUILT

When determining how big you want to make your quilt, how to join your blocks together, and what border to choose, be sure to do your calculations carefully.

While there is no one "standard" quilt dimension for any size of bed, we can give you some guidelines to follow when planning your bed quilt. Here's a chart to help you decide what size of quilt you want to make:

WIDTH RANGES
Twin	Full
63"–81"	78"–96"
Queen	King
84"–102"	100"–118"

LENGTH RANGES
Twin	Full
87"–106"	87"–106"
Queen	King
92"–112"	92"–112"

SASHING
Fabric strips that separate or frame the blocks are called sashing strips. They enhance a quilt design and enlarge the quilt center.

Adjusting the width of the sashing strips is one way to make your quilt larger or smaller. Other ways to alter the finished size of your quilt include:
- Use more or fewer quilt blocks.
- Add or delete sashing strips.
- Select a wider or narrower border.
- Change the layout of the blocks or add setting blocks.

FINISHING THE BORDER
Most quilters prefer to use binding when finishing the border edges of a quilt. However, you can use a blind-hem stitch or face the quilt, if desired.

BACKING AND BINDING
To back a quilt, you simply cut a piece of the fabric you have chosen, making it at least 3 inches larger on all sides than the quilt top. (The larger the quilt, and the more quilting you plan to do, the more extra fabric you should allow on all sides.) If the quilt is larger than the fabric you want to use, you will have to piece the backing to make it the right size.

Layer the top, batting, and backing, with wrong sides of the top and backing toward the batting. Baste the layers together and quilt as desired.

HOW TO BIND THE QUILT
Choose ¼- or ½-inch binding and cut as described above (and long enough to go all the way around the quilt with a few inches to spare).

QUARTER-INCH BINDING—
Cut binding 2 inches wide. Use ¼-inch seam allowances.

HALF-INCH BINDING—
Cut binding 2½ inches wide. Use ¼-inch seam allowances.

Piece the binding as necessary using a diagonal joining seam to reach the required length, pressing seams open. Then press the binding in half (wrong sides together) along the length.

Lay binding along the raw edge of the quilt, folding over the beginning binding edge before stitching (see Diagram 1). Stitch, using the correct seam allowance.

Stop stitching ¼ inch from the corner. Backstitch and break the thread. Fold binding up, as shown in Diagram 2, then down (see Diagram 3), and stitch from edge. Repeat the process at each corner of the quilt. When you return to the starting point, over-lap the end of the binding strip beyond the fold in the first end. Trim the backing and batting even with the edge of the quilt front.

Turn binding up and over the edge to the back of the quilt. Tuck binding in at corners on back to make a miter. Hand stitch the binding to the backing, being careful not to sew through to the front.

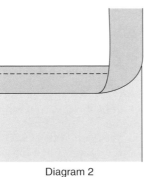
Diagram 1

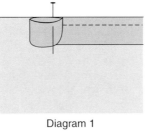
Diagram 2

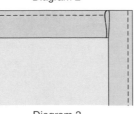
Diagram 3

SELECT A BATTING
A variety of choices are available in batting fiber content, loft, warmth, ease of needling, softness, and washability. The qualities of the batting you use should compliment the nature and future use of your quilt.

CUT BIAS STRIPS
To cut bias strips, begin with a fabric square or rectangle. Use a large acrylic triangle to square up the left edge of the fabric and to draw lines at a 45° angle (see Diagram 1). Cut the fabric on the drawn lines. Handle the edges carefully to avoid distorting the bias. Cut enough strips to total the length needed. Join the strips with diagonal seams to make one continuous binding strip.

Bias Strip Diagram

MAKE MITERED BORDER CORNERS
Pin a border strip to one edge of the quilt top, matching the center of the strip to the center of the quilt top edge. Sew together, beginning and ending the seam ¼ inch from the edge of the quilt top (see Diagram A, *below*). Allow excess border fabric to extend beyond each edge. Repeat with remaining border strips. Press the seam allowances toward the border strips.

Overlap the border strips at each corner (see Diagram B, *top right*). Align the edge of a top border. With a pencil, draw along the edge of the triangle from the border seam to the outside corner. Place the bottom border on top and repeat marking process.

With the right sides of adjacent border strips together, match the marked seam lines and pin (see Diagram C, *right*). Beginning with a backstitch at the inside corner, stitch exactly on the marked lines to the outside edge of the borders. Check the right side of the corner to see that it lies flat. Then trim the excess fabric, leaving a ¼-inch seam allowance. Press the seam open. Mark and sew remaining corners in this manner.

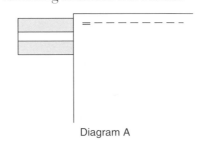
Diagram A

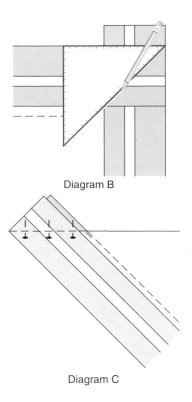
Diagram B

Diagram C

PRAIRIE POINTS
To make prairie points, cut fabric squares as indicated in instructions. Press squares in half diagonally twice, right side out. Using the Steps, *below*, pin the triangles evenly along the edges of the project front with all of the double-folds facing the same direction. Lap adjacent edges, or slip single-folds inside double-folds. Stitch on seam line.

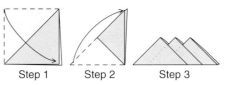
Step 1   Step 2   Step 3

QUILTING STYLES
Outline "In-the-Ditch" Quilting—
Quilting in-the-ditch is a single line of stitching that is done right on the seam line around patches, along sashing and borders, or just outside the edge of an appliqué. The stitches disappear into the seam, making a patch, block, border, or motif stand out from its background.

Single-Outline Quilting—
Single outline quilting is done parallel to and on one side of a seam (or the edge of an appliqué), ¼ inch to ½ inch away or far enough to clear the seam allowance. Quilting can be done closer to the seam (or appliqué edge) if done on the side of the shape without seam allowance.

Double-Outline Quilting—
Double-outline quilting is done parallel to and on both sides of a seam (or the edge of an appliqué), ¼ inch to ½ inch away or far enough to clear the seam allowance.

Echo Quilting—Echo quilting consists of multiple concentric outlines stitched either inside or outside a patchwork piece, appliqué, or quilted motif. The quilting lines are spaced evenly, ¼ inch to ½ inch apart (closer if stitched on the side without seam allowance) and can be expanded to completely fill the foreground or background if desired.

Diagonal Quilting—Diagonal quilting does not follow a motif outline but runs at an angle across part or all of a quilt. It may make use of the squareness of a block because a stitching line is easy to establish by marking from corner to corner, with additional lines parallel to the first if desired. Diagonal quilting can be used on isolated patches or blocks in the quilt center and/or on the border, and if well-planned and stitched over a large grid of squares, the quilted lines can create attractive geometric designs.

Motif Quilting—Motif quilting is a showcase for stitched designs rather than patchwork shapes. A motif is a design not necessarily related to the shape of the fabric piece on which it is stitched nor to any other part or aspect of the quilt top. It can be large or small; simple or complex; straight-edged or curved; single-outlined, double-outlined, or echoed; and used just once or repeated.

Many traditional motifs are available ready-made on templates in a variety of sizes. Most motifs can be enlarged, reduced, rearranged, or otherwise adapted for any plain patch, block, or strip.

Stippling—Stippling is a type of quilting design that can be stitched by hand or by machine. It can take the form of straight rows of stitches regularly placed (lined up or staggered), random zigzags, or random puzzle-like curves. Stippled designs should always be closely spaced.

Allover Designs—Some designs, particularly geometrics, are stitched all over the quilt with no regard to the shapes or fabrics on the quilt top. Allover designs can be stitched from either the quilt top or the backing side.

COLOR AND DESIGN

Make a bed quilt, wallhanging, or other quilting project in colors that coordinate with the room in which it will be used or displayed, or make it in colors that are pleasing to you or to the person who will receive it as a gift.

Use solids, prints, dots, or stripes. Experiment with different colors and combinations of colors, first with colored pencils and paper, then with fabric swatches.

THE COLOR WHEEL

The color wheel can help you understand why some colors work together while others seem to clash. Colors that sit adjacent to one another on the wheel will blend quietly; to enliven a color add one from the opposite side. All colors alter in appearance when placed next to different colors. Any color will gain importance as you add more of it to any arrangement.

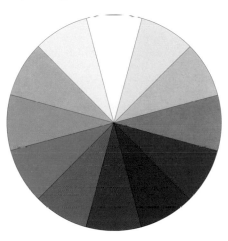

COLOR VOCABULARY

Primary Colors: Yellow, red, blue

Secondary Colors: Orange, violet, green (halfway between primary colors on color wheel)

Tertiary Colors: Yellow-orange, red-orange, red-violet, blue-violet, blue-green, yellow-green (between primary and secondary colors on color wheel)

Neutral Tones: White, gray, black, beige

Tint: Made by adding white to a color (for example, pink is a tint of red)

Shade: Made by adding black to a color (for example, maroon is a shade of red)

Warm Colors: Yellow, orange, red (visually stimulating)

Cool Colors: Violet, blue, green (visually soothing)

Achromatic: Without color; neutral tones

Monochromatic: Shades and/or tints of one color (for example, pink, dusty rose, maroon)

Polychromatic: Several colors, or shades or tints of several colors (for example, salmon, light sea-green, light violet)

Analogous: Two or more adjacent colors on color wheel (for example, yellow, yellow-green, green)

Complementary: Two opposite colors on wheel (for example, red and green)

COLOR SCHEMES

Consider the value of colors (light, medium, or dark) when planning a color scheme. Dark colors seem brighter against a white or beige background. Against a black background, muted colors can have a somber look (as in Amish quilts), and bright, solid colors can appear to shine like stained glass.

Consider also the proportion and placement of the colors and prints, which will have an important effect on a quilt's overall look.

Mix and match color values based on the effect you want. Use high-contrast, solid colors for a bold look and low-contrast, soft prints for a quiet, subdued look.

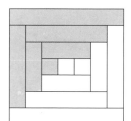

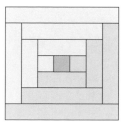

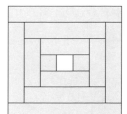

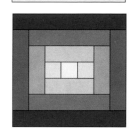

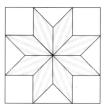

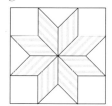

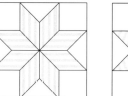

STRIPES

Stripes can be a striking addition to a quilt, but they require special care in cutting and extra fabric to allow for waste. You can use the stripes as guides for straight edges.

PRINTS

Use dense, allover prints for small pieces, as these tend to get lost between the motifs of a sparse print and wind up looking like solids. Small, allover prints can also be used for backing and to camouflage seams and quilting lines.

Use large-scale prints for large pieces or to create different effects on small pieces.

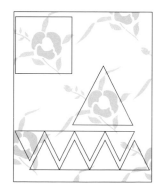

INDEX AND SOURCES

SOURCES
FABRIC
Concord Fabrics, Inc., 1359 Broadway, New York, NY 10018, (212)760-0343.
David Textiles, Inc., 5959 Telegraph Road, City of Commerce, CA 90040, (213)728-3231.
FABRI-QUILT, INC., 901 E. 14th Ave., North Kansas City, MO 64116, (816)421-2000.
Fabric Traditions, 1350 Broadway #2106, New York, NY 10018.
Island Textiles, Inc., 6320 Easton Road, Pipersville, PA 18947, (215)766-8484.
Marcus Brothers Textiles, Inc., 1460 Broadway, New York, NY 10036, (212)354-8700.
P&B Textiles, 1580 Gilbreth Road, Burlingame, CA 94010, (415)692-0422.
RJR Fashion Fabrics, 13748 S. Gramercy Place, Gardena, CA 90249, (800)422-5426.
Robert Kaufman Co., Inc., 129 W. 132nd St., Los Angeles, CA 90061, (310)538-3482.
Rose & Hubert, 1450 Broadway, 20th Floor, New York, NY 10018.
Spring Industries, 420 W. White St., Rock Hills, SC 29730.
V.I.P. Fabrics, 1412 Broadway, New York, NY 10018, (800)847-4064.
Westwood Inc., 1460 Broadway, New York, NY 10036.

SUPPLIES
Batting—Mountain Mist, The Stearns Technical Textiles, 100 Williams St., Cincinnati, OH 45215, (513)948-5276.

Batting, pillowforms—Morning Glory Products, 302 Highland Drive, Taylor, TX 76574, (800)234-9105.
Buttons—JHB International, 1955 S. Quince St., Denver, CO 80231, (303)751-8100; Streamline, Inc., 845 Stewart Ave., Garden City, NY 11530.
Cutting tools, cutting mat, rulers—Omnigrid Inc., 1560 Port Drive, Burlington, WA 98233, (800)755-3530.
HeatnBond Lite Iron-on Adhesive—ThermOWeb, 770 Glenn Ave., Wheeling, IL 60090.
Threads—Coats & Clark, 30 Patewood Drive, Suite 351, Greenville, SC 29615, (864)234-0331.
Quilt thread—DMC, Port Kearney Building 10, South Kearney, NY 07032-0650.
Sewing Machine—Husqvarna Viking Sewing Machine Company, 11760 Berea Road, Cleveland, OH 44111.

QUILT BLOCK AND BORDER DESIGNERS
Antique—36, 80, 90, 128, and 170.
Laura Collins—10, 14, 18, 62, 78, 82, 84, 120, 122, 124, 126, 194, 195, and 197.
Phyllis Dobbs—8, 12, 16, 24, 26, 34, 54, 56, 58, 60, 64, 66, 68, 76, 102, 104, 106, 108, 130, 152, 154, 156, 158, 160, 180, 182, 184, 186, 196, 198, 199, 200, 201, 202, 203, 204, 205, 206, 207, and 211.
Lynette Jensen, Thimbleberries—Appliqué Pansy, page 20.
Jill Mead—70, 110, 162, 164, and 166.
Mountain Mist—1930s Ohio Rose from the Mountain Mist Collection, page 28.
Margaret Sindelar—22, 30, 40, 86, 92, 112, 114, 116, 118, 132, 134, 148, 150, 176, 178, 195, 196, 199, 208, 209, and 210.
Terrece Beesley and Trice Boerens, Studio B—42, 44, 46, 72, 74, 88, 168, 172, and 174.

PROJECT DESIGNERS
Phyllis Dobbs—100 (cushions).
Jill Mead—52 (jacket).
Margaret Sindelar—6–7, 52 (stockings, tote), 53 (valance), 100–101 (basket cover, place mat, tablecloth), 146 (hot pad, tea towel), 147.

QUILTERS
Linda Beardsley, Terrece Beesley, Trice Boerens, Laura Collins, Walinda Doescher, Phyllis Dobbs, Margaret Sindelar, and Jan Temeyer.

PHOTOGRAPHERS
Hopkins Associates and Scott Little

PHOTO STYLING ASSISTANT
Donna Chesnut